Max Stirner on the Path of Doubt

Continental Philosophy and the History of Thought

Series Editors: Christian Lotz, Michigan State University, and
Antonio Calcagno, King's University College
at Western University, Canada

Advisory Board: Smaranda Aldea (Kent State University), Amy Allen (Penn State University), Silvia Benso (Rochester Institute of Technology), Jeffrey Bloechl (Boston College), Andrew Cutrofello (Loyola University, Chicago), Marguerite La Caze (University of Queensland), Christina M. Gschwandtner (Fordham University), Dermot Moran (Boston College and University College Dublin), Ann Murphy (University of New Mexico), Michael Naas (DePaul University), Eric Nelson (Hong Kong University of Science and Technology), Marjolein Oele (University of San Francisco), Mariana Ortega (Penn State University), Elena Pulcini (University of Florence, Italy), Alan Schrift (Grinell College), Anthony Steinbock (Stony Brook University), Brad Stone (Loyola Marymount University)

The Continental Philosophy and the History of Thought series seeks to augment and amplify scholarship in continental philosophy by exploring its rich and complex relationships to figures, schools of thought, and philosophical movements that are crucial for its evolution and development. A historical focus allows potential authors to uncover important but understudied thinkers and ideas that were nonetheless foundational for various continental schools of thought. Furthermore, critical scholarship on the histories of continental philosophy will also help re-position, challenge, and even overturn dominant interpretations of established, well-known philosophical views while refining and re-interpreting them in light of new historical discoveries and textual analyses. The series seeks to publish carefully edited collections and high-quality monographs that present the best of scholarship in continental philosophy and its histories.

Titles in series:
Max Stirner on the Path of Doubt, by Lawrence S. Stepelevich

Max Stirner on the Path of Doubt

Lawrence S. Stepelevich

LEXINGTON BOOKS
Lanham • Boulder • New York • London

Published by Lexington Books
An imprint of The Rowman & Littlefield Publishing Group, Inc.
4501 Forbes Boulevard, Suite 200, Lanham, Maryland 20706
www.rowman.com

6 Tinworth Street, London SE11 5AL, United Kingdom

Copyright © 2020 The Rowman & Littlefield Publishing Group, Inc.

All rights reserved. No part of this book may be reproduced in any form or by any electronic or mechanical means, including information storage and retrieval systems, without written permission from the publisher, except by a reviewer who may quote passages in a review.

British Library Cataloguing in Publication Information Available

Library of Congress Cataloging-in-Publication Data

Names: Stepelevich, Lawrence S., 1930– author.
Title: Max Stirner on the path of doubt / Lawrence S. Stepelevich.
Description: Lanham : Lexington Books, [2020] | Series: Continental philosophy and the history of thought | Includes bibliographical references and index. | Summary: "This book examines how in a series of critical confrontations, Stirner rejected the efforts of his 'Young Hegelian' contemporaries to recast Hegel as a revolutionary. For him, the various apocalyptic declarations of these 'pious atheists,' were only the expressions of adolescent dreams set upon the annihilation of real individuality" — Provided by publisher.
Identifiers: LCCN 2020042404 (print) | LCCN 2020042405 (ebook) | ISBN 9781793636881 (cloth) | ISBN 9781793636904 (pbk)
ISBN 9781793636898 (epub)
Subjects: LCSH: Stirner, Max, 1806-1856. | Hegel, Georg Wilhelm Friedrich, 1770–1831.
Classification: LCC B3153.S754 S74 2020 (print) | LCC B3153.S754 (ebook) | DDC 193—dc23
LC record available at https://lccn.loc.gov/2020042404
LC ebook record available at https://lccn.loc.gov/2020042405

*TO
IRENA*

Contents

Preface	ix
Acknowledgments	xi
Introduction	1
1 The Hostile Brothers	11
2 Stirner as Hegelian	29
3 The Path Ahead	63
4 The First Step	79
5 An Atheistic Turn: Bruno Bauer	91
6 From the God-Man to the Man-God: Ludwig Feuerbach	109
7 The New World as the New Jerusalem: Moses Hess	121
8 A Sudden Turn to Scientific Socialism: Marx and Engels	143
9 The End of the Path	157
Addenda	161

    I: A Review of Stirner's final work:
        DIE GESCHICHTE DER REACTION
    II: A. *The Free Ones*
    II: B. Stirner's Review of Eugene Sue's *The Mysteries of Paris*
    II: C. Stirner's Review of Bruno Bauer's *The Trumpet of the Last Judgment*

Bibliography	201
Index	211
About the Author	213

Preface

This work has a simple intention: to propose that Max Stirner is a legitimate heir to Hegelian philosophy. His major and singular work, *The Ego and His Own*, has often been dismissed as but the eccentric work of a passing figure among the early students of Hegel. But, yet, from its first appearance in the fall of 1844, to the present day, it has provoked constant and heated debate over its significance. For over a century it has remained in print, translated into dozens of languages, and has gathered as much scorn as it has admiration. Its persistent ideological magnetism, either repelling or attractive, has been an enigma—just as the philosophy of his teacher, Hegel. I will maintain that both are linked by a profound dialectical logic, and this logic, so often ignored or misunderstood, which sustains their philosophical vitality and insures the endurance of their thought. Hegelianism, in following its own self-reflecting dialectical logic, reaches a closure in which, as with Heraclitus, the "end and the beginning are one and the same." As Heinrich Heine said, "Our Philosophic revolution is concluded; Hegel has closed the great circle."—and Stirner rests at the point of its closure.

Acknowledgments

Were it not for the intelligent encouragement of Professor William Desmond, a good friend of many years, this study would not have been completed.

My thanks to Amrit Manazak Heer, for his assistance in formatting this work.

Introduction

Some time ago, I happened upon a work by the Marxist scholar, Hans C. Helms.[1] In this study, Stirner is taken as the ideological éminence grise behind a myriad of transient and little-noticed number of "anonymous societies" who devoted themselves to a radical individualism antithetical to the desired world of Marxian collectivism. For Helms, a devoted Marxist, these small groups of Stirnerians, despite their "anonymity," were in part responsible for the dreadful bourgeois era of free-market capitalism which emerged in post-war Germany. Certainly, for the 1945 Marxists, just as those in 1918, the attempt to totally enfold Germany into a "People's Republic" had once again failed, and Helms sees Stirner's heavy, if unnoticed, hand in all of this Capitalistic mischief.

However, for me, the most interesting feature of Helm's book was its bibliography. With a dedication that a Marxian critic of Stirner might not be expected to have, Helms listed hundreds of works, with over ninety pages devoted to the various editions, translations, and commentaries upon Stirner! But even Helm's compilation has been overshadowed by a recent exhaustive bibliography devoted to Stirner, which runs to 325 pages![2] As a recent German work has it, Stirner's work is "Heimlich hit"—a secret best-seller.

These large bibliographies focused on Stirner came as a surprise, for at least in my experience, references to Stirner were few and far between. As an example, in the cloistered groves of academe, the *Philosopher's Index*, philosophy's "preeminent reference resource" has, for many years, listed journal articles drawn from 680 journals, collected from 50 countries. Here, Stirner, just as Engels, plays second fiddle to Marx. Stirner's name appears in the titles of 68 journals and books but is heavily outweighed by Marx, whose name appears in the titles of 2,407 journals and books. Little is heard of Stirner in the groves of the academe. The academic silence concerning Stirner becomes even more audible in that his main work, *Der Einzige und sein Eigenthum*,[3] has appeared in over 100 editions and translated into over 17 languages and literally hundreds of books and articles that deal with Stirner. His work has appeared in such rare expressions as Yiddish, Serbo-Croatian, and Catalan.[4]

Press copies of the *Ego* first appeared in November of 1844, although dated as 1845 on the title page. For almost forty years it seems to have been totally forgotten, then, in 1882 it was unexpectedly re-published. It has not been out of print since that time. The latest English edition, that by the Cambridge University Press, appeared in 1995,[5] and as if to show that Stirner's work is still of interest, a new English translation appeared in 2017, under a new title, *The Unique and Its Property*.[6]

The further tracing of this bibliographic trail supported my early conviction that Stirner was much more than he was usually portrayed: as being merely an early passing figure long lost in the dust of advancing Marxism. His "insignificance" is often noted, although Marx and Engels did devote a large and unpublishable work against him, one which, as Engels had to ruefully admit, devoted more pages against Stirner that Stirner himself had written. Neither their vitriolic criticism, nor that of their followers, was enough to put an end to Stirner. He has remained, as one commentator noted, a "thorn" in Marxian flesh.[7]

Stirner's philosophic equation to Hegel is seldom dealt with, but it alone renders the continuing interest in Stirner intelligible. From the time of its publication, the Ego has defied attempts to comprehend either its persistent influence or meaning. What is not comprehended is that this "absurd" work is the creation of a Hegelian who authentically restates Hegel along the dialectical lines established by Hegel. He is neither an "Old Hegelian" dedicated to the exhaustive autopsy of the Hegelian corpus nor a "Young Hegelian" bent upon employing it to a further purpose. For him, these were false alternatives, with both making claims to independent and positive meaning in themselves. To set up contrary alternatives, such as "Young" or "Old," upon a singular philosophical ground was dialectically false and have rendered efforts to "comprehend" Hegel—as well as Stirner—impossible.

The division of the whole of Hegel's philosophy into two opposing schools of thought is a division made only by reflection, by an abstract sundering of a philosophic totality. Neither the one nor the other either "Young" or "Old" can stand alone. Here the dialectic is at work, wherein the self-contradiction of any initiating point, in this case Hegelianism, is manifested. However, in simply holding to this division, which exemplifies the either/or logic of Aristotle, it was impossible for the logic of common sense to comprehend the essential union of both.

Much of what is understood of the Young Hegelian school, and Stirner, in particular, is drawn from a Marxian viewpoint—and much of that from the 1888 recollections of Engels, *Ludwig Feuerbach and the Outcome of Classical German Philosophy*. It is not unexpected that most political scientists, fixed upon the political effects of "Scientific Socialism," would simply view the contemporaries of the young Marx, such as Moses Hess, Feuerbach, Bauer, or Stirner, as having an interest only for briefly impinged upon the development of Marxist theory. Unhappily, for the Marxists, Stirner's work has always been readily accessible and has an irritant to the collectivist mind. Its basis in Hegelian philosophy has rendered it even more irritating.

Lenin, who knew something of Hegel, once observed that "It is impossible completely to understand Marx's Capital, and especially its first chapter, without having thoroughly studied and understood the whole of Hegel's Logic. Consequently, half a century later none of the Marxists understood Marx!!" Lenin might not be surprised that another century has passed without Hegel being understood by the Marxists or their later various incarnations as "Postmodern Neo-Marxists." A recent example is the academic collection of articles and translations gathered by Saul Newman,[8] a Political Scientist known for having coined the term "Postanarchism" (described as "wedding poststructuralism to anarchism"). Among the eight postmodern essays and translations in the collection, Foucault, Deleuze, Derrida, and Hegel find their places, Hegel being occasionally recognized but seldom discussed. One of the contributors, Riccardo Baldissone, a Research Fellow at the Centre for Human Rights Education at Curtin University, Australia, seems ready to take the plunge into Hegel—if only indirectly:

> I will not construct Stirner's approach and themes as derivative of Hegel or any other previous author. Instead, I will exemplify how Stirner's text modifies our reading of previous philosophical works or, to put it bluntly, how Stirner constructs his predecessors. A most interesting illustration of the effect exerted on Hegel by Stirner is the truly remarkable essay "Max Stirner as Hegelian," which could be also described as Stepelevich's rereading of Hegel after Stirner. However, rather than making Hegel "anticipate" Stirner, I will follow the example of Newman's reversal and I will attempt recalling a Stirnerian moment in Hegel.

What is interesting here, at least to me, is what is so "remarkable" about my essay? The answer is easy enough; I have asserted that Stirner was a Hegelian. This, to be refuted, would require some work to see just where and how Stirner is or is not a Hegelian. But the work is passed off, and Baldissone calls upon Saul Newman for help.[9] Hegelian logic, other than its appearance in "Dialectical Materialism" is seldom dealt with among Political Scientists.

In the contemporary era, the view of the Young Hegelian School seems to have died out, and the former followers of such as Feuerbach and Bauer and are hardly heard, and if so, their voices find only faintly echoed in Critical Theory and other variants upon the themes of Postmodernism. With the exception of such scholars as Saul Newman, Stirner would also have likely continued on in his usual unnoticed way along the path of social theory. A recent example of this lack of attention is to be found in Robyn Marsco's work, *The Highway of Despair: Critical Theory after Hegel*.[10] As described by its publisher, the work

> follows Theodor Adorno, Georges Bataille, and Frantz Fanon as they each read, resist, and reconfigure a strand of thought in Hegel's *Phenomenology of Spirit*. Confronting the twentieth-century collapse of a certain revolutionary dialectic, these thinkers struggle to revalue critical philosophy and recast Left Hegelianism within the contexts of genocidal racism, world war, and colonial domination.

Exactly why "Left Hegelianism" (which is the first label of "Young Hegelianism") was in need of being "recast" in order to deal with the "twentieth-century collapse" of a certain (Marxian?) revolutionary dialectic" is simply left unsaid. I would propose that Stirner's critique created the collapse. Although this is a good scholarly work, it nevertheless might serve as another example, rather subtle, of the Marxian avoidance of Stirner. The avoidance of the disastrous encounter of Young Hegelianism with Stirner had made it quite difficult for contemporary Marxists to account for their later despair.

This avoidance is one reason for the myriad of confusing and often conflicting labels affixed to him. An often-used label is that he is an "Anarchist." It certainly did not help toward the understanding of Stirner when Engels, after briefly considering him a Benthamite, went on to link him to Bakunin.[11] It was thereafter taken as axiomatic among political scientists that Stirner was an "anarchist"—even if he did present a strong argument against Proudhon's slogan that "Property is Theft"[12]—and it was Proudhon who coined the term "Anarchist." On this, George Woodcock, in his extensive work *Anarchism*,[13] noted that Stirner influenced "only a few marginal groups of individualists"[14]). In another study by David E. Apter and James Joll, their 274-page work, *Anarchism Today*,[15] Stirner is only briefly (and barely) mentioned—at one time linking him to Bergson. More recently, in her excellent essay "Why Anarchists Need Stirner,"[16] Kathy E. Ferguson comes directly to the point:

> Stirner is a hard thinker to categorize. He has been called a nihilist, one who advocates "heartless frivolity and criminal irresponsibility" above the necessities of social revolution. Some readers debate, rather ponderously, whether or not he is a psychological egoist. Others find him to be a radical individualist who is "wrong in his fundamental presupposition," about society, or a "radical

nominalist" who launches "a comprehensive attack on the world, generally." Perhaps we can learn from these earnest ventures to eschew the desire to pin Stirner down, and instead let him float a bit.[17]

Professor Ferguson's prudential attitude toward the labeling of Stirner was earlier manifested in her essay "Saint Max Revisited: A Reconsideration of Max Stirner."[18]

Most Political Scientists and historians are, expectedly, not too interested or well-versed in speculative philosophy, particularly Hegelianism. This lack of interest has been noted: "To a historian concerned with the Young Hegelians, the problem of Hegel's philosophy is less acute than for a philosopher specifically concerned with that philosophy."[19]

Marx was the first to see Stirner as an enemy and stigmatized "Sankt Max" as but "the speculative spokesman for the petty bourgeois, a decadent Hegelian boasting over the unrestraint of his self-inflated ego."[20] Marx's view was simply and unquestionably accepted by generations of his followers, and even later critics of Marx, such as Sidney Hook, nevertheless echoed Marx when he condemned Stirner's work as but the "social defense mechanism of a petty bourgeois soul."[21] Others, unsatisfied with this "petty" status, elevated him to the status of "the Grand Bourgeois," or Fascist.[22] Still others, taking an opposite stance, see in Stirner the most articulate defender of individual liberty.[23] He has been labeled an existentialist, a solipsist, an anti-Benthamite, an intemperate capitalist, or—as we might now suspect—an anti-capitalist. For a large spectrum of the opinions regarding Stirner, see Kathy E. Ferguson's article, "Saint Max Revisited: A Reconsideration of Max Stirner."[24] A recent title was affixed upon Stirner by the political scientist, Saul Newman, who understands him as a "proto-poststructuralist."

But, finally, and not unexpectedly, Stirner was once, in 1903, and also in 2018 designated as "Paranoiac."[25]

But despite the difficulties of identifying Stirner's thought, there is a consistent agreement that Stirner be taken as the last of the "Young Hegelians." In this regard, most commentators have agreed with Frederick Engels, who had Stirner concluding the "decomposition process" of the Hegelian School.[26] In the words of a later commentator, David McLellan, Stirner was simply "the last of the Hegelians."[27] Franz Mehring, Marx's biographer, also held the same view: Stirner was "the last offshoot of Hegelian philosophy."[28] Kurt Mautz, who, in 1936, wrote a comprehensive study of the relationship between Hegel and Stirner, described Stirner as "the last metamorphosis of German Idealism."[29] For Fritz Mauthener, Stirner had drawn "The ultimate consequence of the Hegelians [die allerletzen Folgerungen aus der Hegeliei]."[30] But perhaps the French scholar Henri Arvon stated the matter most elegantly, for him Stirner was "le dernier maillon de la chaîne hégélienne."[31] More recently, in proposing that Stirner influenced Nietzsche, Gilles Deleuze observed:

> It is clear that Stirner plays the revelatory role in all this [i.e., the revelation of the nihilism inherent in German philosophy against which Nietzsche struggles]. It is he [Stirner] who pushes the dialectic to its final consequences, showing what its motor and end results are[32]

Indeed, even before he met Bauer, Stirner had already elected himself to that final position—since, as he wrote: "The true tendency of the Hegelian system" [die wahre Tendenz des Hegelschen Systems] was to obtain "the autonomy of free men [die Autarkie des freien Menschen]."[33]

All this would suggest that Stirner's philosophy might well be a logical consequence of Hegelianism. The historian and Hegelian, Johann Erdmann, thought this to be the case, and noted that "Max Stirner is the one who really represents the culminating point of the tendency begun by Hegel."[34] His view was also that of Karl Löwith, who wrote that:

> Stirner's book, *Der Einzige und sein Eigentum* has usually been considered the anarchic product of an eccentric, but it is in reality an ultimate logical consequence of Hegel's historical system, which – allegorically displaced – it reproduces exactly. Stirner himself admits this derivation from Hegel in his discussion of Bauer's Pousane.[35]

I believe that Erdman and Löwith are correct, and I have earlier argued this point—that Stirner is not simply, in a historical sense, "the last of the Hegelians," but that his philosophy is the realization of what is entailed in "being a Hegelian."[36]

From the beginning of my long interest in Stirner, I've always believed that the moral, or if you wish, his "immoral" philosophy, was nothing less than the final and exhaustive expression of Hegel's philosophy. The dark image of Hegel is reflected in Stirner, an image which has fascinated, and often repelled, those who have looked into it. Stirner stands at the end of the path that was followed by Hegel's first radical followers. But he was simply unwilling to continue along that path, which would require him to subordinate himself to their various idealistic "causes," into a denial of actual reality, and to deny "the course of the world." He proved to be a formidable opponent, and none of them were able to avoid him—and so they either silently turned away, as with Feuerbach and Bauer, or declared it was the wrong path, as with Marx, Engels, or Moses Hess. All of these early radicals, with the exception of Marx, are now all but forgotten, yet they yet remain as the sources of the most significant movements of our modern world—evidenced in such ideologies as Marxism, Anarchism, Individualism, and Zionism. For anyone interested in a more detailed look at Stirner's world, a look at his writings as presented in the Appendix to this work might be helpful.

But for all, Old or Young, the road to truth is, just as Plato's "steep and rough ascent" out of the Cave, a difficult and demanding path, which, in his Introduction to *The Phenomenolgy of Mind*, Hegel describes as

> the path of doubt, or more properly a highway of despair. For what happens there is not what is usually understood by doubting, a jostling against this or that supposed truth, the outcome of which is again a disappearance in due course of the doubt and a return to the former truth, so that at the end the matter is taken as it was before. On the contrary, that pathway is the conscious insight into the untruth of the phenomenal knowledge.

On one side there stood a group of his optimistic students, not bound by any fear of doubt, who envisioned the "path" as being much more than merely an intellectual activity, more than a way to theoretically reach "the conscious insight into the untruth of phenomenal knowledge." For them, taking the Path of Doubt meant to give themselves over to doubting the truth of the actual world in which they lived. Doubting was not, as it was with Descartes, a mere intellectual activity, but a serious engagement with the world. Hegel's dialectic would be the way by which to test the "supposed truth" of all that had been dogmatically presented to them as unquestionable. Their absolute doubt would be the antithesis to the accepted values of their world, and from this radical action of questioning and examining, a social revolution would come about, one from which a new order of world would rise into being.

For these radicals, the first critical examination would turn upon the ancient link between Church and State, and this absolute skepticism would be the ground of an ideology of reform. The "Old Hegelians" did not see it this way. For them, comfortable within the secure structures of academic life, only time could test the theory—and it never could, since the truth was impervious to history. There was no "time to change." Philosophy had ended with Hegel, with his unalterable truth. But the Young Hegelians considered history to be the final judge of philosophy, and the rational, the theoretically true, would in time emerge into actual being. The ancient argument between truth and time continued, and since both schools made a claim to be the "true" Hegelians an unsteady and enduring armistice was soon set up, as Karl Löwith has it, between the two "hostile brothers."

Unhappily, for these young critics, the final member of the critical school, Max Stirner, set about—in a most lucid manner—to overturn the logic of Hegel's critics by turning it against them. This is the root of Stirner's philosophical power and his profound ambiguity as a Hegelian. This "negation of the negation" by which he turned against the negative criticisms of Hegel explains the persistence of interest in his thought. It can be maintained that his "nihilism" was the final conclusion and truth of Hegelianism itself, and after him every member of the Young or Old Hegelian schools had little to say, either of him or the positions they had held before his criticism of them. He was indeed, as it will be seen, "The Last of the Hegelians"—both historically and logically.

The great difficulty in comprehending the persistent presence of Stirner follows from his dialectical stance in regard to Hegelianism. He is neither "Young" nor "Old," and his "egoism" can be considered as the "synthesis" of both schools and the recovery of the Hegelianism which had been lost. His work recast the concept of "Absolute Knowledge," which terminated that Hegel's *Phenomenology of Mind* was again realized in Stirner—he is the fate of Hegelianism.

NOTES

1. Hans Günter Helms, *Die Ideologie der anonymen Gesellschaft: Max Stirners "Einziger" und der Fortschritt das demokratischen Selbstbewusstseins vom Vormärz bis zur Bundesrepublik* (Köln: Verlag M. Du Mont Schauberg, 1966).

2. See Bernd Laska, "Max Stirner Archiv Leipzig – Max Stirner." Accessed October 16, 2019. http://www.max-stirner-archiv-leipzig.de/max_stirner.html. For a further exhaustive bibliography, see Trevor Blake. *Max Stirner Bibliography*. 127 House, 2016.

3. In 1907 the first English language translation by Steven Tracy Byington Bynignton was published under the title of *The Ego and Its Own*. It became the standard translation, however, in 1995, a slightly amended translation by David Leopold was published by Cambridge University Press under the title *The Ego and His Own*.

4. Chronologically, first editions have been translated into French (L'unique et sa propriété, 1899), Danish (Den Eneste og hans Ejendom, 1901), Spanish (El único y su propiedad, 1901), Italian (L'unico e la sua proprietà, 1902), Russian (Edinstvennyj i ego dostojanie, 1906), English (The Ego and His Own, 1907), Dutch (De Eenige en z'n Eigendom, 1907), Swedish (Den ende och hans egendom, 1910), Japanese (Yuiitsuslha to sono shoyû, 1920), Serbo-Croatian (Jedini i njegovo vlastništvo, 1976), Catalan (L'únic i la seva propietat, 1986), Hungarian (Az egyetlen és tulajdona, 1991) (second part only), Greek (Ο μοναδικός και το δικό του, 2002), Portuguese (O Único e a sua propriedade, 2004), Polish (Jedyny i jego własność, 2005), Czech (Jediný a jeho vlastnictví, 2010).

5. All citations to the *Ego* will be based upon this recent work. The German text is to be found in the edition of the Carl Hanser Verlag 6. Köln: 1968. It is edited by the Marxian critic, Hans G. Helms, who, on the back cover, heatedly describes the *Ego* as "a justification of Capitalism . . . of falsity and injustice. Even the justification of murder, etc."

6. Max Stirner, *The Unique and Its Property*, trans. Wolfi Landstreicher (Baltimore: Underworld Amusements, 2017).

7. Bernd A. Laska, *Ein dauerhafter Dissident: 150 Jahre Stirners "Einziger" : eine kurze Wirkungsgeschichte* (Nurnberg: LSR-Verlag, 1996).

8. Saul Newman, *Max Stirner* (New York: Palgrave Macmillan, 2011).

9. The reader, curious about "Newman's reversal" is referred to Newman's excellent study, Saul Newman, "Stirner and Foucault: Toward a Post-Kantian Freedom." *Postmodern Culture* 13, no. 2 (May 6, 2003)

10. Robyn Marasco, *The Highway of Despair: Critical Theory after Hegel* (New York: Columbia University Press, 2015.)

11. Karl Marx, *Karl Marx, Friedrich Engels Gesamtausgabe (MEGA)* (Berlin: Dietz, 1975), XXVII, 9.

12. Stirner, *Stirner*, 222 ff.

13. George Woodcock, *Anarchism* (Cleveland: World Publishing, 1962).

14. Ibid., 105.

15. David Apter, and James Joll, *Anarchism Today* (New York: Doubleday, 1972).

16. Kathy Ferguson, "Why Anarchists Need Stirner," in *Max Stirner*, ed. Saul Newman, 167–88 (New York: Palgrave Macmillan, 2011).

17. Ibid., 167.

18. Kathy E. Ferguson, "Saint Max Revisited: A Reconsideration of Max Stirner," *Idealistic Studies* 12, no. 3 (1982): 276–92.

19. William J. Brazill, *The Young Hegelians* (New Haven: Yale University Press, 1970).

20. Marx and Engels, *The German Ideology*.

21. Sidney Hook, *Towards the Understanding of Karl Marx: A Revolutionary Interpretation* (London: Victor Gollancz, 1933), 66.

22. For example, Helms, *Die Ideologie der anonymen Gesellschaft*.

23. Cf. James J. Martin's Introduction to Stirner, *The Ego and His Own*.

24. Ferguson, "Saint Max Revisited," 276–92.

25. Ernst Schultze, "Stirner'sche Ideen in einem paranoischen Wahnsystem," *Archiv für Psychiatrie und Nervenkrankheiten* 36, no. 3 (January 1, 1903): 793–818. This singular study seems to be the only evidence for associating Stirner to Donald Trump, a stretch for even the most dedicated of today's Social Justice Warriors. Hegel, in his Phenomenology, termed them "Knights of Virtue," high-ground moralists whose oppressive standards led them finally to a compromise with the "Way of the World" [Lebenslauf]. As an example of one of these "Knights" at work, see Michael McAnear's strained political efforts in McAnear, "Max Stirner, the Lunatic and Donald Trump."

26. Friedrich Engels, *Ludwig Feuerbach and the End of Classical German Philosophy* (Moscow: Progress Publishers, 1946), 17.

27. David McLellan, *The Young Hegelians and Karl Marx*, 1st ed. (London, Melbourne: Macmillan, 1969), 119.

28. Franz Mehring, *Karl Marx: The Story of His Life* (Ann Arbor: University of Michigan Press, 1962), 104.

29. Kurt Adolf Mautz, "Die Philosophie Max Stirners Im Gegensatz Zum Hegelschen Idealismus," *Philosophical Review* 46, no. n/a (1937): 75.

30. Barnikol and Ott, *Das entdeckte Christentum im Vormärz: Bruno Bauers Kampf gegen Religion und Christentum und Erstausgabe seiner Kampfschrift*, ed. Ralf Ott (Scientia Verlag, 1989), 117.

31. Henri Arvon, *Aux Sources de l'existentialisme: Max Stirner* (Paris: Presses universitaires de France, 1954), 177.

32. Gilles Deleuze, *Nietzsche et la philosophie*. Quadrige Grands textes edition (Paris: Presses universitaires de Fran, 2010), 184–7.

33. Max Stirner, *Kleinere Schriften Und Seine Entgegnungen Auf Die Kritik Seines Werkes, "Der Einzige Und Sein Eigenthum" Aus Den Jahren 1842–1848* (Berlin: John Henry Mackay, 1914), 19ff.

34. Johann Eduard Erdmann. *A History of Philosophy: German Philosophy since Hegel*, trans. Williston Samuel Hough (London: Swan Sonnenschein, 1890), 100.

35. Karl Löwith, *From Hegel to Nietzsche*, trans. David E. Green (New York: Columbia University Press, 1964), 101; Löwith, Karl, *Von Hegel zu Nietzsche* (Hamburg: Felix Meiner Verlag, 1995), 118.

36. Lawrence Stepelevich, "Max Stirner and the Jewish Question," *Modern Judaism* 34 (February 1, 2014): 42–59.

Chapter 1

The Hostile Brothers

G. W. F. HEGEL, 1770–1831

It is characteristic of the division of the Hegelian school into a right wing, composed of Old Hegelians, and a left wing, composed of Young Hegelians, that this division did not result from purely philosophical differences, but political and religious ones. Its form grew out of the political division of the French Parliament, and its content out of the divergent views on the question of Christology.

—Karl Löwith

On October 14, 1806, Napoleon's victory over the Prussian Army at the Battle of Jena put an end to the Holy Roman Empire. On that day, Hegel, then a young and little-known Professor, had just finished writing his major work, *The Phenomenology of Mind*. The book and the battle marked the beginning of the modern age. Stirner was born a few days later when the victorious French Army entered Berlin.[1]

In the Preface to his *Phenomenology*, Hegel set out the character of his age:

> It is not difficult to see that ours is a birth-time and a period of transition to a new era. Spirit has broken with the world it has hitherto inhabited and imagined, and is of a mind to submerge it in the past, and in the labour of its own transformation.... The frivolity and boredom which unsettle the established order, the vague foreboding of something unknown, these are the heralds of approaching change.[2]

The signs that "there is something else approaching" seemed clear enough for Hegel, but the nature of this "something" was never made clear. Even those of his students, who hopefully embarked upon the "Path of Doubt," there seemed little concern about what the nature of this "new era" might be or how their crusade might end—or indeed if a crusade was needed. At the start, it seemed enough to simply declare and pursue their visions of a utopian future, which one described as a world which realized "the ideas of beauty and truth in practical life . . . to bind together, organically, all of the manifestly one sided and limited elements of the life of humanity and bring it into vital cooperation, finally to realize the idea of absolute good and absolute teleology in our world; this is the great task of the future." Or Marx's famous visions of a "Classless Society."

But if, in 1806, he envisioned his age as "a birth-time and a period of transition to a new era," a few years later, in 1820, in another Preface, he discouraged attempts to impose any ideals to bring forth a "new ear." Reality itself, only when "matured" and having "made itself ready," would bring about the ideal—ideals are *ex post facto* and not generated by a philosophic fiat, an "Ought to be."

> Only one word more concerning the desire to teach the world what it ought to be. For such a purpose philosophy at least always comes too late. Philosophy, as the thought of the world, does not appear until reality has completed its formative process, and made itself ready. History thus corroborates the teaching of the conception that only in the maturity of reality does the ideal appear as counterpart to the real, apprehends the real world in its substance, and shapes it into an intellectual kingdom. When philosophy paints its grey in grey, one form of life has become old, and by means of grey it cannot be rejuvenated, but only known. The owl of Minerva, takes its flight only when the shades of night are gathering.[3]

In sum, actual reality is prior to any ideals, for those things that "Ought to be." the "ideal" is merely a possibility, an idea that may or may not come into being, and exists only in the world of mind, and as an ideal it can be only known, but only in the minds of the believer." It is otherwise in the mind of the realist, as in the case of scientific knowledge, such as physics, wherein the observable and measurable are set as the basis of knowledge, a knowledge drawn directly from the actually given, based upon that which is first given to the senses, and any theory will follow from the observation and measurement of the event. It is only in social theory that theories or ideals are proposed that find their only basis in the inner ideal life of the social reformer. In this idealistic dream, they take their theory as the guide to a future more often than not is better than their present reality. With this in mind, their theory will be imposed upon present "realists: by "revolutionary" activity—an often violent overturning of present social life. Unhappily, for these social idealists, this certitude can only be found in the realm of their desires and beliefs—in theory.

Five years prior to the appearance of the *Phenomenology*, Hegel's first book was published, *The Difference Between Fichte's and Schelling's System of Philosophy (Differenz des Fichte'schen und Schelling'schen Systems der Philosophie)*.[4] In it, Hegel, then but a mere unsalaried Privatdocent in Jena University, not only dared to criticize the logic of Johann Gottlieb Fichte but even suggested that it should be replaced with young Hegel's own logic. After this, there was no fundamental change in Hegel's thought regarding his radical recasting of traditional logic, the common logic of "healthy common sense," the logic of Aristotle.

The major theme in Hegel's first work is its incisive critique of Fichte's "Philosophy of Identity," which he considered to have failed in its effort to present a coherent philosophical system. The fundamental reason for this being is that Fichte, as so many past philosophers, relied upon the traditional logical forms inherited from Aristotle. The persistent errors of philosophical thinking could only be remedied by replacing these forms of "reflective" logic with Hegel's own dialectical or "speculative" logic. In his unconscious acceptance of the logic of "reflection," Fichte had made a major error, for this logic, which is based upon the unexamined and "undeniable" axioms, such as "A = A"—which re-appears as Fichte's "Ego = Ego"—will inexorably lead to unquestionable "either-or" dichotomies which will ensure that no coherent philosophical system can ever be developed—either by Fichte or anyone else. But for Hegel, the rigid and absolute dichotomy still remained, only that, for Fichte, the proposed "synthesis" (a monism) took place only within the consciousness of the subject. It was a dogmatic egoism which simply posited ego itself as the singular ground from which issues the seeming contradiction between self and world. However, for Fichte, this confrontation is merely apparent, as the contradiction between self and world is merely a creation of the ego itself. For Hegel, such a dogmatic idealism, which would maintain that the separation between self and world is merely a contradiction that has been generated by consciousness itself, is no more feasible than the opposite point of view, dogmatic materialism.

For Hegel, "Monism" was the original sin of philosophy. It remains as the fundamental logical error which, in dogmatically positing a singular thing, drawn from either the "ideal" or the "real" order, posits it as the ground upon which a comprehensive philosophic system can be developed. It cannot be done simply because it cannot comprehend the "other"—depending upon which singular thing is chosen, which is to be the "thesis" (taken from either the ideal or the "real" world), the other remains as its contradictory, its "antithesis."

Fichte, as Kant, as most other German philosophers, also chose to be "Idealists," but Hegel decided to try to pass between the horns of the Idealist-Materialist dilemma and looked for a middle ground. He found the path had been earlier suggested by the ancient philosopher Heraclitus, the "Obscure." In his *Lectures on the History of Philosophy Lectures on the History of Philosophy*, he credited Heraclitus with setting a new logical frame upon which he developed his own logic:

> The advance requisite and made by Heraclitus is the progression from Being as the first immediate thought, to the category of Becoming as the second. This is the first concrete, the Absolute, as in it the unity of opposites. Thus with Heraclitus the philosophic Idea is to be met with in its speculative form; the reasoning of Parmenides and Zeno is abstract understanding. Heraclitus was thus universally esteemed a deep philosopher and even was decried as such. Here we see land; there is no proposition of Heraclitus which I have not adopted in my Logic.[5]

Here then is the essential principle of dialectical logic: that the "unity of opposites"—or the reconciliation of contradictories—is the ultimate speculative truth, and contradiction is not to be rejected but rather accepted. The foundation of either/or logic, that which finds itself expressed in the Cartesian "mind-body" problem, as well as in Boolean computer logic in which switches are either "on" or "off" (there is no middle ground), finds its grounding in the teachings of the Eleatics. But Hegel turned to Heraclitus, the contemporary of Parmenides, to find another logic, and with it understood that the idea of "Nothing" was as necessary as the idea of "Being" to generate the reality of "Becoming," a reality which was by its very definition contradictory—it was and it was not.

> In Becoming, the Being which is one with Nothing, and the Nothing which is one with Being, are only vanishing factors; they are and they are not so[6]

That reality is in a constant state of change, of becoming, is the central ontological principle of Hegelianism. It militates against any fixity or stability in the real as well as the ideal order—both of which are congruent "realities." Dialectical logic is both the cause and effect of this ontology, a logic which refuses to accept the concept that reality is one and unchanging, refusing, in fact to accept the position of the Eleatics, a position which was immanent in the dominating the logic of Aristotle, in which the "Principle of Identity," that A = A, was unassailable. Hegel's logic, in theory, was set against the "given," realities fixed and constrained in their definitions, and in practice, meaning that all now "given" will, in the course of becoming (history) vanish. It is a revolutionary logic.

> It is not too much to say that Hegel performs a revolution in logic. We see that Hegel proposes a new conception to replace the one that goes back to Greek antiquity.... The Hegelian logic is no longer the generalized form of abstraction as it was during some two millennia from Aristotle to Kant.[7]

Hegel's "new conception" of logic could also serve as a basis of actual revolution, and Lenin praised Alexander Hertzen (1812–1870) who "rose to a height which placed him on a level with the greatest thinkers of his time. He assimilated Hegel's dialectics. He realized that it was "the algebra of revolution."[8] However, it is most important to realize that the progressive view of dialectical logic places the articulation of the elements, commonly stated as "thesis," "antithesis," and "synthesis" upon a temporal or historical frame. This reading characterized the Young Hegelian view, and led inexorably to holding that the present time was but a "thesis," which, in the course of time would generate its antithesis, generally identified as the "revolutionary" overthrow of the given (thesis) and the coming into being of a higher "synthesis." This final historical moment would be taken as the necessitated termination of the historical process. That the present moment or state of reality, might actually be the completed expression of history, was dismissed by the revolutionary if the present moment seemed to be illogical or unreasonable—and it always seems so to the revolutionary mind. An example of this historical reading of the dialectic is found in the mind of Engels, in which the historical antithetical moment, or revolution is presently necessitated:

> In the course of development, all that was previously real becomes unreal, loses it necessity, its right of existence, its rationality. And in the place of moribund reality comes a new, viable reality—peacefully if the old has enough intelligence to go to its death without a struggle; forcibly if it resists this necessity. Thus the Hegelian proposition turns into its opposite through Hegelian dialectics itself: All that is real in the sphere of human history, becomes irrational in the process of time, is therefore irrational by its very destination, is tainted beforehand with irrationality, and everything which is rational in the minds of men is destined to become real, however much it may contradict existing apparent reality. In accordance with all the rules of the Hegelian method of thought, the proposition of the rationality of everything which is real resolves itself into the other proposition: All that exists deserves to perish.[9]

Engels wrote this in 1886. However, the seeming nihilistic element of Hegel's philosophy was not so evident in 1818 when he was invited to assume the Chair of Philosophy at the University of Berlin, a chair once held by Fichte. Shortly thereafter, in 1820, Hegel, perhaps following the dialectical ambiguity of his own logic, or out of prudence, evidently concurred with the rationality of the established order by writing his *Philosophy of Right*. It seemed to confirm his conservative political views, but it might immediately be noted that the *Philosophy of Right* has been the only source for those who would take Hegel as a conservative thinker.[10]

The appeal of the work to the conservatives within the Prussian government is obvious. It ensured that Hegel would avoid any official objections to his philosophy during the course of his tenure. He had not only blunted any fears that his philosophy was a matter of political concern but even went to assert the legitimacy of "modern states"—although it was not clear that he had the given Prussian State in mind:

> The state is the actuality of concrete freedom. . . . The principle of the modern states has prodigious strength and depth because it allows the principle of subjectivity to progress to its culmination in the extreme of self-subsistent personal particularity, and yet at the same time brings it back to the substantive unity [of the state].[11]

In sum, the "modern state" is the reconciliation, the synthesis, as it was of two apparent opposites: "self-subsistent personal particularity" or autonomous individuals with the "substantive unity" of the state, a compromise, as it were, between anarchy and totalitarianism. However, the ambiguity of this particular reconciliation became evident when it was asked if the Prussian monarchy was in fact a "modern state," a "true" or "rational" state deserving to be accepted as a "real state." The theoretical debate soon evolved into a dangerous political debate. As one historian stated the issue,

> The famous principle of Hegel that "what is real is rational and what is rational is real" could be interpreted in two different ways. A static construction served as a justification for all existing institutions. This was the view taken by the right-wing Hegelians who defended the rationality of the status quo by the reality of its existence; the pious romantic-conservatives and their allies, however, were not interested in the rational justification of ancient institutions and privileges. And when left-wing Young Hegelians used the dynamic explanation of Hegel's principle to denounce all "reality" of today as the "irrational" of tomorrow, Hegelianism was declared a dangerous and subversive philosophy by the religious conservatives.[12]

Conservative authorities, in both Church and State, tended to agree with the thinking of the German historian Henrich Leo (1799–1878), who held that Hegel was creating "the most dangerous enemies of Christian society."[13] Not unexpectedly the thought emerged among them that dialectical logic might well serve to transform the repressive forces holding back a new age. The force of his "mystical" doctrines, such as the present actuality of the Absolute Spirit, which could be taken as God, literally "converted" his students into disciples. As a recent commentator on the effect of Hegelianism wrote: "to become an authentic Hegelian," it was necessary that "a person had to undergo an existential transformation, a philosophical 'rebirth'."[14] An example of this 'rebirth' is evidenced in the testimony of Bruno Bauer (1809–1882). "Hegel alone has given back peace and certainty to my unsteady spirit. From the first moment I heard them, his lectures held me chained and seemed to present nothing new but only the explanation of that of which knowledge is inherent in each of us."[15] Wilhelm Vatke (1806–1882), later a theology Professor at the university, was even more impressed by Hegel's lectures. As he wrote to his brother, "You will think I am insane when I tell you that I see God face to face, but it is true. The transcendent has become immanent . . . Oh, if I could only describe to you how blessed I am."[16]

As a recent biographer of Hegel observed, regarding the widespread reverence accorded to Hegel, it was "clear that Hegelianism had become something more than just an academic doctrine.[17] In fact it had become a religion.

Ernst Wilhelm Hengstenberg (1802–1869) was a German Lutheran churchman and neo-Lutheran theologian and leader of Berlin's orthodox clergy. He well understood the threat of Hegelianism, and had earlier warned his fellow clerics that it was possible "that this devotion to Hegelian philosophy will in the near future develop into a much more diabolical force than the declining rationalism. . . . It is our holy duty to watch out and to attack immediately."[18]

As if in confirmation of Hengstenberg's warning, in the year before Hegel's death, one of his young followers, Ludwig Feuerbach (1804–1872), revealed the effects of Hegel's "diabolical force" in a lengthy and provocative essay, "Thoughts on Death and Immortality."[19] The essay clearly bears the thought which, from its first clear expression in the Preface to the *Phenomenology* until his final lectures, directed Hegelianism: that the World Spirit is now at a critical turning point, and that what has been given is but the thesis to a new age, an age which is to be taken as opposed to the old—the same thought is found in Feuerbach's *Thoughts on Death and Immortality*. The translator and commentator of this work have expressed its central theme:

> Feuerbach is certain that Hegel's philosophy contains nothing less than the seeds of a new epoch in world history . . . the new epoch can be established only by direct attack; in order to be effective enough to uproot the old assumptions and become humanity's new mode of perception.[20]

Adding to his popularity among his liberal acquaintances, there was his revolutionary logic, which powered his whole philosophy, a logic which required the "overthrow" of the given—which, to his students at that time and place, was the "given" of an orthodox Pietism, and a divinely established monarchy—neither of which had any claim upon either reason or reality. But during his lifetime, Hegel's personal reputability, just as his philosophy, seemed distant from any suggestions that his thought might be a danger to the established order. That was to change.

From the beginning of his teaching career in Jena until the final year of his life, Hegel envisioned his philosophy as "the inward birth-place of the spirit which will later arrive as actual form" and that this demand was "the demand of all time and of Philosophy. A new epoch has arisen in the world."[21] It is evident that Hegel considered his own thought to be the long-awaited arrival of Spirit as "actual form," and he concluded his comprehensive history of philosophical thought, not with a resume of his own thought, but with a final command—a "summons" to his students:

> I have tried to develop and bring before your thoughts this series of successive spiritual forms pertaining to Philosophy in its progress and to indicate the connection between them. This series is the true kingdom of spirits, the only kingdom of spirits that there is— . . . This long process is formed by the individual pulses which beat its life; they are the organism of our substance, an absolutely necessary progression, which expresses nothing less than the nature of spirit itself, and which lives in us all. We have to give ear to its urgency—when the mole that is within forces its way on—and we have to make it a reality. It is my desire that this history of philosophy should contain for you a summons to grasp the spirit of the time [Zeitgeist], which is present in us by nature, and—each in his own place—consciously to bring it from its natural condition, I.e., from its lifeless seclusion, into the light of day."[22]

In this final statement, the essentially revolutionary character of his "summons" is undeniable, and as his students thought the same, Stirner cites Hegel's "summons" in his review of Bauer's *Trumpet of the Last Judgment*. So also did his opponents. Hegel's disciples, mainly young theological students with a weak hold upon doctrinaire belief, were now given the idea that they were called upon bring forth a "new epoch" in the world. They had been invited, if not commanded, to become the first disciples of the Absolute Spirit, which had become incarnate in the philosophy of Hegel.

During his time at the university Hegel's strong personality and the support of few, but important, liberal officials held his conservative enemies at bay. Among one of the most important supporters was Karl von Altenstein, Prussian Minister of Culture, who since 1817, had supported Hegel's appointment to the Professorship of Philosophy, as was also the case with the powerful Minister of Education, Johannes Schultz. Despite his admitted difficulty in comprehending Hegel's philosophy, Altenstein loyally continued, until his death in 1840, to support Hegel. There seemed to be little to worry about, for at the time of his death, Hegel, and his philosophy, was held in high regard, enjoying both political and academic support. It was a good time to be a Hegelian, and as a contemporary historian described it, "One was either a Hegelian or a barbarian, idiot, laggard and hateful empiricist . . . when in the eyes of the Prussian ministry of culture and learning it was considered nearly a crime not to be a Hegelian."[23]

The division of Hegelian philosophy is based on its own logical premise that everything contains its own negation. Given this premise, a question emerges: is Hegelianism itself subject to its own logic? It would seem so, as it should contain its own negation. So, the question as to the future of this Hegelianim was to be read became a divisive issue upon its founder's death. Would it divide into two schools of thought? Might it well be lost and absorbed into a new "Philosophy of the Future"?[24]

If this is the case, does it mean that "Hegelians" are just as philosophically obsolete as "Platonists"? Hegel's answer to this question was ambiguous, or at least was seen as such by his immediate followers, who soon after his death expectedly divided into two schools. They were in agreement that there is but one fundamental philosophy, and after centuries of development, it finally manifested itself in Hegelianism. The history of philosophy is but the record of the advance of that philosophy to its own maturity, and so it is similar to the process wherein "the man, the youth, and the child, are all one and the same individual," so all previous philosophies can be said to have come to arrive at a final result in the maturity of Hegelianism.[25] However, for his followers, this conclusion still left open the question of what is to be done with this "true theory"?

Those who maintained the independence of Hegelianism as a theoretical knowledge independent of the course of history have been termed "Old Hegelians." Directly after Hegel's death, they immediately set about to compile his writings and lecture notes into a canon. This task, along with the explication of their meaning, into what might be termed a "midrash," has continued until the present. Most conservative Hegelians are, just as their ancestors, mainly found populating academic departments, and share their common interest in various learned societies. It is not, of course, expected that they fully agree on every point, but they do agree, as much as philosophers can agree, that Hegelianism is to be accepted as the true and final philosophy, and they will abide by Hegel's dictum that philosophy must avoid the "desire to teach the world what it ought to be"—and so avoid turning "Hegelianism" into a progressive ideology subordinated to social-political forces.

At the time of Hegel's tenure at the University of Berlin, the study of theology was an absolute requirement for entering into clerical duties, either pastoral or academic, but there was yet another requirement: political correctness. The connection between orthodox Christian faith and Prussian political conservatism had been established two decades earlier, in 1815, a "Holy Alliance" between the emperors of Russia, Austria, and the King of Prussia. With it, the link between theological orthodoxy and governmental authority was firmly established. Theological issues were no longer, as they had been mistakenly perceived just prior to the religious and cultural revolution of the Reformation, as mere "parsons' quarrels" (Pfaffengezank), but were seen as sources of political disturbance. The link between faith and political life was needed to support the unstable balance of forces in Metternich's Europe, particularly in Prussia, where it was required that theological matters be carefully monitored and that the political leaning of theology teachers be seriously examined prior to their appointments by the government. Needless to say, politically conservative theological professors found favor. It soon accounted for the growing political power of the Evangelicals, but it also served to drive some of the most talented libera students to leave their careers. Among them were such as Ludwig Feuerbach and Bruno Bauer. They, just as many other theological students, reacted to the Evangelical threat, and within a decade, in prestigious universities as Halle or Berlin, studies had lost many of their students. At the University of Halle, which in 1828 had 900 theology students, over half of them were lost by the 1840s, and at the University of Berlin, which in 1830 had counted 641 students, only 214 were enrolled in 1847. The other universities reflected these same losses.[26]

In July 1830, a year before the death of Hegel, a popular revolution in France finally put an end to the Bourbon monarchy, and Charles X was replaced by his cousin, Louis Philip. Two years later, In June of 1832, another uprising, led by the liberal factions attempted to depose the new King. This revolution soon provoked a series of anti-monarchist uprisings throughout Europe. In Brussels and the Southern Provinces of the United Kingdom of the Netherlands, further revolts led to the establishment of the Kingdom of Belgium. The example of the July Revolution also inspired unsuccessful revolutions in Italy as well as the November Uprising in Poland, which led to the exile of a future leader of the Young Hegelians, August von Cieszkowski. Fearful of their own future, the orthodox religious leaders and political conservatives of Prussia became even less tolerant of any philosophical doctrines, such as Hegelianism, which seemed—even if ambiguously—to support both heresy and political revolution.

Unhappily for the established school, the Chair of Philosophy at the University of Berlin remained vacant for four years after the death of Hegel. It was finally filled by Georg Andreas Gabler (1786–1853), an early student and enthusiastic admirer of Hegel. However, he displayed as little talent as he did presence and was hardly a substitute for Hegel. Gabler joined the other followers of Hegel, who, shortly after his death, bravely tried to defend his dialectical speculations against the growing threatening charge that it was incompatible with Christianity, a charge which has yet to be clearly refuted. In 1836 Gabler wrote two vague defenses of "the true philosophy," *De verae philosophiae erga religionem Christianam pietate and die Übereinstimmung der Hegelschen Philosophie mit den christlichen Religionsdogmen nachzuweisen*. But the successor to Hegel proved himself simply unable to assure the orthodox Pietists that Hegelianism was not a dangerous doctrine. He later failed in his effort to defend dialectical logic from the Aristotelean criticisms of Friedrich Adolf Trendelenburg (1802–1872). One of the leading figures among the academic Hegelians, Philip Konrad Marheineke (1780–1846), even went so far as to revise the hegelian mantra as to the identity of reason and reality by making the compromising statement, "The Church is the truth of the State, the State is the reality of the Church."[27]

Nevertheless, to his followers, Hegel's unexpected death did not seem to imply either the death of his philosophy or a threat to their careers. The academic followers retained, and acted upon, what Frederick Forster 1791–1868 had said in the course of his eulogy at Hegel's funeral. He had envisioned his academic colleagues to the followers of Alexander, whose vast Kingdom, upon his death, had been divided among his "Satraps." The Hegelians would be the governors of the provinces of an intellectual Kingdom, and it was only left to them to "confirm, proclaim and strengthen the Kingdom of Thought." In short, there were no more intellectual worlds to conquer.[28] The division of the Kingdom was parceled out by the gathering of writings, a "Nachlass," containing all of the material both previously published along with his own lecture notes and student notes. Each subject would be edited by a specific authority in the field. The project began immediately, and by 1845 the project was completed. It ran to twenty volumes. Since then, several revised and even more complete editions have appeared, and the latest and final collection, edited and fully annotated, has been compiled by the Hegel-Archiv at the University of Bochum. This edition of the *Werke* runs to over forty volumes and is a weighty testament to Hegel's reputation. The names of those who first diligently compiled his works and notes have largely been forgotten, but they were the major Hegelians of the times. Of them, Karl Löwith noted:

> The majority of the editors of Hegel's works were Old Hegelians in the original sense of the school founded by Hegel, von Henning, Hötho, Forester, Marheineke as well as Henrichs, C. Daub, Conradi and Schaller. They preserved Hegel's philosophy literally, continuing to reproduce it in a uniform manner

beyond the period of Hegel's personal influence. For the historic movement of the nineteenth century they are without significance.[29]

Within a few decades, the Hegelian historian, Karl Rosenkranz, noted, with some dry wit, that he was indeed "the last of the Mohicans." It was not until almost a half century later that the school re-surfaced in England in the modified form of "neo-Hegelianism." Still confused by Hegel, the English schools turned to "Analytic" Philosophy for clarification.

During his thirteen years at the University of Berlin, Hegel's strong personality and the support of few, but important, liberal officials held his conservative enemies at bay. Among one of the most important supporters was Karl von Altenstein (1770–1840), Prussian Minister of Culture since 1817, who had supported Hegel's appointment to the Professorship of Philosophy. There was also the support of the powerful Minister of Education, Johannes Schultz (1786–1869). Despite his admitted difficulty in comprehending Hegel's philosophy.[30] Altenstein, until his death, loyally continued to support Hegel. Unhappily, for the Hegelian students and academics, Altenstein died in 1840, and Schultz resigned his post. A new Culture Minister was appointed, Theodore von Eichhorn (1732–1827), who was just as hostile to the Hegelian school as his close friend, the theological leader of the Pietist faction, Ernst Wilhelm Hengtenberg (1802–1869). This removal of bureaucratic support would likely have ensured the final passage of the school's waning influence, but the death of the Prussian King Frederick Wilhelm III, who was not particularly hostile to Hegelian philosophy, inflicted a "coup de grâce" that ended the vitality of Hegelianism in Prussia. Upon his death, the Crown Prince ascended the throne as Frederick Wilhelm IV. He neither understood nor supported Hegelian philosophy, and shortly upon gaining the Crown, the young romantic and reactionary monarch defined himself as a "Christian Monarch" and took it upon himself to put an end to "the dragon seed of Hegelian Pantheism."[31] In proof of this, he called upon the aging Friedrich Schelling, Hegel's old rival, to lecture in Berlin.

Anyone who had expected Schelling's inaugural lecture to set forth some striking new path for the future of philosophy could not but be disappointed. Little is to be found of significance in his mainly rhetorical exercise, and he manages to avoid mentioning Hegel, although Fichte and Schleiermacher are praised for their contribution to the "renown and legacy" of German philosophy. However, as to the present state of affairs, Schelling asks and answers his own question: "Should now this long renowned movement end with a shameful shipwreck, with the destruction of all great convictions and even philosophy itself? Never!"[32] It was not long before Bakunin drew his conclusion. In a letter to his brother, he characterized Schelling as being nothing less than a "miserable, living-dead romantic." (Letter to Paul Bakunin, November 7, 1842).

Kierkegaard, just as Bakunin, had eagerly awaited Schelling's arrival in Berlin. His reaction to the tepid first lecture was tepid. However, his reaction to the second lecture was an Epiphany: "The embryonic child of thought leapt for joy within me, as in Elizabeth, when he mentioned the word "actuality" in connection with the relation of philosophy to actuality."[33] But in time, after dutifully attending thirty-six of Schelling's lectures, Kierkegaard reached a breaking point. "Schelling jabbers intolerable twaddle. I think that "I'll go completely silly if I keep listening to Schelling." He finally stopped listening on February 3, 1842. A few weeks later, his feelings had not changed: "Schelling talks endless nonsense both in an extensive and an intensive sense. I am leaving Berlin and hastening to Copenhagen, but not, you understand, to be bound by a new tie, oh no, for now I feel more strongly than ever that I need my freedom . . . I do owe Schelling something. For I have learned that I enjoy traveling."[34]

Looking upon themselves as the heralds of the "new age," the Young Hegelians, just as the "Illuminati" or the "Cognoscenti" of earlier generations, considered themselves as a community of dedicated intellectuals who scorned the accepted orthodoxies their time. They were all young. The aged Schelling was a disappointment. Arnold Ruge and Ludwig and Feuerbach were the oldest participants in the Young Hegelian movement, both in their thirties when they produced their most important works. David F. Strauss wrote the *Leben Jesu* in 1835 when he was but twenty-seven years old; Bruno Bauer was twenty-eight years old in 1837 when he first met Marx, then nineteen years old, and Friedrich Engels was twenty-four when he met Marx for the first time. Cieszkowski was twenty-four when he wrote the *Prologemena zur Historiosophie*, and Moses Hess was twenty-five when he wrote *Die heilige Geschichte der Menscheit*. Stirner was thirty-six years old when *Der Einzige und Sein Eigentum* was published. They seemed not particularly surprised nor frightened by the angry public reaction to their programs, and all displayed the common confidence of most reformers and revolutionaries—in this case, a confidence that bordered upon arrogance. Hegel had earlier forewarned them as to how "Healthy Common sense" [*Gesundmenschenverstand*] would respond to their unorthodox speculations—their future plans: Common sense cannot understand speculation; and what is more, it must come to hate speculation when it has experience of it; and, unless it is the state of perfect indifference that security confers, it is bound to detest and persecute it.[35] And this was the case. The Young Hegelians, who chose "the path of doubt" experienced the punishments of "common sense," and were often exiled, or jailed, and their works censored. Almost all of them were doomed to have suffered the loss of any future hopes for either social acceptance or professional careers. The academically protected Old Hegelians chose not to take that path and sought an "Accommodation" with the conservatives.

The first generation of the radical theorists had directly witnessed Hegel's victorious campaigns upon the fields of speculation and so were prepared to join battle with the irrational forces they saw stifling their world. Certainly, the reality of their time appeared to be fraught with political fantasies and religious illusions. The reactionary residue of Medieval Europe, restored to life with the fragile 1815 Congress of Vienna, still held sway. For them, that in Germany the link still remained unquestioned that orthodox Church and the divinely appointed monarchy were congruent was clear evidence of the irrationality of the real—at least it so seemed to the growing numbers of the reformers and revolutionaries of the time—among whom were the first generation of Young Hegelians. Given the circumstances, it was not long before the radical disciples of Hegel broke away from his apparent theoretical quietism and enthusiastically set about, as would be expected of young disciples, to save the flawed world in which they lived. Their decision required a dangerous missionary effort to declare their "cause" among those who needed to be saved—even if they refused salvation. As Engels had it, "In the place of moribund reality comes a new, viable reality—peacefully if the old has enough intelligence to go to its death without a struggle; forcibly if it resists this necessity."[36] In sum, The Young Hegelians were fixed upon an eschatological view of human history which, similar to the original Judeo-Christian, envisioned the future, after an apocalyptic revolution, in which the Coming of the Kingdom of God (in this case, Man) would be realized. However, unlike Christian eschatologically, the "beyond" was identified, not with a distance Heaven in space, but with the future. The Messianic message was common, with the leader of the Berlin Young Hegelians, Bruno Bauer, even taking the title of "The Messiah of Atheism." Most, with the exception of Stirner, had been theological students and lived and thought out their prophetic visions immersed in the heavy Pietistic atmosphere of Berlin. They went on their apostolic journeys with confidence that the new "Man" of the future would soon be revealed. But all of the Young Hegelians had their own similar enthusiastic programs for just what the present portended. And they set about proclaiming their new gospel. But, as Karl Löwith wrote of their calls to join in the pursuit of their millennial causes, that "their writings are manifestos, programs, and theses, but never anything whole, important in itself. . . . Whoever studies their writings will discover that, in spite of their inflammatory tone they leave an impression of insipidity."[37]

Stirner was the exception. He took Hegel seriously, and took his dictum that the "Rational is Real and the Real is Rational" as a fact. Actual reality was not to be set apart from reason, as something that had to be "rationalized" but as a realistic and present "given." He resolutely avoided programs and cast his judgment upon these disciples of a higher cause in his major work. His heretical acceptance of the presence, set out on the very first page of *Der Einziger*, "exploded like a bomb shell among the ranks of his former comrades-in-arms."[38]

> What is not supposed to be my concern [Sache]! First and foremost, the good cause [Sache], then God's cause, the cause of mankind, of truth, of freedom, of humanity, of justice; further, the cause of my people, my prince, my fatherland; finally, even the cause of Mind, and a thousand other causes. Only my cause is never to be my concern. Shame on the egoist who thinks only of himself![39]

With Max Stirner, the "Path of Doubt" had become a dead end. No longer would any idealistic reformer be safe from his scorn. The high humanistic intentions of both Bauer and Feuerbach wilted, with neither able to either counter or continue their critical roles as atheistic leaders, and Marx and Engels, having "settled accounts with their philosophic consciousness"— which meant only that they discarded any further philosophic reflections, went on to fame as the "Fathers of Scientific Socialism."

For Bakunin, who, as Engels had it "had taken much from Stirner" the logic of the path ended into a nihilism, but none of the Young Hegelians, despite their various readings of Hegel, ever abandoned his logic, and all confidently entered onto his "Path of Doubt," and set themselves against "common sense" and the conventions of their times—and all paid a heavy price—but none of them ever turned against Hegel. Even Karl Marx, in 1873, a decade before his death, noted that he had always considered himself as being "the pupil of the mighty thinker."[40] But on this matter, both he and Stirner were again in agreement, yet Stirner was the better pupil, for he did more than just "stand Hegel on his head" but, as Gilles Deleuze wrote, "It is he [Stirner] who pushes the dialectic to its final consequences, showing what its motor and end results are."[41]

NOTES

1. Much of Alexander Kojève's extraordinary and influential theory rests upon the profound connection he found between Hegel and Napoleon. Stirner, however, is left unmentioned Kojève, Introduction to the Reading of Hegel.

2. Georg Wilhelm Friedrich Hegel, *Phänomenologie Des Geistes* (Hamburg: Felix Meiner, 1987). Further citations will refer to both this text and the English translation, Georg Wilhelm Friedrich Hegel, *Phenomenology of Spirit*, trans. A. V. Miller (Oxford, UK: Oxford University Press, 1977).

3. Georg Wilhelm Friedric Hegel, *Philosophy of Right*, trans. T. M. Knox (Oxford: Oxford University Press, 1952), 12–13.

4. Georg Wilhelm Friedric Hegel, *The Difference between Fichte's and Schelling's System of Philosophy*, trans. H. S. Harris and W. Cerf (Albany, NY: State University of New York Press, 1977).

5. Georg Wilhelm Friedric Hegel, *Lectures on the History of Philosophy, Volume 1*, trans. E. S. Haldane (Lincoln, NE: University of Nebraska, 1995), 279.

6. Georg Wilhelm Friedric Hegel, *The Encyclopaedia Logic: Part I of the Encyclopaedia of the Philosophical Sciences with the Zustze*, trans. T. F. Geraets, W. A. Suchting, and H. S. Harris (Indianapolis: Hackett, 1991), 145.

7. Tom Rockmore, *Before and after Hegel: A Historical Introduction to Hegel's Thought* (Indianapolis: Hackett, 2003), 113.

8. Vladimir Ilyich Lenin, *Collected Works*, Vol. 18 (Moscow: Progress Publishers, 1975), 18:25–31.

9. Engels, *Ludwig Feuerbach and the End of Classical German Philosophy* [Need Page Number (in 'Part I: Hegel')].

10. See Jacques d' Hondt, *Hegel in His Time* (Lewiston, NY: Broadview, 1995), 29.

11. Hegel, *Philosophy of Right*, 160–1.

12. Robert M. Bigler, *The Politics of German Protestantism: The Rise of the Protestant Church Elite in Prussia, 1815–1848* (Berkeley: University of California Press, 1972), 188.

13. Ibid., 82.

14. John Edward Toews, *Hegelianism: The Path toward Dialectical Humanism, 1805–1841* (Cambridge: Cambridge University Press, 1985), 90ff.

15. Bauer Bauer, "Lebenslauf," in *Bruno Bauer: Studien Und Materialien*, ed. Ernst Barnikol. Assen: Van Gorcum, 1972. Cited in Harold E. Mah, *The End of Philosophy, the Origin of "Ideology": Karl Marx and the Crisis of the Young Hegelians* (Berkeley: University of California Press, 1987), 46.

16. Cited in Toews, *Hegelianism: The Path toward Dialectical Humanism, 1805–1841*, 91.

17. Terry Pinkard, *Hegel: A Biography* (Cambridge: Cambridge University Press, 2001), 660.

18. Mah, *The End of Philosophy, the Origin of tantismrm,*" 48.

19. Ludwig Feuerbach, *Thoughts on Death and Immortality*, trans. James A. Massey (Berkeley: University of California Press, 1981) [Feuerbach, Gedanken Uber Tod Und Unsterblichkeit.].

20. Feuerbach, *Thoughts on Death and Immortality*, xxi.

21. Hegel, *Lectures on the History of Philosophy*, Volume 1, 55.

22. Georg Wilhelm Friedrich Hegel, *Lectures on the History of Philosophy, Volume 3*, trans. E. S. Haldane (Lincoln, NE: University of Nebraska, 1995), 553.

23. Rudolf Haym, *Hegel Und Seine Zeit* (Berlin: Rudolph Gaertner, 1857), 4.

24. Feuerbach, *Principles of the Philosophy of the Future*. Trans. Manfred Vogel (Indianapolis, IN, Hackett Classics, 1986).

25. See Stefano Franchi, "Telos and Terminus: Hegel and the End of Philosophy," *Idealistic Studies* 28, no. 1/2 (1998): 35–46.

26. See Bigler, *The Politics of German Protestantism*, 122.

27. Ibid., 80. Cited in Löwith, *From Hegel to Nietzsche*, 58.
28. Toews, *Hegelianism: The Path toward Dialectical Humanism, 1805–1841*, 204.
29. Löwith, *From Hegel to Nietzsche*, 51.
30. Bigler, *The Politics of German Protestantism*, 79.
31. Pinkard, *Hegel: A Biography*, 268.
32. Friedrich Wilhelm Joseph von Schelling, *Erste Vorlesung in Berlin. 15. November 1841* (Stuttgart: Cotta, 1841), 20.
33. Søren Kierkegaard, *Journals and Papers*. Vol. 5 (Indianapolis: Indiana University Press, 1978); Søren Kierkegaard, *Søren Kierkegaards Skrifter*, ed. Niels-Jorgen Cappelorn. Vol. 19 (Copenhagen: Gad, 1997), 19:235.
34. Kierkegaard, *Journals and Papers*, 5:201.
35. Hegel, *The Difference between Fichte erence persBerlin. 15. November 1841E*, 99–100.
36. Friedrich Engels, *Ludwig Feuerbach and the End of Classical German Philosophy*. Moscow: Progress Publishers, 1946 [Need Page Number (in 'Part I: Hegel')].
37. Löwith, *From Hegel to Nietzsche*, 64.
38. Sidney Hook, *From Hegel to Marx* (Ann Arbor: University of Michigan Press, 1962), 173.
39. Max Stirner, *The Ego and Its Own*, ed. David Stirner, trans. Steven Tracy Byington (Cambridge, England; New York: Cambridge University Press, 1995), 5.
40. Karl Marx, *Capital* (London: Penguin, 1976), 103.
41. Deleuze, *Nietzsche et la philosophie*, 184–87.

Chapter 2

Stirner as Hegelian

I am the creative nothing [das schferiche Nichts],
the nothing out of which I myself as creator create everything.

Johann Caspar Schmidt, who later wrote under the pseudonym of Max Stirner, was born in Bayreuth, on October 25, 1806. Less than two weeks earlier, Hegel had sent the final draft of his Phenomenology to a publisher.

We have no clear image of Stirner's appearance, and his biographers can only rely upon the two rough sketches drawn by his one-time friend, Frederick Engels. Equally, there is also no complete or clear image of Stirner's life. His only biographer, the minor poet and novelist, John Henry Mackay (1864–1933) had chanced upon Stirner's name, which was mentioned in Langes' History of Materialism. Upon reading Stirner's work, Mackay immediately became Stirner's devoted admirer and set about writing a biography of his hero. Mackay's poetic inclinations often took precedence over his study, and although he lived close enough to the time of Stirner to interview those who had known Stirner, his work often veered off into being an undocumented hagiography rather than a documented biography.[1] The Mackay biography is not quite, as Hans G. Helms wrote, "about the worst ever written," it nevertheless contains a great deal of significant information about Stirner that would otherwise be lost. In any case, it is enough to come to a firm history of his life. Overall, he led an obscure and quite pathetic life, darkened by a series of pathetic events, and had he not written *The Ego and His Own*, he would hardly deserve a footnote in any history of the period.[2] But as this singular work alone has exercised such a deadly and corrosive effect upon all of the theories and programs of Hegel's first followers, it alone has ensured his presence in any history of philosophy.

Figure 2.1 Max Stirner. Drawn from memory, Federick Engels, London, 1892.

In the first year of his life, his natural father, Johann Schmidt, died. Stirner's mother soon remarried a middle-aged Pharmacist, Heinrich Ballerstedt. Shortly after her re-marriage, the young mother and her son moved to his home in the small city of Kulm, on the Vistula, far from their first home and family in Bayreuth. The young mother, perhaps grieving over the deaths of her first husband, the loss of her own home, and the death of her young daughter, drifted slowly into insanity, which lasted the rest of her life. She died, hospitalized, in Berlin in 1859, three years after the death of her son. Alone, with a mother whose mind might have been exhibiting the early signs of her insanity, and an aging step-father, his early life could not have been a happy one.

In 1818, when he was twelve years old, he was sent back to Bayreuth to live with his uncle. Why he was sent away from Kulm to return to his first home is unknown, but the next eight years of Johann's life was spent in Bayreuth. During this time, it seems likely that he might have first encountered

Hegelianism during his school years at the prestigious Imhof Gymnasium in Bayreuth, where he was recognized as an excellent student. George Andreas Gabler was then its Rector, the same Gabler who finally assumed the chair of philosophy at the University of Berlin that was vacated upon Hegel's death. Johann proved to be an excellent student and graduated from the Gymnasium in 1826 with a high grade. While at the Gymnasium he received the nickname "Max Stirner, likely by reason of his high forehead [Stirn]—it has also been taken to mean, rather fittingly, that he was a "highbrow."

Directly upon graduation from the Bayreuth Gymnasium, he enrolled at the University of Berlin as a student of Philosophy, and not Theology, as was the case with Bauer, Feuerbach, and many other of the "Young Hegelians." His biographer, Mackay, summed up these first years:

> Schmidt studied in the first of his four semesters in Berlin: Logic with Heinrich Ritter, the philosopher known by his independent historical-philosophical research; General Geography with the philosopher's namesake, the great geographer Carl Ritter; and Pindar and Metrics with Bockh, the famous rhetorician and researcher of antiquity. His second semester was dedicated to philosophy: Ethics with Schleiermacher, the "greatest German theologian of the century," and above all Philosophy of Religion with Hegel-with Hegel, whose tremendous, then still unbroken, influence on the whole thinking of that time was such that we today can hardly have any kind of correct concept of it. In the next winter semester Schmidt went to further lectures: he heard History of Philosophy and Psychology, and Anthropology or Philosophy of the Spirit with the same admired man. Besides that, he 37 again attended the lectures of Bockh and Carl Ritter: the former on Greek Antiquity, the latter on Geography of ancient Greece and Italy. And, so as not to neglect his theological studies, he heard Marheineke, the orthodox teacher of the Hegelian right, on Dogmatics and on the significance of the new philosophy in theology. Likewise in the last, the fourth semester, theology came first: Neander, the church historian and opponent of Strauss, taught Church History and Christian Antiquity; Marheineke taught the Theological Encyclopedia and Church Symbolism. Thus the industrious student attended up to 22 lectures a week, and in just four semesters in Berlin he must have laid a firm foundation for his later knowledge.[3]

It is not recorded that his response to these lectures was as enthusiastic as those of Wilhelm Vatke, who saw "God face to face" when Hegel lectured, or Bauer being mesmerized by them, but it might have well been the case. Certainly, his response to Hegel's lectures on the Philosophy of Mind definitively determined the course of his mature thought.

In the fall of 1828, Stirner was forced to leave the University of Berlin to study at the University of Erlangen, where he could live with relatives. In that fall semester Stirner attended the lectures then being presented by the Hegelian philosopher Christian Kapp. After three years, time mostly spent in Kulm caring for his Mother; he returned once again to Berlin, where he would spend the rest of his life. In Berlin he continued his philosophical studies, among them a two-semester course on Aristotle conducted by the Hegelian philosopher Karl L. Michelet (1801–1893). In 1842, two years prior to the publication of *The Ego*, he attended a class taught by Karl Werder on Hegel's Logic. It was an extraordinary class, which had such as Frederich Engels, Michael Bakunin, Soren Kierkegaard, and Ivan Turgenev—and perhaps August von Cieszkowski—as its members.[4]

Stirner was not an unknown among them, as Engels, then Stirner's close friend ("düzbruder") recalled that they had discussed Hegelian dialectic on many occasions.

> We discussed a great deal concerning Hegel's philosophy, and at that time he had made the discovery that Hegel's Logic began with an error: Being [*Sein*], which proved itself as Nothing [*Nichts*], and so set itself in opposition to itself, could not be the beginning; the beginning must be something that is in itself the immediate, the naturally given unity of Being and Nothing out of which the first contradiction develops. According to Stirner this was "It [*Es*]" (it snows, it rains), something that is and is also yet Nothing. Yet, afterwards he seemed to come to the conclusion that the "It" was, in fact, just as much nothing as Being and Nothing.

A few lines after this recollection of their mutual interests, Engels noted:

> Stirner has experienced a rebirth through Bakunin, who was also in Berlin at that time, and sat before me with four or five Russians in a row attending Werder's logic class (1841/42). The harmless, merely etymological Anarchy (i.e., the absence of a state power) of Proudhon could never have led to the anarchistic doctrines of the present, had not Bakunin assimilated a good part of Stirner's "uprising" [*Emporung*]—so unique that no two of them can tolerate the other.[5]

That Stirner and Engels, along with Bakunin, would have attended Werder's class seems to be the case. All seemed to have shared, in a greater or lesser degree Werder's own view—that "Nothing," absolute negation, was the fundamental ground of Hegelian Logic.

It can be said that Stirner's formal acquaintance with Hegelian philosophy was much more extensive than that obtained by any of the Young Hegelians, and it was informally advanced among the radical non-academic circles which gathered in Berlin during the 1840s—among whom Hegel's philosophy was always favorite discussion topic. On the point of Stirner's understanding of Hegel, R. W. K. Paterson observes in an otherwise critical study that he displayed a

> detailed familiarity with the crucial philosophical literature of the day. From the internal evidence of Der Einzige, it is clear that he was conversant with Hegel's Phenomenology of Mind, with his Encyclopedia of the Philosophical Sciences, his Philosophy of Right, and his published lectures on the philosophy of History. . . . From the works directly cited or discernibly used in the writing of Der Einzige alone, it is indisputable that Stirner had prepared himself for his comprehensive evaluation of existing German ideology by massive researches into the distinctive complexion of the major philosophical coalitions of the day."[6]

Stirner, always frail, was a bit ill while taking the examination for a teaching certificate, and in 1834, after seeing to it that his mother was placed in Berlin's Charitie Hospital, Stirner finally had some time to prepare for a licencia docente, which, the equivalent of a Doctorate, would allow him to teach at the university level. Always frail, and a bit ill while taking the examination for the examination, his bad luck continued. As it happened, his examiner was Adolph Trendelenberg (1802–1872), a famed Aristotelean logician and a persistent and dedicated opponent of Hegel's logic. Not unexpectedly Stirner failed the examination, being judged deficient in the science of logic—that logic being Aristotelean rather than Hegelian. Consequently, he only was able to obtain a limited licencia docente, which forced him for the next year to serve as an unpaid teacher. But even after this year of teaching internship in the Berlin Konigliche Realschule, he was still unable to obtain any salaried teaching position. In the winter of 1837, whether out of need, or love, or both, he married his landlady's daughter, Kunigunde Burtz. Unhappily, his young wife died in childbirth, along with the infant. In 1839, he finally found a paid teaching position in Berlin—at a certain Madame Gropius' school for wealthy girls. He held the post for the next five years, until late 1844, when *The Ego* was published. During these years he became a frequent visitor to a well-known gathering place for the "Vormarz" radicals, Hippel's Weinstube on Friedrchstrasse.[7] Among the publicists, politicians, academics, and other liberal groups who gathered to protest the conservative grip upon both Church and State were many Young Hegelians, who proudly named themselves as "The Free Ones [Die Freien]." Bruno Bauer was the nominal leader of the informal group, who, along with his brother Edgar, more or less presided over the usual weekly gatherings. The publicist Arnold Ruge, known for provoking arguments which were often as noisy and inconclusive as they were bitter, seemed always in attendance.

Among the "regulars" at these meetings were Friedrich Köppen, Dr. Arthur Muller, Moses Hess, Ludwig Buhl, Adolf Rutenberg, Eduard Meyen, Julius Faucher, and Frederick Engels—his close friend at the time. Occasional visitors included the poets Herwegh and Hoffman von Fallersleben, as well as Ludwig Feuerbach and the radical anti-Christian writer, Wilhelm Jordon. Engels had some small talent for sketching, and one of his rough depictions of a disputation initiated by Arnold Ruge has survived. It is one of the two images we have of Stirner, both by Engels. In this one, a quiet observer of the noisy scene stands apart, smoking a cigarette. It is Stirner. In 1842, Stirner wrote a small article defining and defending the "Die Freien."[8]

Prior to the appearance of *The Ego*, Stirner was a minor figure among Berlin's radical Young Hegelians. He had, since 1841, written a number of small and generally unimpressive articles and reviews, most of which appeared in the short-lived Rheinische Zeitung, a newspaper now remembered only by reason of Marx's tenure as its editor. Stirner's obscure status at the time found a brief illustration as he was mentioned in Engel's mock-epic poem of 1842, Der Triumph des Glaubens. The poem was written to mark Bruno Bauer's return that year to Berlin after having lost his licentia docendi at Bonn by reason of his atheism. It affords an interesting glimpse, through the eyes of young Engels, of Berlin's "Free Ones." In the strained exuberance of over 700 heroic couplets, most of which celebrate Bauer, Stirner receives mention in ten lines, even less than that accorded such forgotten "Freien" as Friedrich Köppen and Eduard Meyen.

Look at Stirner, look at him, the peaceful enemy of all constraint.
For the moment, he is still drinking beer,
Soon he will be drinking blood as though it were water.
When others cry savagely "down with the kings"
Stirner immediately supplements "down with the laws also."
Stirner full of dignity proclaims; You bend your willpower
   and you dare to call yourselves free.
You become accustomed to slavery Down with dogmatism, down with law.[9]

Engels, who was then a close personal friend, a Duzbrüder of Stirner, later noted that he "had obviously, among the 'Free Ones' the most talent, independence, and diligence."[10] Later, Engels, after Marx had died, recalled that Stirner was "a good fellow, far from being so bad as he made himself out to be in his Einzigen."[11] As to how Stirner considered the "Free Ones," his letter defending their activities appears in the Addenda to this work.

During his time as one of the "Free Ones," Stirner met and married Marie Dähnhardt (1818–1902), to whom he dedicated *The Ego*. She later gained recognition as an early leader in the woman's suffrage movement. Maria had received a small inheritance upon the death of her father, but within three years they had separated and her money had gone. Stirner had ineptly squandered her inheritance to set up a small milk delivery business, which immediately failed. This loss became a bit of a joke among his colleagues. And so it was, that ironically, he was not, despite his later translations of Adam Smith and J. B. Say, much of a capitalist entrepreneur. For that matter, Marx, despite that he had never worked for a wage during his lifetime, became the revered leader of the working class.

In November 1844, Stirner's major work made its appearance. *The Ego and Its Own* has always been a work that might be described as an "enigmatic curiosity"—as a repellent to some as it is attractive to others. This was so even before it appeared in the bookstores of Berlin. As it had been published in early November 1844 by Otto Wigand, the Leipzig publisher known for his daring sponsorship of such radical works as Feuerbach's Essence of Christianity, Stirner's work was to be examined by Prussian censors before its distribution. Prepared to defend both public morals and political stability, the regional director of the Prussian censorship bureau in Leipzig set about putting a stop to any clandestine distribution of *The Ego*. However, the director had only managed to gather up 250 copies of the one thousand published copies before his decision to review the work was overruled. Two days after he had started his task, in early November 1844, the censor was suddenly informed by the Saxon Minister of the Interior that the book was simply "too absurd" to be hindered from distribution. The grounds for his rather unexpected decision were to be made public—but never were. And so, *The Ego* was distributed without any further official difficulties. Stirner's biographer, Mackay, suggests that Stirner had "tricked" the state by presenting his thought as "absurd" and so "whereas the most harmless scribbling was outlawed, he most radical and "most dangerous" book of that and all time was allowed to go unhindered from hand to hand—then and still today."[12] Doubtless, there are, then and still today, those who would agree with the Interior Minister that the book is indeed "too absurd." Restoration Marxists, such as György Lukács, Jacques Derrida, and Jürgen Habermas, repeatedly employ the term "absurd" when treating of Stirner's work. Lukacs, in *The Destruction of Reason*, writes of the Hegelian tendency to abstraction, which "reaches its climax which tilts over into the absurdly paradoxical with Stirner,"[13] and Habermas writes of the "absurdity of Stirner's fury." On variant Marxist readings of Stirner, see *Bernd A. Laska: Max Stirner Ein dauerhafter Dissident.*[14] Modern restoration Marxists, just as the restored Bourbon Monarchists, seem to have "learned nothing and forgotten nothing."

It might be mentioned that the most available recent English edition of The German Ideology has continued the Marxian tradition of ignoring this section of the work. The 700 or so page manuscript was reduced to 212 pages by simply eliminating the section dealing with Stirner.[15] A case in point regarding traumatic Marxian memory loss when it comes to Stirner would be Cesare Luporini's 1977 Italian translation of The German Ideology. [L'ideologia tedlesca] Although Stirner is the constant subject of over 300 pages of criticism, Luporini, in his seventy-nine-page "Introduction," somehow manages to mention Stirner less than a dozen times—and then but briefly.

The Ego was well-received among Stirner's acquaintances, with Arnold Ruge, who once was Marx's editorial associate, in the Deutsch-Fransocsis er Jahnbook (a brief association that ended in a long bitterness) wrote that the work was "a good criticism of Communism."[16] Shortly after, in a letter to his mother, he commented that the book was "the most readable work on philosophy that had ever been written in Germany."[17] Anyone familiar with nineteenth-century German philosophical writings might well agree with Ruge. As one recent commentator has it, "Almost every feature of his writing seems calculated to unnerve"[18]—and it certainly continues to do so. The book was widely reviewed and attracted attention from such leading figures as Bettina von Arnim (1785–1859), the doyenne of the Berlin literati, and Kuno Fischer (1824–1907), later a distinguished neo-Kantian historian of philosophy. The book also generated responses from many of its left-Hegelian, targets such as Bruno Bauer, Ludwig Feuerbach, and Moses Hess, all of whom ventured into print in order to defend their own views against Stirner's polemic. The book, however, was neither a popular nor a financial success, and any hopes that it would generate some royalties soon faded. It would be almost forty years after his death, in 1882, that a second edition unexpectedly appeared. It has since never been out of print. Stirner had left his teaching post shortly before the book was published. By 1846, having exhausted much of his second wife's inheritance, his life spiraled down into deeper poverty, marked by social isolation and financial precariousness. He remained detached from contemporary events—he seems, for example, to have largely ignored the revolution of 1848—and his daily life was one of routine and economic hardship. Stirner continued to write intermittently, but commentators have generally found his later work to be of little independent interest (i.e., apart from its uncertain potential to illuminate *The Ego and His Own*). He translated into German some of the economic writings of Jean-Baptiste Say (1767–1832) and Adam Smith (1723–1790) and wrote a series of short journalistic pieces for the *Journal des oesterreichischen Lloyd*, *Rheinische Zeitung*, and the *Leipziger Allgemeine Zeitung*. Some of his essays were published and have been translated, such as his *Das unwahre Princip unserer Erziehung* [The False Principle of our Education] and *Kunst und Religion* (Art and Religion). None, however, display the literary power and intent of his Eingige. In 1852, he contributed some material to a History of Reaction,[19] which mainly consisted of excerpts from other authors, including Edmund Burke (1729–1797). Stirner's main strategy for economic survival in this period seems to have involved changing addresses in order to evade his creditors, although he does not appear to have moved quickly enough to avoid two brief periods in a debtors' prison in 1853 and 1854. It was no time to be poor in Berlin, which had its full share of unemployment, overpopulation, homelessness, and poverty. Marx, who also suffered in London, even though it is possible that Stirner had died of starvation. He did not, but given the dreadful living conditions at the time, it was not inconceivable.[20]

In May 1856, still living in reduced circumstances in Berlin, Stirner fell into a "nervous fever," possibly after being stung in the neck by a Wasp or other insect. Following a brief remission, he died on June 25. Having neither money, nor reputation, nor position, he died as he lived—without notice. His funeral, in 1856, was attended by only two of his old friends, Adoph Rutenburg and Bruno Bauer. His friends had gathered enough money to purchase a second-class grave for him, which cost only a few dollars, a burial more pathetic than sad. But it time, as his work began to be noticed and appreciated, his grave in Berlin's Sophenkirkhof was marked with an impressive marble plaque—which happened to be very close to Marx's memorial, the "Berlin Wall." At his death, his mother still lived as a patient in Berlin's Charitie Hospital. Whatever inheritance she might have had from her late husband was received by the state at her death. Her son had always tended to his mother during her long mental illness, and his delay in taking his doctoral examination was likely due to the time needed to bring his mother to Berlin for medical care—actions hardly to be expected from a "nihilistic egoist."

There is a stark contrast between the often dramatic of Stirner's best-known work, on the one hand, and, on the other, the rather less sensational and more muted events of his personal life. On this, his biographer, John Henry Mackay, emphasized the "ataraxic" dimension of *The Ego* as the authentic embodiment of the emotional detachment required by the egoist to avoid being enslaved by his own passions and commitment.

The Ego has a singular and rather simple theme: that the modern replacement of "God" with "Humanity" was nothing more than a bit of dialectical sleight-of-hand, generating a new human God even more inhuman than the old:

> one thing certainly happened, and visibly guided the progress of post-Christian history: this one thing was the endeavor to make the Holy Spirit more human, and bring it nearer to men, or men to it. Through this it came about that at last it could be conceived as the "spirit of humanity," and, under different expressions

like "idea of humanity, mankind, humaneness, general philanthropy," appeared more attractive, more familiar, and more accessible.[21]

Modern readers hoping to understand *The Ego* are confronted by several obstacles, not least the form, structure, and argument, all of which make it difficult to read, if not to understand, Stirner's book. It is crowded with aphorisms, emphases, hyperbole, and neologisms, and the logic which leads to his conclusions is often unlike the conventional form, as he often approaches a claim that he wishes to endorse by exploiting words with related etymologies or formal similarities. For example, he associates words for the property (such as "Eigentum") with words connoting distinctive individual characteristics (such as "Eigenheit"), which promotes the Hegelian claim that property is expressive of personality. The rejection of conventional forms of intellectual discussion is linked to Stirner's own Hegelian understanding of the congruency of language and rationality. Some are not pleased by his style, as George Santayana, who in the heat of pre-WWI anti-German sentiment, held that Stirner's work was but

> A bold, frank, and rather tiresome protest against the folly of moral idealism, against the sacrifice of the individual to any ghostly powers such as God, duty, the state, humanity, or society; all of which this redoubtable critic called "spooks" and regarded as fixed ideas and pathological obsessions.[22]

Others, such as the American literary critic, James Huneker, held *The Ego* to be "compulsively readable."[23] He was more than seconded by the American individualist, James L. Walker, who admired Stirner at the expense of Nietzsche: "In style Stirner's work offers the greatest possible contrast to the puerile, padded phraseology of Nietszche's Zarathustra and its false imagery."[24] The earliest remark upon this style was made by Arnold Ruge, Marx's passing associate, who declared that Stirner was responsible for "the first readable book in philosophy that Germany has produced."[25] His judgment is perhaps too generous, but there has been little doubt as to Stirner's mastery of language.

His unusual style reflects the conviction that the fluid mental acts of logic and thought, once willfully fixed, are transformed into the permanent dictatorial tyrants of their own creators. In this, he is in agreement with Hegel and Heraclitus, both of whom hold the priority of Becoming over Being. It is only the fixed thoughts and dogmas generated in the minds of individuals which sustain the traditional standards religion and government, and these standards are ultimately grounded in the idea that there is somewhere an absolute truth, a "divine" truth, existing beyond the mind of the individual who has created that idea. This conception of an unrealizable absolute and eternal truth makes its first appearance in Hegel's Phenomenology of Mind—it is the creation of the "unhappy consciousness." It is the dialectical resultant of the Stoic consciousness, which finds its solace only in its withdrawal from reality. This unhappiness reappears in the modern obsession as some form of social or political "alienation," salvation from which requires a revolution. Only after this will come some form of heavenly future in which the "truth" and the "real" will be finally realized. But for Stirner, a "revolution" was just that—a re-cycling of what was given either politically or socially, the results having little to do with individual needs. The release from the unhappy consciousness requires a radical personal revolution, an insurrection, a "standing up" for oneself—Egoism.

> Revolution and insurrection [Empörung] must not be looked upon as synonymous. The former consists in an overturning of conditions, of the established condition or status, the state or society, and is accordingly a political or social act; the latter has indeed for its unavoidable consequence a transformation of circumstances, yet does not start from it but from men's discontent with themselves, is not an armed rising, but a rising of individuals, a getting up, without regard to the arrangements that spring from it. The Revolution aimed at new arrangements; insurrection leads us no longer to let ourselves be arranged, but to arrange ourselves, and sets no glittering hopes on "institutions." It is not a fight against the established, since, if it prospers, the established collapses of itself; it is only a working forth of me out of the established. If I leave the established, it is dead and passes into decay. Now, as my object is not the overthrow of an established order but my elevation above it, my purpose and deed are not a political or social but (as directed toward myself and my ownness alone) an egoistic purpose and deed.
>
> The revolution commands one to make arrangements, the insurrection [Empörung] demands that he rise or exalt himself [empor-, aufrichten]. What constitution was to be chosen, this question busied the revolutionary heads, and the whole political period foams with constitutional fights and constitutional questions, as the social talents too were uncommonly inventive in societary arrangements (phalansteries and the like). The insurgent strives to become constitutionless.[26]

In 1827, his first year at the University of Berlin, Stirner heard Hegel lectures on the Philosophy of Mind.[27] The experience of hearing these lectures had a deep and lasting effect upon the intellectual formation of young Stirner. Although he had attended Hegel's lectures on the Philosophy of Religion and the History of Philosophy, it was the lectures on the Philosophy of Mind upon which almost all of the concepts which determine the nature of Stirner's singular work *The Ego and His Own* can be found. In these lectures the young student was introduced to the famous dialectic earlier formed in Hegel's Phenomenology of Spirit, that which held between Master and Slave [Herrschaft und Knechtschaft]" The description of the struggle for recognition which established the division between the two, between Lord and Serf, would find expression in the struggle that Stirner envisioned occurred between the "Owner" and the "Owned," between himself as a unique Ego, the Einzige, and his expression, his property, his world, his Eignentum.[28] The outcome of this battle determines who will either rise to freedom and mastery and be the owner or those who will be enslaved. This primal struggle to gain recognition and freedom is central to the understanding of Hegel,[29] and it formulates the whole of Stirner's view of individual and social history. It is, for the combatants, a life-threatening encounter, a "life and death struggle: either self-consciousness imperils the other's life, and incurs a like peril for its own."[30] Stirner, who as a youth, had experienced the battle, understood it well, and agreed with Hegel. It was a battle in which one could only be defeated or victorious—"Victory or defeat—between the two alternatives the fate of the combat wavers. [Siegen oder Unterliegen—zwischen beiden Wechselfällen schwankt das Kampfgeschick.] For Hegel the struggle was resolved in the rising consciousness of the stoic mind, an inward acceptance, an "atarxia" and in this Stirner followed Hegel. Stoicism was a necessary stage marking the emergence of the individual from the struggle, but the stoic shape of consciousness will give way to the skeptical mind, which then advances to the unstable "unhappy consciousness [unglückliches Bewusstsein]" of the religious mind. It is only after this unhappy shape of consciousness is overcome by reason that absolute self-affirmation is reached. Stirner restated the Hegelian pattern of the battle throughout *The Ego*, and the deadly struggle between the Master and Servant will find its expression not only on the level of the individual but within the total social and cultural world as well:

> Political liberalism abolished the inequality of masters and servants: it made people masterless, anarchic. The master was now removed from the individual, the "egoist," to become a ghost—the law or the state. Social liberalism abolishes the inequality of possession, of the poor and rich, and makes people possessionless or propertyles. . . . But, since the master rises again as state the servants appears again as subject [aber der Herr als Staat wieder aufersteht so erscheint der Diener als Untertan wieder].[31]

As Hegel once confessed to being the spiritual son of Goethe, it is appropriate for Stirner to use a line from Goethe to both begin and to end his book: "Ich hab' mein' Sach' auf Nichts gestellt,"[32] which translates into "I have set my cause upon nothing." We can now say that it is more than a bit of literary decoration, for it encapsulates the view of both Hegel and Stirner in regard to the fundamental nature of pure subjectivity. The opening lines of *The Ego* are directly followed by a brief and striking prefatory declaration of his egoism, in which all "causes" [Sache] other than those given toward his own self-interest, are rejected. From this point, the book immediately proceeds to its first chapter, A Human Life [Ein Menschenleben], and with this the central theme of *The Ego* is set out. It is telling that at the very onset of "A Human Life" there is a passage which cannot but be taken as autobiographical. It reflects Stirner's own experience, but can lend itself to the human struggle for individual freedom:

> Behind the rod, mightier than it, stands our—obduracy, our obdurate courage. By degrees we get at what is back of everything that was mysterious and uncanny to us, the mysteriously-dreaded might of the rod, the father's stern look, etc., and back of all we find our ataraxia—our imperturbability, intrepidity, our counter forces, our odds of strength, our invincibility. Before that which formerly inspired in us fear and deference we no longer retreat shyly, but take courage. Back of everything we find our courage, our superiority; back of the sharp command of parents and authorities stands, after all, our courageous choice or our outwitting shrewdness. And the more we feel ourselves, the smaller appears that which before seemed invincible. And what is our trickery, shrewdness, courage, obduracy? What else but—mind ! [Geist]

If one seeks the emotional ground upon which found later expression throughout Stirner's works, it is in this statement. It is his stoic "ataraxia," his stoic response to the "mysteriously dreaded might of the rod"—for "the more we feel ourselves, the smaller appears that which before seemed invincible." The egoist Stirner had come to himself—and he was never intimidated by either the Old or the New God.

The first chapter of *The Ego* can only be understood by seeing the hand of Hegel in its creation, as both share the same quadratic pattern; There are four distinct ages in the course of human life: childhood (Kinde), adolescence (Jüngling), maturity (Mann), and old age (Greis), and each age will manifest a clear and specific attitude toward the relationship between the individual and their world. Hegel and Stirner not only agree to the same quadratic pattern but even as to the way which each age will look upon the world in which they live. Stirner's Menchenleben is the mirror of Hegel's "der natürliche Verlauf der Lebensalter"—the natural course of individual history.

For both, the first stage of human life begins with the consciousness of the child, an age of innocent inner peace, a period of acceptance and unreflective activity. Hegel described the mind of a child as "mind wrapped up in itself" ["in sich eigehüllten Geiste"] and "a time of natural harmony." Stirner restates this:

The fairest part of childhood passes without the necessity of coming to blows with reason . . . and we are deaf to good arguments and principles.[Die schönste Kindheit geh vorüber, ohne daß Wir nötig hätten, Uns mit der Vernunft herumzuschlagen . . . und gegen die guten Gründe, Grundsätze, u.s.w. sind Wir taub.].allem finder Wir Unsere—Ataraxie]

For Stirner, the first threat to the mind of the child is cast in the form of a concrete physical enemy—a form that demands obedience under the threat of physical punishment. It is only after this enemy is overcome by the stubbornness of the child [its Trotz or Eigensinn] that the emergence of the stoic consciousness takes place. This consciousness is marked by the Stoic Ataraxia, which no longer cares for the threats or promises of the physical world. It has overcome the world—for "back of all we find our ataraxia—our imperturbability, intrepidity, our counter forces, our odds of strength, our invincibility."

The first stages of the Slave's [Knecht] development of self-consciousness are found in the slave's (or child's) display of reluctance, an obstinacy, toward fulfilling the commands of the Master [Herr]. The passage from childhood to maturity and freedom, as given in either Hegel's Lebenslauf or Stirner's Ein Menschenleben is first manifested in childish obstinacy [Trotz], which is merely resistant to the threats of the other, now finds itself confronted by another thereat, this born in its own mind—the abstract ideals of the adolescent mind. It suffers under, as Hegel understands it, the domination of "Ideals, Imaginations, Oughts, Hopes, etc." [Ideale, Einbildungen, Sollen, Hoffnungen, u.s.f.]. In short, for Stirner, just as Hegel, the end of childhood brings forth another, and even more powerful, enemy than the physical—abstract "Ideals."

In Stirner's "Ein Menchenleben" this might be said to be the first movement of consciousness that rises up against the "gefürchtete Macht der Rute, der strengen Meine des Vaters." This first movement is to be seen in the child's obstinacy [Trotz]. Hegel understands the slave's stubborness [Eigensinn] as a "freedom, which still remains placed within slavery" ["ein Freiheit, welche noch innerhalb der Knechtschaft stehen bleibt."]. This obstinacy or stubbornness is not independence, but it does prefigure the coming of the stoic mind. When this stage is reached, there is a consciousness of one's freedom from physical determination, an Ataraxia which is merely the subjective mind knowing itself not to be of the physical world. The refusal to obey parental authority [Herrschaft] signals the coming of the adolescent mind. Developed Stoicism is only the consciousness of one's freedom from all physical coercions; it is a negative freedom, a freedom from an actual encounter with the corporeal world. The identity of the child with the sensuous world has been lost, and a new world of mind has been obtained. However, it only the beginning of the path that consciousness must take on its journey to realized freedom. It must first pass over into skepticism and then into the "Das unglückliche Bewusstsein." It is only after this final and tormented "shape of consciousness" is negated and transcended (aufgehoben) that the freedom of reason will be realized. I would propose that this long phenomenological passage, Hegel's "highway of despair and path of doubt" was followed to its final conclusion by Stirner. But whether or not this passage from childhood to adolescence, as given in Hegel's Lebenslauf or in Stirner's "Ein Menschenleben" is or is not accomplished with a struggle, it arrives at a new threat to conscious freedom. This new threat is expressed, as Hegel understands it, as the domination of "Ideals, Imaginations, Oughts, Hopes, etc." [Ideale, Einbildungen, Sollen, Hoffnungen, u.s.f.]" In short, for Stirner, just as Hegel, the end of childhood brings forth yet another, and more powerful, enemy than the physical—abstract "Ideals." And so,

> As in childhood one had to overcome the resistance of the laws of the world, so now in everything that he proposes he is met by an objection of the mind, of reason, of his own conscience. [Hätte man in der Kindheit den Widerstand der Weltgesetze zu bewältigen, so stößt man nun bei allem, was man vorhat, auf eine Einrede des Geistes, der Vernunft, des eignene Gewissens.][33]

Both stoic and adolescent are locked in a world of their own making, in a world created when a painful physical reality has been rejected. But then it follows that these "free" thoughts turn themselves against the very mind which gave them birth. They alienate themselves from the mind which produced them and set themselves in opposition to that mind. (The theme of estrangement [Entfremdung] is not uncommon among the Young Hegelians.) Henceforth, as Stirner notes, "Our course of action is determined by our thoughts (ideas, conceptions, faith) as it is in childhood by the commands of our parents" [Unser Thaten richten sich nach Unsern Gedanken (Ideen, Vorstelllungen, Glauben), wie in der Kindheit nach den Befehlen der Eltern"]. However, in this very overcoming, in which the stoic is cast back into their own thoughts of the world, abstract thought becomes the new reality—thoughts which are necessarily opposed to the actuality of the physical world. The stoic consciousness plays the same role in the historical passage from slavery to final reason and freedom that the young adolescent plays in the phenomenological passage to maturity.

Just as the stoic, the adolescent consciousness rejects the sensuous world in favor of the world of thought. From this rejection there naturally follows a critical attitude toward that rejected object-world of childhood. In short, the innocent Kind has developed into the critical and often rebellious Jüngling. Here are Stirner's words concerning the mind of the Jüngling:

Mind is the name of the first self-discovery, the first undeification of the divine; that is, of the uncanny, the spooks, the "powers above." Our fresh feeling of youth, this feeling of self, now defers to nothing; the world is discredited, for we are above it, we are mind. [Geist heißt die erste Selbstfindung, die erste Entgötterung des Göttlichen, d.h. des Unheimlichen, des Spuks, der 'obern Mächte.' Unserem frischen Jugendgefühl, diesem Selbstgefühl, imponiert nun nichts mehr: die Welt ist in Verruf erklärt, denn Wir sind über ihr, sind Geist.]

In Hegel's words:

> The content of the ideal imbues the youth with the feeling of the power to act; he therefore fancies himself called and qualified to transform the world, or at least to put the world back on the right path from which, so it seems to him, it has strayed.[34]

This "Jugendgefühl" as "Selbstgefühl" which places the youth from the standpoint of "the heavenly" forms a major basis of his critique of the Young Hegelian "praxis" as an adolescent project—a dangerous enthusiasm only to be understood as such by the mature individual.

For Stirner, as well as Hegel, the clearest expression of that adolescent "feeling of the power to act" that fancies itself able to "transform the world" could be found in lesser or greater degree within every radical revolutionary to be found in history, and Stirner perceived it most clearly among his contemporaries, the "Junghegelianer"—and they were young and inspired:

> To bring to light the pure thought, or to be of its party, is the delight of youth; and all the shapes of light in the world of thought, like truth, freedom, humanity, Man, illumine and inspire the youthful soul.[35]

Hegel shared Stirner's doubts as to the youth of his own time, particularly those whose revolutionary enthusiasm had been justified by the emotional addresses of Professor Fries during the 1818 Wartburg Festival. It was a prelude to the 1848 German Revolution, and Fries shallow doctrine was simply based upon "the brew and stew of the "heart, friendship, and inspiration." The excited students had been easily led by Fries to set their abstract ideals in opposition to the concrete demands of actual reality:

> At first (i.e. especially in youth) a man chafes at the
> idea of resolving on a particular social position, and looks
> upon this as a restriction on his universal character and as a
> necessity imposed on him purely ab extra. This is because his
> thinking is still of that abstract kind which refuses to move

beyond the universal and so never reaches the actual. It does
not realise that if the concept is to be determinate, it must
first of all advance into the distinction between the concept
and its real existence and thereby into determinacy and
particularity (see §7)—It is only thus that the concept can win
actuality and ethical objectivity.[36]

In short, abstract idealism must come to terms with actual reality, but for the youth this is but a welcome compromise, a descent into cynicism, for if you just compare a man with a youth, and see if he will not appear to you harder, less magnanimous, more selfish. Is he therefore worse? No, you say; he has only become more definite, or, as you also call it, more "practical." But the main point is this, that he makes himself more the center than does the youth, who is infatuated about other things, for example, God, fatherland, and so on.[37]

With Hegel, manhood emerges when the youth finally recognizes "his true relation to his environment, recognizing the objective necessity and reasonableness of the world as he finds it—a world no longer incomplete" ["zu dem wahrhaften Verhältniß, der Anerkennung der objectiven Nothwendigkeit und Vernüftigkeit der bereits vorhandenen, fertigen Welt"]. If, however, the youth does not accept the painful transition into the life of a philistine[38] and so "concern himself with details" the youth will fall into a "hypochondia," obsessive anxiety which can last a lifetime. This persistent mental illness and the absence of any specific political details in respect to their high ideals gave Stirner grounds for his criticism of the various Young Hegelian "programs"

Stirner's own statement of the distinction between the adolescent and the mature adult is clearly drawn from Hegel, and Stirner is in full agreement that:

The man is distinguished from the youth by the fact that he takes the world as
it is, instead of everywhere fancying it amiss and wanting to improve it, model
it after his ideal; in him the view that one must deal with the world according to
his interest not according to his ideals, becomes confirmed. [Den Mann scheidet
as vom Jünglinge, daß er die Welt nimmt, wie sie ist, statt sie überall im Argen
zu wähnen und verbessern, d. h. nach seinem Ideale modeln zu wollen; in ihm
befestigt sich die Ansicht, daß man mit der Welt nach seinem Interesse ver-
fahren müsse, nicht nach seinen Idealen.][39]

In Stirner, the dialectic by which this level is reached is fully Hegelian and triadic in character, which is evident in Stirner's development of "Ein Menchenleben." To state it, perhaps too concisely, it runs this way: the thoughtless child is innocently lost in the physical realities of the world, but in time passes into the antithesis of childhood, adolescence. This shape or form of consciousness discovers the realm of thought, ideas which had never occurred in childhood. Ideas are set, as ideals, against the actual physical world and are taken as realities—yet to be realized. Childhood and youth stand in antithetical opposition, but again, in time, the mature consciousness emerges. The "Man" comes into being, and this being is the synthetic moment of its prior stages. The mature individual was nothing less than the individual which became fully himself and recognizes "the objective necessity and reasonableness of the world as he finds it," Stirner adds that this is to take the world as his own property [Eignentum]:

My power is my property.
My power gives me property.
My power am I myself, and through it am I my property.[40]

In form, Stirner's dialectical development of individual self-consciousness is similar to Marx's own "scientific socialism" in which primitive Communism, private property, and Communism are the three historical stages of material progress. Not unexpectedly, Stirner's triad was rejected as but unscientific idealism.

For both Stirner and Hegel human maturity develops into a final closure with the death of the aged individual, the Gris. This final stage of life, as the fourth stage, seemingly violates the omnipresent triadic formulation, the fourth stage, that of the Gris, the "Old Man." For Hegel this final age is a time of withdrawn serenity and the ending and beginning of a new cycle. It was not lost on Stirner that Hegel ended his Lebensalter by placing the ages within a circle which opened and closed with the Gris would return to the kind: "The sequence of ages in man's life is thus rounded into a notationally [conceptually] determined totality of alternations generated which are produced by the process of the genus [Man] with the individual.[41] Human history would also close, and the cycle of its life would repeat itself—but at an other, dialectically determined, level. I would propose that Stirner, who modeled human history upon individual history would initiate a level that would transcend the Modern Age, perhaps the Post-modern age, which gives support for the Saul Newman's description of Stirner as a "proto-post modernist."

Although Stirner follows Hegel in considering old age, Greis, as the fourth and final stage of human life, he does not, as Hegel, give any description of that final age. He merely passes by the subject by remarking, in the final sentence of Ein Menschenleben "Finally, the old man? When I become one, there will still be time enough to speak of that." One cannot but wish that he had been allowed time to "speak of that." But even if there were enough time, would Stirner have spoken of that fourth age? Perhaps not, simply because it was the fourth age. After all, the Hegelian dialectic is a triad, as the old formula has it: thesis, antithesis, and synthesis. The triadic dialectic of Childhood, Adolescence, Manhood is almost too perfect to lost with the addition of a fourth age—so Mann must be the last level to discuss. I would suggest that the reason that Hegel did not avoid the quadratic pattern of "ein Lebenslauf," and so went on to discusses the Greis is to be found in his first description of that pattern as "der natürliche Verlauf der Lebensalter"—it is "natürliche" and not dialectical. The four-fold pattern is, for Hegel, a natural ordering, such as North-South-East-West, and although subject to the dialectic is distinct from the triadic dialectic in that its middle term, the antithesis, is divided into two opposing poles. The complex explanation which Hegel presents for a tetradic development within nature is set out in the Introduction to his Naturphilosophie. However, whether or not Hegel employs a triadic dialectical analysis upon "der natürliche Verlauf der Lebensalter," it seems that Stirner did. In any case, the triadic formulation infuses the whole of Stirner's work and gives it internal unity and cohesiveness without which, or without being recognized, makes the work "absurd."

The introductory triad of "Ein Menchenleben," Childhood—Adolescence—Maturity, is the paradigm upon which the whole of Der Einziger und Sein Eigenthum is grounded. That it expressed the total course of human history was noted by Karl Löwith, who contended that Stirner's book, "is in reality an ultimate logical consequence of Hegel's historical system, which—allegorically displaced—it reproduces exactly."[42]

Stirner recognized "the world as it is," and it would have to be "dealt with" in the light of his interests—not in the light of what Hegel termed adolescent "Ideals, imaginary reality, shoulds, hopes, etc." [Ideale, Einbildungen, Sollen, Hoffnungen, u.s.f.]. If it happens that what one wants is prevented by what is, then one might well have to do without it, as a stoic might recommend, but in any case, at least individuals need not enslave themselves to such vapid abstractions as, "Freedom," "Justice," Equality, and so on.

In that same significant winter semester of 1827, Stirner had also attended Hegel's lectures on the Philosophy of World History. The thought that world and individual history are congruent, that one mirrors the other, dominates the formation of Der Einzige und Sein Eigentum. Löwith's "allegorical displacement" is the linking of the stages of individual human life to the stages of universal human history. Given this, the first chapter of Der Einzige, "A Human Life" sets the schemata for the whole work. History begins with the childhood of the "Ancients," who, both obedient and innocently satisfied with their world, accord their lives with the given, the traditional. However, this early period ends with the coming of the modern age, which corresponds to the adolescence of world history, a time which begins, as it does with both Hegel and Stirner, with the coming of Christianity. It is a time of unhappy idealism, in which the world is found "wanting," a time in which either the world is to be abandoned for an ideal world, or is to be simply rendered into a new world. But, in the course of time, another level of consciousness emerges, that of the mature mind in which the world is taken as it is, not as the child would take it, but as the "Man" would deal with it—in his own interests. It is the age of human "Ownership" of the world. The final level of both history and individual development is set forth as the time in which the individual, "The Unique One," is expressed. This is the statement of Stirner's own "unique" personality, which is to be taken as the model of the fully conscious and self-reliant mind. The fully mature mind is not distracted from itself and in this regard "unique" [Der Einzige] and "owns itself" [sein Eigentum] unlike either the mind of the child or the youth it does not take its stubbornness as freedom and is free from the oppression of ideals and causes [Sachen].

The idealistic and reforming youthful consciousness, manifested in any judgment, in ethics, in social life, in politics or in philosophy, is indeed a destructive force.—and it dominated Young Hegelianism.

In the final chapter of his work, Stirner takes up the problem of overcoming the antithesis holding between the childish mind and that of the adolescent in a desire to bring forth a reconciliation, a synthesis, in which the mature consciousness unites reality and reason are united, in which "the real is rational and the rational is real."

> The opposition of the real [the child mind as thesis?] and the ideal [the adolescent mind as antithesis?] is an irreconcilable one, and the one can never become the other ... The position of the two is not to be vanquished otherwise than if some one annihilates both. Only in this "some one," the third party, does the opposition find its end. "Der Gegensatz des Realen und Idealen ist ein unversöhnlicher, und es kann das eine niemals das andere werden ... Der Gegensatz beider ist nicht anders zu überwinden, als wenn man beide vernichtet. Nur in diesem "man," dem Dritten, findet der Gegensatz sein Ende; sonst aber decken Idee und realität sich nimmermehr].

This "some one" is Stirner. He takes himself to be the one who "annihilates both." This understanding of himself as the annihilator of both antithetical parties, the child-like ancient world, and the adolescent post-Christian modern world, is both the negation and the completion of world history. It is the maturity of history, and it will follow upon this negation of both Old and Young Hegelianism that Stirner's Egoism emerges as the conclusion and completion of Hegelianism itself.

Der Einzige und sein Eigentum begins and ends with the same declaration: Ich hab' Mein' Sach' auf Nichts gestellt—"I have set my cause on nothing." This is the central thought of Stirner's work, and it is not a "nihilism," but simply the rejection of all idealistic causes and programs that demand the devotion and sacrifice of individual interests such as "the good cause [Sache], then God's cause, the cause of mankind, of truth, of freedom, of humanity, of justice; further, the cause of my people, my prince, my fatherland; finally, even the cause of Mind, and a thousand other causes."

It was in these same provocative 1827 lectures on the Philosophy of Spirit that Hegel introduced Stirner to the close relationship between "fixed ideas" and insanity. Hegel displayed a quite advanced understanding of the treatment of the mentally ill, and during the course of his lectures, openly expressed his appreciation of his contemporary Philippe Pinel (1745–1826), a French physician who had developed a humane treatment of mental illness. Pinel, who later earned the title "Father of modern psychiatry," stressed the role that fixed ideas [Idée fixe] played in mental illness. Hegel fully agreed with him. For Hegel, although rationality was covert in a deranged mind, it could be brought out by in treatment, since "a skillful psychiatrist is able to develop sufficient power to overcome the particular fixed idea" (it is the merit of Pinel, in particular, to have grasped his residue of rationality in lunatics as the foundation of treatment).[43] In this regard, Hegel observed that the insane mind

> when it is engrossed with a single phase of feeling, it fails to assign that phase its proper place and due subordination in the individual system of the world which a conscious subject is. In this way the subject finds itself in contradiction between the totality systematized in its consciousness, and the single phase or fixed idea which is not reduced to its proper place and rank. This is Insanity or mental Derangement.[44]

Stirner saw in this "fixed idea" as that same paralyzed adolescent idealism which Hegel had seen as expressed in a life-long mental illness—a "hypochondria." It was a common personal malady which had infected the whole of human history—a moral illness caused by the presence of "fixed ideas." It was the most persistent of human afflictions and the cause of every ideological fantasy:

> Do not think that I am jesting or speaking figuratively when I regard those persons who cling to the Higher, and (because the vast majority belongs under this head) almost the whole world of men, as veritable fools, fools in a madhouse. What is it, then, that is called a "fixed idea"?[eine fixe Idee] An idea that has subjected the man to itself. When you recognize, with regard to such a fixed idea, that it is a folly, you shut its slave up in an asylum. And is the truth of the faith, say, which we are not to doubt; the majesty of the people, which we are not to strike at (he who does is guilty of—lese-majesty); virtue, against which

the censor is not to let a word pass, that morality may be kept pure;—are these not "fixed ideas"? Is not all the stupid chatter of most of our newspapers the babble of fools who suffer from the fixed idea of morality, legality, Christianity, and so forth, and only seem to go about free because the madhouse in which they walk takes in so broad a space? Touch the fixed idea of such a fool, and you will at once have to guard your back against the lunatic's stealthy malice. For these great lunatics are like the little so-called lunatics in this point too—that they assail by stealth him who touches their fixed idea. They first steal his weapon, steal free speech from him, and then they fall upon him with their nails. Every day now lays bare the cowardice and vindictiveness of these maniacs, and the stupid populace hurrahs for their crazy measures. One must read the journals of this period, and must hear the philistines talk, to get the horrible conviction that one is shut up in a house with fools. "Thou shalt not call thy brother a fool; if thou dost ... "But I do not fear the curse, and I say, my brothers are arch-fools. Whether a poor fool of the insane asylum is possessed by the fancy that he is God the Father, Emperor of Japan, the Holy Spirit, or whatnot, or whether a citizen in comfortable circumstances conceives that it is his mission to be a good Christian, a faithful Protestant, a loyal citizen, a virtuous man - both these are one and the same "fixed idea." He who has never tried and dared not to be a good Christian, a faithful Protestant, a virtuous man, and the like, is possessed and prepossessed [gefangen und befangen] by faith, virtuousness, etc. Just as the schoolmen philosophized only inside the belief of the church; as Pope Benedict XIV wrote fat books inside the papist superstition, without ever throwing a doubt upon this belief; as authors fill whole folios on the state without calling in question the fixed idea of the state itself; as our newspapers are crammed with politics because they are conjured into the fancy that man was created to be a zoon politicon—so also subjects vegetate in subjection, virtuous people in virtue, liberals in humanity, without ever putting to these fixed ideas of theirs the searching knife of criticism. Undislodgeable, like a madman's delusion, those thoughts stand on a firm footing, and he who doubts them—lays hands on the sacred! Yes, the "fixed idea," that is the truly sacred![45]

Those who accept the fixed idea that "Truth" is a property of something or someone else have simply given themselves over to a foreign master; they are "possessed" rather than being their own owner [Einzelner]. Adolescent idealism finds its final expression if left unchecked by reality, in the insanity of self-imposed servitude. The mature and sane mind accepts its ownership of itself, and as self-possession, it is, as Stirner has it, "Egoism." It is the only possible choice if servitude to another's truth or ideals is to be avoided. Needless to say, his moral position has never been popular, since "egoism" is a pejorative term, and it has been, from the beginning, either ignored or rejected. Socialists, as well as all moralists, share the same opinion that self-interest is to be taken as a threat to both morals and community values—which indeed it is.

When it comes to the issue of property [Eigentum], which dominates almost the whole of *The Ego*, Stirner is again in full agreement with Hegel. For both, the property is the external expression of personal freedom, and its placement in the title, Der Einzige und sein Eigentum indicates its importance to Stirner. For both, "property" is more than merely the physical possession of an external object, but is also the whole range of the intellectual characteristics of an individual, in short, their ideas, and even their will. For Hegel, "the three intolerable vows of poverty, chastity, and obedience" were devised not only to separate individuals from physical property but of their emotional life as well as their freedom of will.[46]

For Stirner, the "Einziger," translated, the "Ego," is a unique and separate personality, essentially distinct from all others. The title of his work might be translated as "the Owner and His Ownership," but the most recent English translation bears the more familiar title, *The Ego and Its Own*.[47]

In his lectures on the Philosophy of Mind, Hegel is concise when it comes to discussion the issue of property, with only four paragraphs given over to the matter (488–491). There are none of the expected student notes [Zusätze] found in the earlier parts of the work. However, enough is given to confirm their absolute congruence of both on the meaning of property. There is a more extensive discussion of property found in Hegel's Philosophy of Right, of which Stirner was familiar[48] and which reinforces their agreement.

In the first paragraph, under the heading, "Eigentum" (paragraph 488), in his Philosophy of Mind, Hegel sets out the relationship between liberty [Freiheit], and the individual:

> Mind, in the immediacy of its self–secured liberty, is an individual, but one that knows its individuality as an absolutely free will: it is a person, [Einzelner] in whom the inward sense of this freedom, as in itself still abstract and empty, has its particularity and fulfilment not yet on its own part, but on an external thing. This thing, as something devoid of will, has no rights against the subjectivity of intelligence and volition, and is by that subjectivity made adjectival to it, the external sphere of its liberty – possession [Besitz].

This same sense is present in the Philosophy of Right:

> The rationale of property is to be found not in the
> satisfaction of needs but in the supersession of the pure
> subjectivity of personality. In his property a person exists for
> the first time as reason. Even if my freedom is here realised
> first of all in an external thing, and so falsely realised,

nevertheless abstract personality in its immediacy can have no
other embodiment save one characterised by immediacy.[49]

There is also complete agreement on the matter of "communal" vs. "private" property. Hegel presents the rationale for the priority of private property:

> In property my will is the will of a person; but a
> person is a unit and so property becomes the personality of
> this unitary will. Since property is the means whereby I give
> my will an embodiment, property must also have the
> character of being 'this' or 'mine'. This is the important
> doctrine of the necessity of private property. While the state
> may cancel private ownership in exceptional cases, it is
> nevertheless only the state that can do this; but frequently,
> especially in our day, private property has been re-introduced
> by the state. For example, many states have dissolved the
> monasteries, and rightly, for in the last resort no community
> has so good a right to property as a person has.[50]

This positing of property as being a "this" or "mine" is central to Stirner and forms the basis of his critique of Communism, which, as an ideal, will appropriate his personal property for the benefit of the state, in which all property becomes "communal"—and no longer "mine."

Both stress the essential relationship between private property and the freedom of individual expression. Here it is of interest to note that Hegel not only admired but understood the economic theory of Adam Smith,[51] the expression of it in the freedom of the individual. Stirner shared that interest in that he translated Smith's work into German. It was published in three volumes in 1846–1847, and it became the standard for the next century. That he was aware of Smith's economic theory even before he wrote *The Ego* is suggested in his observation that "He who in a pin factory only puts on the heads, only draws the wire, works, as it were, mechanically, like a machine; he remains half-trained, does not become a master."[52]

The vitriolic criticism of Der Einzige by the team of Marx and Engels would certainly be provoked by such passages as:

> Communism, by the abolition of all personal property, only presses me back
> still more into dependence on another, namely, on the generality or collectivity;
> and, loudly as it always attacks the "state," what it intends is itself again a state,
> a status, a condition hindering my free movement, a sovereign power over me.
> Communism rightly revolts against the pressure that I experience from individual proprietors; but still more horrible is the might that it puts in the hands
> of the collectivity.[53]

The abolition of all personal property will end in the creation of an individual who possess, if even that, only their own body, the covert intent of Communism is to make "them all "ragamuffins [Lumpen]"; all of us must have nothing, that "all may have."⁵⁴ The "all" here is the abstract universal, the "community." Stirner's "Lumpen" soon re-appeared in the first chapter of The Communist Manifesto:

> The "dangerous class," [lumpenproletariat] the social scum, that passively rotting mass thrown off by the lowest layers of the old society, may, here and there, be swept into the movement by a proletarian revolution; its conditions of life, however, prepare it far more for the part of a bribed tool of reactionary intrigue.

For Stirner, this is the expected rage of a frustrated adolescent whose idealism is being born in the form of a violent revolution. Putting this rage as mildly as possible, he noted:

> All attempts to enact rational laws about property have put out from the bay of love into a desolate sea of regulations. Even Socialism and Communism cannot be excepted from this.⁵⁵

The modern age, for both Hegel and Stirner not only begins with the advent of Christianity, but still remains within its ideological grasp.

As to Stirner's "Nihilism" it should be understood directly that it is in no way the Nihilism of Bakunin. There is nothing in Stirner's writings that come close to the radical program expressed by his statement, as "The urge to destroy is also a creative urge."⁵⁶

This "popular but inaccurate description of Stirner as a 'nihilist'"⁵⁷ was not only stimulated by Engels but has endured with such studies as that of R. W. K. Paterson, *The Nihilistic Egoist: Max Stirner*. The linking has been heavily criticized⁵⁸ as it runs counter to the whole trajectory of *The Ego*, which is an overall critique of the covert religiosity of political and social liberalism, such as set forth by Bakunin: "We must not only act politically, but in our politics act religiously, religiously in the sense of freedom, of which the one true expression is justice and love."⁵⁹

The term "Nihilism" dates back to the Middle Ages, where it was applied to heretics. It still retains much of that meaning, although the term now immediately evokes images of bomb-throwing anarchists. This recent meaning developed during the pre-revolutionary times of nineteenth-century Russia, when the term merely signified the skeptical individualism of such as Dmitry Pisarev (1840–1868), who admired Stirner. All came to an end when the "Nihilists" were taken as those who conspired in the 1881 Assassination of Czar Alexander II (1881). They did not, but political as well as clerical authorities are usually indifferent to the labels they affix upon their enemies.

Stirner's work is decidedly not a call to any form of "world-transforming" praxis, as would be more or less the case with all of the other Young Hegelians. What sets Stirner apart from the Hegelians of both the Right and the Left, or the Old and the Young, and has made him a most difficult subject for classification is that Stirner is neither, but merely one who has accepted the moral consequences of what is involved in being a "Hegelian." He was not an "academic" or "Old" Hegelian, engaged in the false infinity of a Misrah of interpretations, nor a "Young" Hegelian, set upon the applying Hegelian theory (necessarily modified) to solve various social or personal problems. If anything, Stirner might be labeled a "Quietist"—a sin that Marx considered mortal.

There would be, of course, a seemingly counter-reference to this antinihilistic reading in citing Stirner's remark, found at the very beginning of *The Ego*, that

> If God, if mankind, as you affirm, have substance enough in themselves to be all in all to themselves, then I feel that I shall still less lack that, and that I shall have no complaint to make of my "emptiness." I am not nothing in the sense of emptiness, but I am the creative nothing [das schöpferiche Nichts], the nothing out of which I myself as creator create everything.

The nature of this "creative nothing" that is Stirner's ego is taken up again when he compares his own pure subjectivity, his unique ego, with that which Fichte presented:

> When Fichte says, "The ego is all," this seems to harmonize perfectly with my thesis. But it is not that the ego is all, but the ego destroys all, and only the self-dissolving ego, the never-being ego, the—finite ego is really I. Fichte speaks of the "absolute" ego, but I speak of me, the transitory ego.[60]

Or again,

> Fichte's ego (Ich) is also . . . outside me, for every one is an ego; and if only this ego has rights, then it is "the ego" (das Ich), and not I. But I am not an ego along with other egos, but the sole ego (das alleinige Ich): I am unique (Ich bin einzig). Hence my wants and my deeds are also unique; in short, everything about me is unique. And it is only as this unique being that I take everything as my own, as I set myself to work, and develop myself, only as this unique being. I do not develop mankind or man, but as I, I develop—myself (als Ich entwickle Ich—Mich). This is the meaning of the Unique One (Dies ist der Sinn da—Einzigen).[61]

Spinoza's dictum "**omnis determinatio est** *negatio [All determination is negation]*" is at the metaphysical basis of Stirner's principle that he is unique and indefinable. Logically, as Spinoza has it, anything to be defined must be set within a limiting, a negating context. As an example, a triangle" is defined as "*A plane figure that has three straight bounding sides.*" The general context is the genus, in this case, "a plane figure," this is its "class," which is itself within the class, of figures," which itself in a class, and so on, to an indefinable infinity—to the "creative nothing" which defines Stirner. But this "nothing" is not in a defining genus, as it cannot limit another; it is "unique." In short, He is a negative being who determines himself as such.

Fichte, as Hegel presents him, is a "dogmatic" idealist who attempted to posit the empirical "other," the "Anstoss," and ultimately all of the objective world, as being nothing other than the self-limiting creation of *The Ego* itself. This fixed and defined "Ego" is not that of either Hegel or Stirner. In that same series of 1827 lectures on the Philosophy of Mind, which so powerfully influenced the work of Stirner, Hegel understood individual self-consciousness as the result of the negation or internal sundering of a given unreflective consciousness into a self-reflective conscious. The dialectical course is evident, in which the antithetical development to self-reflection is a negative act, a "creative nothing." In Hegel, the identity of the self with itself, as self-consciousness, is

> absolute negativity—for whereas in Nature the intelligent unity has its objectivity perfect but externalized, this self-externalization has been nullified and the unity in that way been made one and the same with itself.[62]

In sum, the external world (in which the self is to be found) exists as an externality, which is negated with the advent of self-awareness. It is the expected dialectical movement of "negating the negation," from which the unity of the self, in the very division of the self, finds expression:

> In the formula $I = I$, is enunciated the principle of absolute Reason and freedom. Freedom and Reason consist in this, that I raise myself to the form of an $I = I$, that I know every thing as mine, as "I," that I grasp every object as a member in the system of what I myself am, in short that I have in one and the same consciousness myself and the world, that in the world I find my self again and, conversely, in my consciousness have what is.[63]

"To know every thing as mine" is a phrase that one might expect to find in *The Ego*, but the same thought is also found in Hegel, in a concluding passage of the Phenomenology:

> This last shape of Spirit—the spirit which at the same time gives its complete and true content the form of the Self and thereby realizes its Notion as remaining in its Notion in this realization—this is absolute knowing. . . . The nature, moments, and movement of this knowing have, then, shown themselves to be such that this knowing is a pure being-for-self of self-consciousness; it is "I," that is this and no other "I" (es ist Ich, das dieses und kein anderes Ich), and which is no less immediately a mediated or superseded universal "I." Consciousness has a content which it differentiates from itself; for it is pure negativity or the dividing of itself (denn es ist die reine Negativität oder das sich Entzweien), it is self-consciousness. This content in sundering itself is the "I," for it is the movement of superseding itself or the same pure negation that the "I" is [dieselbe reine Negativitat, das Ich ist].[64]

The "nothingness" of the self, being only abstract subjectivity in itself, must find its dialectical complement in another "nothingness"—that is, in abstract objectivity or mere "thinghood." For both Hegel and Stirner the interaction of these two empty abstractions initiated between the indeterminate freedom of subjectivity and the indeterminate necessity of pure objectivity, that is, indifferent matter (gleichgültigen Dinge), comprises the whole of actual becoming. Neither self, nor thing, separated in abstraction, can claim actual being.

Of particular interest here in the comparison of both is not only Hegel's description of this "I" in terms of its "nothingness" but also the uniqueness of this entity, as "this and no other 'I'"—an Einziger. The self cannot be defined.

> What Stirner says is a word, a thought, a concept; what he means is neither a word, nor a thought, nor a concept. What he says is not the meaning, and what he means cannot be said. The unique . . . has no content; it is indeterminacy in itself; only through you does it acquire content and determination. There is no conceptual development of the unique; one cannot build a philosophical system with it as a "principle," the way one can with being, with thought, with the I. Rather it puts an end to all conceptual development [Begriffsentwicklung]. . . . With the unique, the rule of absolute thought, of thought with a conceptual content of its own, comes to an end, just as the concept and the conceptual world fades away when one uses the empty name: the name is the empty name to which only the view can give content.[65]

At the onset of his rejoinder to his critics, Stirner takes up a key factor in all of his philosophy, the indefinable meaning of the term "Einzigen," which appears in the title of his main work in which he terms himself Der Einzige. Stirner is clear: the word "Einzigen" can only be spoken or written but cannot be employed as a logical predicate. As a reference to a "this" it is only able to be pointed out or indicated. It cannot be defined. The term is what in classical logic would be termed a "flatus vocis," a word that indicates but does not define:

Stirner's view regarding the impossibility of defining "Der Einzige" is fully in accord with a fundamental principle of classical Logic:

> It should first be noticed that definition is never of an individual, but always of what is universal, predicable of individuals—whether it be what we call their "kind," or some state or attribute of them, or relation in which they stand. For what is defined is thereby marked off and fixed in our thought as a determinate concept; but the individual is made the individual he (or it) is by an infinity of attributes; he is as it were the perpetual meeting-place of concepts; we can neither exhaust what is to be said of him, nor make a selection, and declare that this is essential to him, and that unessential. Moreover, even if we could, we should still only have settled what he in fact is, but a second person also might be; for every concept is universal. What makes him this individual and not another we should not have defined, nor could we.[66]

But, yet, despite the logic, Stirner's critics have all proposed a definition for the Einziger. This, for Stirner, was a futile exercise, as a universal cannot be predicated of a unique individual, such as himself, as "this individual," this "Einziger."

Again, just as with Hegel, a positive note of creativity follows immediately upon the discernment of the negativity inherent in the activity of the conscious ego: "I am not nothing in the sense of emptiness, but I am the creative nothing, the nothing out of which I myself as creator create everything."[67]

This creative aspect of that "reine Negativität, die Ich ist" is also set forth by Hegel, as in this passage which tells of how Spirit, or Mind, comes to itself and has won its freedom in "the immediate unity of self knowledge":

> In this knowing, then, Spirit has concluded the movement in which it has shaped itself, in so far as this shaping was burdened with the difference of consciousness [i.e. of the latter from its object], a difference now overcome. Spirit has won the pure element of its existence, the Notion, The content, in accordance with the freedom of its being, is the self-alienating Self [sich entäussernde Selbst] or the immediate unity of self knowledge. The pure movement of this alienation [Entäusserung], considered in connection with the content, constitutes the necessity of the content. The distinct content, as determinate, is in relation, is not "in itself"; it is its own restless process of superseding itself, or negativity; therefore negativity or diversity, like free being, is also the Self; and

in this self-like form in which existence is immediately thought, the content is the Notion [Begriff].[68]

The Self, through its own negation, freely creates itself. As with Stirner, "It is only as this unique being that I take everything as my own, as I set myself to work, and develop myself. The tracing of how the self, or Spirit, develops itself is described in the Phenomenology of Mind—a work which has been described as a Bildungroman.[69] It is also quite possible to describe *The Ego* as a Bildungsroman, in which I set myself to work, and develop myself, only as this unique being. I do not develop mankind or man, but as I, I develop—myself (als Ich entwickle Ich—Mich). This is the meaning of the Unique One (Dies ist der Sinn da—Einzigen)."[70]

Stirner's thought can be taken as the expression of what is entailed in "Absolute Knowing." As a Hegelian, Stirner would be expected to assume that this absolute knowing, in which the odyssey of consciousness comes to an end, would indeed be the Hegelian consciousness. His particular apprehension consisted of taking the "we" of Hegel's Phenomenology—that constant observer who traces the course of consciousness from its beginning in sense-certainty to its conclusion in absolute knowledge—as himself. His "Egoism" is nothing more than the truth of his Hegelianism.

As Hegel, Stirner took himself at standing "at the boundary of a period"[71]—at the boundary between Hegel and Hegelianism. For Hegel, our age is "a birth-time and a period of transition to a new era," and this new age, for Stirner, was separated from the old by

> A vast interval.... In the old I go toward myself, in the new I start from myself; in the former I long for myself, in the latter I have myself and do with myself as one does with any other property—I enjoy myself at my pleasure. I am no longer afraid for my life, but "squander" it.[72]

In his Hegelian role of "freeing determinate thoughts from their fixity," he would press beyond the "pious atheism" and humanistic liberalism of such as Feuerbach and Bauer, beyond those whom Hegel described as "beautiful souls [die schöne Seele]"—those among whom Stirner has often mistakenly been placed. These contradicted atheistic souls, fixed in the painful penultimate shape of consciousness before it obtained Absolute Knowing, locked in the shape of religious consciousness and seeing themselves in alien form, were unable to reconcile their ideals to the reality of the given world. For Hegel, "This 'beautiful soul' . . . being conscious of this contradiction in its unreconciled immediacy, is disordered to the point of madness [zur Verrüktheit zerrütet]"[73] It is mired in the "hypochondria" of the adolescent. In short, it is the mind of the frustrated revolutionary idealist and reformer, who, driven to seek an ideal "better world" (be it present in either Heaven or in a future world), was nevertheless forced to live in the actual world. The desire for what "ought to be" might begin with a benign idealism, but, if pursued, it inexorably leads to revolutionary terror and final madness. It is a mind of the adolescent grown old, unable to surmount its infatuation with "Ideals."[74]

Soon after the appearance of *The Ego*, three formidable critics presented their case against Stirner. His reply to them appeared in Stirner's first and final answer to his numerous critics appeared in 1845 as a fifty-page article in the third issue of *Wiegands Vierteljahrsschrift*.[75] He began his response by naming not only the journals in which their criticism appeared but who they were:

> The following three notable writings have come out against The Unique and Its Property: 1) Szeliga's critique in the March edition of the "Northern German Gazette"; 2) "On the Essence of Christianity in Relation to the Unique and Its Property" in the latest volume of *Wigand's Quarterly Review*; 3) A pamphlet, "The Last Philosophers," by M. Hess Szeliga presents himself as a critic, Hess as a socialist and the author of the second piece as Feuerbach.[76]

For Stirner, these contemporaries had taken Hegel's "Path of Doubt"—but not to its final end in a self-affirming realism, but rather into the dead end of liberal idealism. They had merely hidden threadbare theism under the costume of atheistic modernity and then the old God was brought on stage as the "New Man." It was left to Stirner to reveal that this new "supreme being" would prove to be more of a threat to individual freedom than the old God had ever been. He set out this intention in the first page of *The Ego*

"Man is to man the supreme being," says Feuerbach.
"Man has been discovered," says Bruno Bauer.
Let us take a more careful look at this supreme being and this new discovery. Stirner's "more careful look" was that of a Hegelian on "the Path of Doubt."

NOTES

1. The excellent recent translation of Mackay's work by Hubert Kennedy, *Max Stirner: His Life and His Work* (Concord, CA: Premptory Publications Concord, 2005), with its informative introduction is recommended.

2. There are many numerous and more or less detailed biographies of Stirner available, among them would be the lucid and concise biography found in David Leopold's Introduction to the Cambridge edition of *The Ego and His Own*.

3. Kennedy, *Max Stirner: His Life and His Work*, 37–38.
4. See author's article, "*Hegelian Nihilism*: Karl Werder and the Class of 1841," *Philosophical Forum* 46, no. 3 (2015): 249–73.
5. Letter of Engels to Max Hildebrand, October 22, 1889.
6. Patterson, *The Nihilistic Egoist: Max Stirner*. (Hull, University of Hull, 1971), 37.
7. See Robert J. Hellman, *Berlin: The Red Room and White Beer: The "Free" Hegelian Radicals in the 1840s* (Washington: Three Continents Press, 1990).
8. See Addenda for translation of article.
9. Arvon, *Aux sources de Islation of articler: Stirner*, 14.
10. Letter of Engels to Marx, November 19, 1844.
11. Letter of Engels to Max Hildebrand, October 22, 1889.
12. Kennedy, *Max Stirner: His Life and His Work*, 127.
13. *The Destruction of Reason*, trans. Peter R. Palmer (Merlin Press, 1980), 254–55. see Bernd A. Laska, *Max Stirner Ein dauerhafter Dissident: 150 Jahre Stirners "Einziger" : eine kurze Wirkungsgeschicht e* (Nurnberg: LSR-Verlag, 1996).
14. Nürnberg: LSR-Verlag 1996.
15. Karl Marx, and Friedrich Engels, *The German Ideology* (New York: Electric Book Company, 2001).
16. Letter to Frobel, December 6, 1844.
17. Letter to Frobel, December 17, 1844.
18. David Leopold, *The Ego and His Own*, (Cambridge: Cambridge University Press, 1995), xiii.
19. See Addenda for details.
20. MEW, 37, p. 293.
21. Ego, p. 86.
22. George Santayana, *The German Mind: A Philosophical Diagnosis* (New York, 1968), 99.
23. James Huneker, *Egoists: A Book of Supermen* (New York, 1932), 356.
24. *Introduction to The Ego and His Own* (New York, 1918), x.
25. Ruge to his mother, December 17, 1844, in *Briefwechsel und Tagebuchbluchbl aus den Jahren 1825–1880*, ed. Paul Nerrlich (Berlin, 1886), 1, 386
26. Ego, 187, 218.
27. Hegel, *Philosophy of Mind*. Translated by W. Wallace, A. V. Miller, and Michael Inwood. (Oxford: Oxford University Press, 2007).
28. *Phenomenology*, par 430–35.
29. As seen in Kojeve see footnote 37.
30. *Phenomenology*, par 432.
31. Ego, p. 85 in Leopold pdf issue of Ego, also in 170 Einziger.
32. Goethe (1749–1832) wrote the poem "Vanitas! Vanitatum Vanitas!" in 1806 as a parody of the church hymn "Ich hab' mein' Sach' Gott heimgestellt" ("I have placed all I have with God") by Johann Pappus (1549–1610). Hegel and Goethe were well aquainted.
33. Ego, p. 3 in Leopold PDF.
34. Para 396.

35. Ego, 6.
36. Hegel's *Philosophy of Right*, 197.
37. Ego, 6.
38. Zu, p. 396.
39. Ibid.
40. Ego, 166 in Leopold text.
41. Zu, p. 396.
42. *From Hegel to Nietzsche*, trans. David E. Green (New York: Doubleday, 1967), 101; Von Hegel zu Nietzsche (Stuttgart: Kolhammer, 1958), 118.
43. Phil of Mind, para 408, p. 137.
44. para 408.
45. Wheels in Head badly translated Sparren, p. 25 Leopold PDF.
46. *HegelLeopold PDF badly transla*, Volume 1, Ch. 3.
47. Modified somewhat from the original title, *The Ego and His Own*, by its editor.
48. The Philosophy of Right is discussed in Bauer's Trumpet of the Last Judgement, which Stirner had reviewed—see Addenda.
49. Para 41.
50. Para 46 Phil of Right.
51. James P. Henderson and John B. Davis Adam Smith's Influence on Hegel's *Philosophical Writings Journal of the History of Economic Thought* 13, no. 2 (Fall 1991): 184–204.
52. Ego, 69. A "pin factory" served Smith as an example of the division of labor.
53. Ego, 151.
54. Ego, 67.
55. Ego, 150.
56. Drawn from his 1842 work, The Reaction in Germany, "We exhort the compromisers to open their hearts to truth, to free themselves of their wretched and blind circumspection, of their intellectual arrogance, and of the servile fear which dries up their souls and paralyzes their movements. Let us therefore trust the eternal Spirit which destroys and annihilates only because it is the unfathomable and eternal source of all life. The passion for destruction is a creative passion, too!"
57. https://plato.stanford.edu/entries/max-stirner/by D Leopold
58. https://www.panarchy.org/schiereck/stirner.pdf
59. Ibid.
60. p. 105 Leopold PDF.
61. Ego, 318; Einzige, 406
62. *Philosophy of Spirit*, para 381
63. Para 424.
64. *The Phenomenology of Spirit*, trans. A. V. Miller (Oxford 1979), 485–6; Phänomenologie des Geistes, hrs. J. Hoffmeister (Hamburg, 1952), 556–7. Hereafter Phenomenology or Phänomenologie.
65. *Stirnerno Critics*, trans. Wolfi Landstreicher (Berkeley: Cal Press, 2012), 55.
66. H. W. B. Joseph, *An Introduction to Logic* (Oxford: University Press, 1916), 81–82.
67. Ego, 324; Einzige, 412.

68. *Phenomenology*, 490–91; *Ph 90menology* , 561–62.

69. See Josiah Royce, *Lectures on Modern Idealism* (New Haven: Yale University Press, 1919), 147–55; cf. John Dobbins and Peter Fuss, "The Silhouette of Dante in Hegel's Phenomenology of Spirit," *Clio* 11, no. 4 (Summer 1982): 387–413; and Jacob Loewenberg, *Hegelnberg, ob Loewen* (La Salle, IL: Open Court, 1965).

70. Ego, 318; Einzige, 406.

71. Ego, 282; Einzige, 358.

72. Stirner footnote 153.

73. *Phenomenology*, 407; *Ph7; menology.*, 470.

74. On the madness of "The Beautiful Soul," see Daniel Berthold-Bond, *Hegel Daniel Berthold-Bon* (Albany: SUNY Press, 1995). For the parallel views of Hegel and Stirner on the adolescent and reforming mind, see the author's article, "Ein Menschenleben," in *The New Hegelians: Politics and Philosophy in the Hegelian School*, ed. Douglas Moggach (Cambridge: Cambridge University Press, 2006), 3.

75. It was reprinted in Mackay's Klinerer Schriften and has been translated into English by Wolfi Landsctricher as Stirner's Critics, LBC Books & CAL Press, 2012. It might be noted that this translation is excellent and the book a fine introduction to the Ego.

76. "Szeliga" was considered a defender of Bauer; his full name was Franz Zychlin von Zychlinsky. He was first a contributor to Bruno Bauer's radical periodicals of 1843–1846 and then of two ultraconservative studies, the Geschichte des 24. Infantrieregiments (1854/1857), and Das preussische Offizierskorps als Erzieher des Volkes (1962). He distinguished himself on the battlefields of 1849, 1866, and 1870, and becoming the highest decorated General of Infantry. When he died in 1900, the Kaiser ordered three days of mourning.

Chapter 3

The Path Ahead

AUGUST VON CIESZKOWSKI, 1814–1894

We thus announce a new era for philosophy.... The future fate of philosophy in general is to be practical philosophy or, to put it better, the philosophy of praxis, whose most concrete effect on life and social relations is the development of truth in concrete activity.

Hegel's warning words, in the *Preface* to the *Philosophy of Right*, to the philosophical activists who desired "to teach the world what it ought to be" was more or less ignored, as it still is, by them. The young students of Hegel, excited by the French Revolution of 1830, which was soon followed by the impotent philosophical leadership of such as George Andreas Gabler were impatient for change and could hardly be expected to wait any longer, "until reality has completed its formative process, and made itself ready." They were ready. Then, in 1838, at the moment in which all revolutionary action would seem to be without any philosophic justification, a small work by a young and aristocratic exile from Poland radically changed the whole framework of Hegel's philosophy of history—and with this, Hegel's eager disciples were given a philosophical weapon that made social revolution not only possible but rational.

August von Cieszkowski's first book, written when he was twenty-four years old, was published in 1838,[1] exactly one decade before *The Communist Manifesto*. It bore the imposing title *Prolegomena zur Historiosophie* [Prolegomena to the Wisdom of History]. It now seems a rather ambitious project to be handled in 150 pages, but yet this "small book" is, "at least as far as the notion of praxis is concerned, ... the most brilliant and the most important single text published between Hegel's death in 1831 and the *Philosophic and Economic Manuscripts* [1844] of Marx."[2]

Count Cieszkowski was born in 1814 at his family estate near Warsaw. His future inclination to aesthetic evaluations was foreshadowed by his father, whose interest in the fine arts manifested itself in an extensive collection, as well as long-established friendships with such artists as the sculptor Canova and the painter Monti. In 1831, young Cieszkowski left a dangerously revolutionary Warsaw for the more philosophic Berlin, intending to study under Hegel. But he, as well as the young David Strauss, arrived in Berlin to the sad news of Hegel's sudden death. Unlike Strauss, who left Berlin in disappointment the following year, Cieszkowski stayed at the University of Berlin for the next three years, apparently finding the inheritors of Hegel's philosophy to his liking. In any case, all of his instructors had been the students of Hegel: Karl Michelet, Karl Werder, Heinrich Hotho, Eduard Gans, Leopold Henning, and Johann Erdmann.

Complementing his education with travel, usual at the time, he visited France and England, where he observed, earlier than Engels, the problems of early capitalism. In 1838 he received his doctorate from Heidelberg, not from Berlin as one would expect. However, as Marx's later experience at Jena indicates, receiving a doctorate from a university that one had never attended was not impossible at the time. In that same year, his *Prolegomena zur Historiosophie*, written earlier in Paris, was published in Berlin. The following year his *Du credit et de la circulation* instituted a series of economic studies, *De la paine et de l'aristocratie moderne* (Paris, 1844), *Zur Verbesserung der Lage der Arbeiter auf dern Lander* (Berlin, 1845), and *Du credit agricole mobilier et immobilier* (Paris, 1847). All of these economic studies reflect the influence of Saint-Simon and Fourier and as early as the *Prolegomena*. Cieszkowski laudes rier for taking "a significant step" in the direction of infusing "organic truth in reality."—Cieszkowski's interests went beyond both economics and philosophy to create his most popular work, the Ojcze-Nasz (Paris, 1848), the Our Father, whose philosophical piety gathered many readers and appeared in several editions and translations. This work, as well as his critique of Michelet's lectures, Gott und Palingenesie (Berlin, 1842), resists easy classification, perhaps by reason of what Löwith would term their "Slavonic" character, a syncretic spirit which could join the Hegelian Geist to the Christian Logos by means of a "philosophy of action."[3]

Before his death in Posen, in 1894, Cieszkowski's energies were still unexhausted by a prolific writing career and had extended into the fields of publishing and politics. In effect, his life mirrored his doctrines, enthusiastically directed to the remodeling of human nature. At eighty, he traveled to Paris in order to attend an electro-technical congress, a final sign of both his vitality and extensive concerns. In his last years, he was honored by all of Poland's political and literary communities. All in all, it had been a good life, but in retrospect, it appears that his most certain claim to that continued scholarly attention, which passes for immortality rests upon the merits of his earliest work, the *Prolegomena*.

While still a student in Berlin, Cieszkowski's intelligence brought him to the attention of both Michelet and his friend, Werder. Michelet—described by Bruno Bauer as "the youngest of the old Hegelians"—became Cieszkowski's lifelong friend, and as early as 1836 both were exchanging letters over the forthcoming *Prolegomena*.[4] By 1843, their friendship and shared professional outlook occasioned their founding of the *Berlin Philosophic Society*, and both edited its journal, *Der Gedanke*. However, it would seem that it was the Dozent Werder who played a central role in communicating Cieszkowski's novel ideas to the Berlin circle of Young Hegelians.

Karl Werder and Bruno Bauer had both been appointed privatdozents in theology at the university in 1834. Friendly, and sharing the ever-growing dangers of being a Hegelian during those years, they found some pleasure in the like-minded company that gathered at Stehey's conditori. It was called the "Doktorsklub," and, in 1837, its informal circle accepted a new member, Karl Marx, sponsored by the publicist Adolf Rutenberg. Marx and Werder shared common interests in both logic and literature. Marx, who was to take Gabler's logic in the summer of 1838, and hoped to write a text on that subject, would certainly find Werder informative—although knowing what we do of Marx's temperament, he must have felt discomfited by the early appearance of Werder's text in logic. Marx was also interested in poetry and would later see his poetry appear for the first time in the Berlin Young Hegelian journal *Athenaeum*. Werder's successful play-writing must have attracted Marx, as it later did Engels. In time, Werder's attention was directed almost exclusively to the study of drama, but at the time he would have known Marx his concerns would have been in large measure those shared by all the members of the club—the reasonable disposition of that unstable mixture of theology, philosophy, and politics which comprised the Hegelian estate.

Although Michelet had exchanged letters with Cieszkowski regarding the *Prolegomena*, it was Werder who received the galley proofs for correction. He was impressed enough by what he read to lecture upon Cieszkowski's ideas for a full semester in 1838.[5] It seems likely that Marx must have been acquainted with these ideas, at least from the introduction of an enthusiastic Werder, if not from a reading of the slim, 157-page work itself. In a letter to Engels, dated January 12, 1882, Marx recalled that he had once met Cieszkowski in Paris in 1844. He ironically noted that although the Polish count had "bewitched" him he had no desire to read his "sins." However, Marx nowhere refers in his writings to work, and although a case has been presented which would prove an indirect influence,[6] conclusive evidence that would absolutely prove Marx's direct indebtedness to Cieszkowski is still lacking.

As might be expected, Cieszkowski's work came to the attention of Berlin's active Russian colony, which would soon number among its members the novelist Turgenev and his friend Bakunin. Determined to understand Hegelianism, Bakunin arrived in Berlin in the summer of 1840 and enrolled in Werder's course. Impressed by Bakunin's "recklessness," which he found refreshing in comparison to the general stolidity characteristic of his regular students, Werder became friendly with both Bakunin and his Russian circle. The Russian salon of Mme. Varvara was honored by Werder's recitation of the first act of his play, *Columbus*—the same play which led Engels to remark that Werder had "discovered the deep of negation."

The Russian revolutionary, Alexander Herzen, had met the young Bakunin for the first time in Moscow during the winter of 1839. A few months earlier, Herzen had written an enthusiastic letter to a friend concerning the *Prolegomena*: "I ordered the work, and imagine my joy: on every essential point I was, to an amazing degree, in accord with the author."[7] Certainly, it seems likely that Herzen discussed Cieszkowski with Bakunin, and so prepared him for his amiable meetings with both Werder and Ruge.

Ruge, whose editorial career intersected with that of Marx in the course of publishing the short-lived *Deutsch-Französische Jahrbücher*, had earlier published a favorable review of the *Prolegomena* in his *Hallische Jahrbücher*. He must have indicated to Bakunin, as well as Marx, how Cieszkowski's ideas represented an "essential progress" in man's understanding of history.[8]

At least there can be no doubt of the relationship holding between Cieszkowski and Moses Hess. Hess openly admired the contribution made by Cieszkowski to the further development of Hegelianism into a program for social and political action and declared that only two works existed which forced an awakening from the sleep of theory to the life of practice—his own *Heilige Geschichte der Menscheit* (Stuttgart, 1837) and the *Prolegomena*. Hess must have conveyed his respect for the "geistvolle Cieszkowski" to both Marx and Engels. It is interesting to note that in 1862, more than twenty years after his praise of the *Prolegomena*, Hess solicited and won a corresponding membership in the Berlin Philosophic Society. His contributions were published in *Der Gedanke*, the same journal established and edited by Cieszkowski and Michelet.

The work appeared in the same year that the publicists Ruge and Echtermeyer established the Hallische Jahrbücher "to prepare the way for the Young Hegelian apocalypse."[9]

Indeed, it was an auspicious time for the appearance of a work which claims, with uncommon assurance, to have solved the mystery of mankind's future. In that decade which began with the portentous July revolution, and within its first five years had recorded the deaths of Hegel, Goethe, and Schleiermacher—all departing with small hope for man's future—Cieszkowski's confidence as to the successful outcome of the human enterprise stood in striking contrast to the doubts and complaints of his contemporaries. Immerman's novel of 1835, *Die Epigonen*, gave voice to those contemporary confusions:

> A desolate tottering and vacillation, an aimlessness and ridiculous pretension of seriousness, a sense of striving—to what goal we do not know—a fear of terrors so ghastly that they have no form—It is as if mankind, buffeted about in its little ship by an overpowering sea, suffers from a moral seasickness whose end is scarcely in sight. . . . We are, to express our affliction in one word, epigones; and we bear the burden which is the heritage of those born too late.[10]

The first forceful paragraph of the *Prolegomena*, with its secure vision and optimism, could undoubtedly cure that "moral seasickness," or at least its symptoms—which might be all that matters.

> Mankind has finally reached a stage of consciousness that can now perceive the laws of its own proper progress and development as the essentially real determinations of God's absolute thought, as the manifestation of objective reason in world history, and not as the monstrous self-delusions of eager spiritualists.[11]

In the *Prolegomena* a central theme is introduced which dominates the Young Hegelian movement; Cieszkowski declares that "we have still not reached the end of history" (4), and he, for one, rejects a Hegelian role which would limit him to merely musing over past events. In his later work, Gott und Palingenesie, Hegel's "Owl" metaphor is developed to Cieszkowski's advantage, with a further Nietzschean suggestion that weakness rather than wisdom accounted for the pessimism of Hegel: "The Owl of Minerva likes to hide in her dark corner,—but our coming Athena will go forth as an eagle with powerful wings and eyes that can endure sunlight . . . away with the Owl!"[12]

However, all of the Young Hegelians, in order to be Hegelians and yet not be forced to accept its bitter consequences, sought, if not an outright flaw, then some "incompleteness," which permitted their ideas to act therapeutically upon the fundamentally healthy corpus of Hegeianism. In retrospect, only Stirner and Kierkegaard seemed willing to let the system, in Cieszkowski's words, "either commit suicide or child-murder."[13]

In Cieszkowski's judgment, presented in the opening pages of his *Prolegomena*, Hegel's error was rudimentary. He had failed to apply his dialectic to world history, and instead of the familiar and compelling employment of the triad to the subject, Hegel looked to a quadruple schema for a principle of order. "Hegel divided the whole course of world history until our time into four great epochs, which he designated as the Oriental, Greek, Roman, and Christian-German world." Unhappily, this tetrachotomous division is appropriate only to the realm of nature, "where the second moment breaks again into itself and by that act the totality appears as a quadruple reality," and since "world history is not a development of nature," Hegel's historical system is necessarily inadequate. As "the highest process of the Spirit can in no way participate in the fated activity of the external world," the confusion of both makes a science of world history impossible. Only one course is possible if a science of world history is to be established: to understand history as the manifestation of the triadic dialectic of the Spirit. Because such a science takes full cognizance of the movement of the Spirit, which is not constrained to "the fated activity of the external world," it cannot take human freedom into account, and "freedom opens the door to the future."

In this, Cieszkowski is at one with the Young Hegelians on which the dialectical triad, of thesis, antithesis, and synthesis, is forced upon a historical framework, in which the present, as thesis, gives rise to a self-generated revolution, its antithesis, and after this struggle to "negate the negation," the desired final moment finally appears—the synthesis. His terminating historical moment must logically be "higher" and "better" than all which has preceded it. To Stirner, it was nothing less than the religious dream of the coming of a Heavenly World, for Marx, the advent of a "Workers' Paradise."

The future had not concerned Hegel. Indeed, he had once mentioned, in passing, that it did belong to a distant North America. But even within the same passage in which North America is characterized as "the country of the future," Hegel felt immediately constrained to introduce a cautionary note:

> Prophecy is not the business of the philosopher. In history we are concerned not with what belongs exclusively to the past or to the future, but with that which is, both now and eternally—in short, with reason. And that is quite enough to occupy our attention.[14]

Among the Young Hegelians, it was left for Stirner to dismiss the "new age" as but a covert and reactionary restatement of the "old." He was, just as Hegel, not disposed to give himself over to apocalyptic visions. But although he was, as a Hegelian, still prone to deal in triads, as found in the format of his major work *The Ego and His Own*, he is yet very clear that his own triadic division of history into "The Ancients," "The Moderns," and "The Free" does not suggest any future project.

> The ancients and the moderns having been presented above in two divisions, it may seem as if the free were here to be described in a third division as independent and distinct. This is not so. The free are only the more modern and

most modern among the "moderns," and are put in a separate division merely because they belong to the present, and what is present, above all, claims our attention here. I give "the free" only as a translation of "the liberals," but must with regard to the concept of freedom (as in general with regard to so many other things whose anticipatory introduction cannot be avoided) refer to what comes later.[15]

But, for Cieszkowski, "if it lies within the power of reason to seize upon the essence of God, of freedom, and of immortality, then why should the essence of the future remain outside of this power?" For him, there was no absolute reason to prevent a knowledge of the essence, if not of the particulars of the future. That speculative knowledge—would be a proper foreknowledge (*praescientia*), and not merely a series of "particular predictions, an auguring of the future (*praesagium*)."

> The totality of world history is fully and absolutely grasped under the speculative trichotomy. However, in order not to damage the freedom of its development, no part of history, such as the past, but rather the totality must be speculatively and organically comprehended. Now the totality of history must include both the past and the future, the traversed and yet to be traversed ways, and so arises the first demand upon speculation: to vindicate the essence of the future. (Prologomena 7–8)

Hegel, by reason of the "retrospective" cast of his speculations, was silent over the future. Unable to comprehend the organic character of world history, he had naturally "spoken not a syllable over the future in all of his works." But the science of the future is "the real experience of philosophy," for upon it rests the understanding of what mankind can obtain for itself as well as an insight into how the "steady [gesetzte] realization" of these human possibilities can take place (Prologemena, 11).

Having now determined the method as well as "the possibility of knowing the future, we can pass over into reality, i.e., we must indicate how consciousness really comes to appropriate this knowledge for itself." At this point, the gnostic perspective which dominates the work is revealed: "The future can, in the main, be determined by three means: through feeling, through thought, and through the will" (*Prolegomena*, 15). These three factors of feeling, thought, and will form the ideological grid upon which is erected a new vision of world history, the new division which replaces the old Hegelian fourfold schema. The replacement, with its rigid reliance upon a trichotomous division, develops a system decidedly more "Hegelian" in appearance than the original. This appearance brings to mind Bauer's remark that "the younger these old Hegelians are, the older they seem to be."[16]

As the *Prolegomena* develops its theme, the three factors are seen to be serially revealed and perfected as the three great epochs of that developing organism called world history—the ancient, the Christian-Germanic (or Christian-modern), and the future. It was a compelling historical frame, as the "fantasy of a third and most glorious dispensation had . . . , over the centuries, entered into the common stock of European social mythology."[17] Hegel had earlier noted that the triadic logic was often considered, because of its opposition to the ordinary either/or logic of common sense to be "the same as what, in special connection with religious experience and doctrines, used to be called Mysticism"[18] This logic that found its place in the Prologomena's triadic progression of history was no doubt enhanced by its subtle evocation of the "Third Reich," that "Kingdom of the Holy Ghost" which Joachim of Flores (1145–1202) predicted was to follow after the Abraham's "Kingdom of the Father" and the Christian "Kingdom of the Son." The persistence of this apocalyptic paradigm is not surprising, not only if considering the great number of discontented students of theology in Germany at the time of the Young Hegelians, but also, among all of the Young Hegelians, with the exception of Max Stirner, a new age did seem imminent. It was now the time, as their book titles declared for *The Philosophy of the Future*[19] and *The Philosophy of the Deed*.[20] This eschatology is pervasive, as in Marx's "scientific socialism." In this, revolutionary history is set forth in three ages: primitive communism, class society, and final communism. The new age will be one in which the Utopian "Classless Society" will have displaced the alienating and evil age of Capitalism—that "false consciousness" which perversely worships the "divine power of money."[21] The triad is still present in such Hegelian theorists as Alexander Kojève, who considered history as falling into three stages, the first, that of the "Master," the second, that of the "Slave," and the third, and final stage, the "Modern," in which there are neither Masters nor Slaves, but only "Citizens."[22] It was left for Stirner to dismiss the "new age" as but a covert and reactionary restatement of the "old."

The first epoch of history, the ancient world, had its modus cognoscendi in feeling [Geftilhl] and was forced to seek its meaning and its future in the equivocal pronouncements of the seer and prophet. This world passed into the Christian-Germanic epoch of Cieszkowski, as the ancient prophetic world ended with its fulfillment in the coming of Christ, who realized all prophecies.

As the antithesis of the ancient period, the modem world has embraced abstract thought as its noetic medium. This "second determination" [of Geist] is reflective, thoughtful, conscious, and necessary; for the most part grasping the generalities of thought, of laws, of essentials, it produces the philosopher of history (16). Now, to employ a comparison suggested by Cieszkowski, as the Prophet Daniel appeared to signal the doom of the ancient world, so he also stands at the close of the second great era, preparing his readers for the advent of the future epoch, a new time that will fall under the domination of human will. It might be remarked here that it is not unusual for the one claiming the role of an Apocalyptic Prophet to suggest that they might also be prepared to be taken as a world-saving Messiah.[23]

Heralding the time in which humans will assume ascendancy over that immediate grasp of being given in sensation and that reflected and mediated reality given to the thinking subject, Cieszkowski's views apparently echo those of Fichte. But whatever his relationship to Fichte, there is no question that Hegel's doctrine regarding the will is rejected by Cieszkowski. In this regard he notes that "according to Hegel the will is only a special mode of thought [;] this is a false apprehension" (120). Going beyond a mere rejection of Hegel, Cieszkowski elevates the will to a status transcending even autonomy and grants it the role of primal mediator of all being, positing the will as the synthetic moment of all noetic acts, as the term of all historical activity. Past history, up to and including the speculative system of Hegel, has manifested two aspects of the dialectical trichotomy, a perceptive thesis—the ancient world—and a reflective antithesis—the Christian-modern world. The present moment is prepared for the synthetic movement of history, the time of willing and doing. In sum, "what perception portended, and wisdom has understood, remains still for the absolute will to realize; and this is in a word the new direction of the future" (29). "Absolute will" is more than the simple practicality of the past and the activity of the ancients in the world and is to be understood as "post-theoretical Praxis, ... the true synthesis of the theoretical and the immediately practical, in which *doing* [Thun] is above all the true substantial synthesis of being and thinking (18).

Certainly, the distinction between Praxis and the "immediately practical" [*unmittelbar Praktischen*] is to be found in Marx's early writings, particularly in the *Theses on Feuerbach*. Further, Cieszkowski's notion of a future in which man will become "the conscious director [*Werkmeister*] of his own freedom" (20) seems equally proto-Marxian. In this context it is worth citing Cieszkowski both as to the nature of this promising future as well as the "necessitated passage" of its birth:

> To realize the ideas of beauty and truth in practical life ... to bind together, organically, all of the manifestly one sided and limited elements of the life of humanity and bring it into vital cooperation, finally to realize the idea of absolute good and absolute teleology in our world; this is the great task of the future. But in order to accomplish this task, in order to open the new period ... another people's movement [Volkerwanderung] is necessary. ... The new Volkerwanderung must be a reaction against the earlier, and so go forth from civilized people in order to inundate the remaining barbarian races. The first Volkerwanderung had carried the raw power of nature victoriously over the still developing strength

of the Spirit; but even so this victory served only to regenerate Spirit itself. Now, however, the power of Spirit will move against the power of nature, and the victory of Spirit will serve to regenerate nature. . . . This revenge of the world-spirit, i.e., the second Völker-wanderung will be the necessitated passage [unentbehrlicher Ubergang] to the third period (29–30)

With this declaration, Messianic Marxism, Polish Millennialism,[24] and German Cultural Chauvinism[25]—these and perhaps other forms of political spiritualism could find one of their ideological ancestors in Cieszkowski's development of the *Dritte Periode*.

For the next dozen pages which conclude the first chapter of the *Prolegomena*, the "third period" theme is deepened and repeated, with its inevitable realization placed in the hands of a special people in cooperation with "great men," these latter patterned after Hegel's "world-historical" individuals.

Alexander Herzen, despite his praise of Cieszkowski's work, was mistaken as to its title, referring to it as the *Prolegomena zur Historiographie*.[26] It is a mistake of some importance in that the term "Historiosophie" is a calculated neologism, and Cieszkowski considered its meaning important enough to direct the concluding page of the first chapter to its signification. In brief, as Hegel had elevated what had been mere Philosophy into a Wisdom, *Sophie*, so Cieszkowski will raise Philosophy of History into the Wisdom of History, *Historiosophie*. This new historical wisdom will understand the "speculative development of World History in its organic ideality, just as Hegel has understood the History of Philosophy.

The second chapter, "Categories of World History," reflects upon the three principal categories of human knowledge, logic, physics, and the pneumatic—this last moment relating to psychology and anthropology—in the light of their concrete interdependence in history. As Hegel had locked the particular developments of philosophic history into an intelligible scheme, so Cieszkowski attempts the same with the particulars of world history or at least suggests the lines upon which such an attempt must proceed.

It can be noted that the ordering of the three chapters which comprise the work is tenaciously Hegelian. In this, Cieszkowski is at one with the later members of the Young Hegelian school, such as Feuerbach, whose work *The Essence of Christianity* is faithful to the tripartite division even unto the ordering of their subject matter.

The first chapter of the *Prolegomena* developed "the formal side of history as an ideal totality subject to systemization" (43) with this being followed by an antithetical second chapter which considers the "content of history." On the grounds that world history was the stage in which the "doing" of the Spirit rendered all that was possible actual, the second chapter indicates the interdependency of historic events. In short, as the first chapter discovered the abstract and formal "how" of history, the second is left "to determine the specific 'what' of history." (44) Not unexpectedly, the synthetic final chapter will concern itself with the "why."

Of these chapters, it is the short second which is unquestionably the least convincing—if not the least interesting—of all. Here is reason enough to accept Walter Kühne's judgment upon Cieszkowski's thought: that it is more of a theosophy than a philosophy.

The lengthy third chapter is introduced by a few lines from Goethe's Faust, concluding with the prescient words, "In the end will be the deed!" This wholly apposite declaration sets the tone for the final "synthetic" chapter, in which the general course of history, now established within a dialectical pattern, is confidently presaged. Having, in the first chapter, described history in its tripartite expression as ancient, Christian-modern, and the future, and further proceeding to indicate, with full credit to Spinoza, that the particulars of that history are organically related—that "world history is the sensorium commune of the universe" (45), Cieszkowski is prepared to "finally question regarding the why, i.e., the absolute teleology of world history in general" (46).

The future, dialectically evolved out of the past two moments of history, reveals a simple goal for mankind: the creation of the universal good. The ancients merely created particulars, the moderns understood the universal, and the future will create the universal. The evolution began with man and nature confronting one another in apparent contradiction and then passed into a period of their particular coaction, which resulted in the creation of the beautiful, the work of art. In this ancient stage, "inwardness [the concept] corresponded to externality [objectivity], but only as the special, as the direct *thisness* [*Dieses*] of being, as particularity." The second epoch of history witnessed the decline of the artist and the emergence of the philosopher, the ascendancy of truth over beauty, of universality over particularity. This was "the stage of truth, which reversed the correspondence of objectivity to the concept—where objectivity was no longer the receptacle of unification, but rather generality itself; no longer *Dieses*, the thing, etc., but generic reality, essence, the idea" (47). In this modern period the mind of man simply reflects objectivity, a truth which finds necessity in itself because it reflects the necessity of nature itself. To employ scholastic terminology, one might say that in the passage from the ancient to the modern world man's noetic emphasis has changed, granting epistemic priority to logical rather than ontological, created truth.

In sum, in the ancient stage of history, the intellect of man informed the world, creating particular works of art. In the second stage, the world informed the intellect, producing general truths. The third, synthetic, stage, will see the creation of nature by man and man by nature, "the highest identification of conception with objectivity," in which "internality and externality will appear as concrete individuality, in which that individuality is simple self-activity" (48).

This final salvatory message, predicting an end to the chasm which now separates objectivity from subjectivity, one soon to be bridged by aesthetic praxis, readily brings to mind Marx's early writings, particularly the *Manuscripts of 1844*. However, discovering solutions to an incomplete Hegelianism which would render the future both intelligible and bearable was a commonplace pursuit of the Young Hegelians. Still, it was only Cieszkowski, followed shortly by Hess,[27] Marx, and Bakunin, who cast his answer in terms of objective human activity, of praxis, of world creation:

> In the future, philosophy must permit itself to decay, to be transformed in principle, for as the poetry of art passed into the prose of thought, so must the philosopher step down from the heights of theory into the field of praxis. Practical philosophy, or more exactly stated, the Philosophy of Praxis, which would realistically influence life and social relationships, the development of truth in concrete activity—this is the overriding destiny of philosophy. (129)

This comprehension of world history as the organic yet serial progress of consciousness in relationship to objectivity, the ascent from particular feeling through abstract thought to creative will "is actually the long awaited discovery of the Philosopher's Stone." At this point, Cieszkowski is prepared "to demonstrate the wonders which lie in the power of this stone (131). However, before revealing these wonders, Cieszkowski touches upon the specific means which must be taken if they are to be realized in the future. The task is given to philosophy, whose "next fate is to popularize itself... it must render its profundities shallow (131). This in order to bring the masses into that state of consciousness necessary for them to embark upon the new [*Völkerwanderung*].

The methodological character of this vulgarization of philosophy was not lost upon the Old Hegelians,[28] as well as some of the Young Hegelians, such as Bauer and Stirner. Nevertheless, on this matter it would appear that Cieszkowski's program has been victorious—at least if Marx's program is granted: "Philosophy can only be realized by the abolition of the proletariat, and the proletariat can only be abolished by the realization of philosophy."[29]

Despite the yet unfinished popularization of philosophy, Cieszkowski was assured that the time for the birth of a new world was near at hand, for contemporary revolutionary movements, signs of "fermentation, even putrefaction" were heady indices that mankind was even then "entering into an epoch of creativity" (122). It would also be the epoch of wonders, such as "the true rehabilitation of matter," in which "sensible appearance will lose its worthlessness" by reason of being infused with creative thought, praxis. This new relationship of man to nature does not mean "a reversion and decline to a life of nature, but a drawing forth and elevation of natural life to our own." This new naturality will ultimately lift itself "to a yet richer artistic life [Kunstlebenj]" (144).

Further, the new age will not only see man and nature reconciled, but men acting in concord with one another. Men will lose their egoistic isolation and win altruistic sociality:

> Man will exchange his previous abstractness and will kat' exochên to a social individual. The naked I will lose its generality and fix itself to an existentially complete [concreten verhaltnissreichen] person. (133)

Naturally, all present moral relationships, such as the family and civil society, will undergo radical transformations, which will rid them of their present "onesidedness and limitations." And as the past has only known two abstract moral institutions, the Roman legal structure and the Christian Church, the future will bring forth a new "concrete sphere" of morality, which will both purge and perfect these earlier forms of ethical life.

Two visions, one concerning the future of the state and the other concerning the future of mankind, conclude Cieszkowski's speculations and the *Prolegomena zur Historiosophie:*

> The state will lose its abstract and separate character and will become the bond between mankind and the concrete family of people. The natural state of people will pass into a social state, and the law of the people [Völkerrecht] will perfect itself ever more fully into a moral code of the people [Völkermoral] and a morality of the people [Völkersittlicheit]. Finally, mankind itself, which even now might not yet consider itself a community, will then gather together into a real and living organism of humanity, which might well be called, in its highest sense, a church.

No one among the Young Hegelians could have expressed the millennial expectations of that early post-Hegelian world better than Cieszkowski, and all of them, with the exception of Stirner, accepted them. And he was not at all sanguine about the future—which would be his future:

> The men of the future will yet fight their way to many a liberty that we do not even miss. What do you need that later liberty for? If you meant to esteem yourself as nothing before you had become a human being, you would have to wait until the "last judgment," until the day when man, or humanity, shall have

attained perfection. But, as you will surely die before that, what becomes of your prize of victory?[30]

In short, what does this future "perfection" mean to the present individual? Stirner never mentions Cieszkowski.

NOTES

1. For a comprehensive history of Cieszkowski, see André Liebich, *Between Ideology and Utopia: The Philosophy and Politics of August Cieszkowski* (Dordrecht, 1979).
2. Lobkowicz, *Theory and Practice: History of a Concept from Aristotle to Marx*, 194. On the particulars of Cieszkowski's revision of Hegel, see author's "Making Hegel into a Better Hegelian: August von Cieszkowski," *Journal of the History of Philosophy* 25, no. 4 (April 1987).
3. Löwith, *From Hegel to Nietzsche*, 144.
4. Walter Kühne, "Neue Einblicke in Leben und Werke Zieszkowskis," *JahrbiJcher für Kultur und Geschichte der Slaven* 6 (1930): 55.
5. Reinhard Lauth, "Einflusse slawischer Denker auf die Genesis der Marxschen Weltanschauung," *Orientalia Christiana Periodica* 21 (1955): 414.
6. Ibid., 399–450.
7. Cited by Alexandre Koyre, *Etudes sur l'histoire de la pense'e philosoplzique en Russie* (Paris, 1950), 189.
8. *Hallische Jahrbücher* (1839), 475.
9. Arnold Ruge, *Aus fruherer Zeit* (Berlin, 1862-67), IV, 445.
10. Karl Immerman, *Werke*, ed. R. Boxberger (Berlin, n.d.) V, 123. Cited by William J. Brazill, *The Young Hegelians* (New Haven: Yale University Press, 1970), 10.
11. *Prolegomena*, 1.
12. *Gott*, 21.
13. *Prolegomena*, 6.
14. Philosophy of History, ?
15. Ego, 56
16. *Hegels Lehre von der Religion und Kunst* (Aalen, 1967), 5.
17. Norman Cohn, *The Pursuit of the Millennium: Revolutionary Millenarians and Mystical Anarchists of the Middle Ages* (London and Oxford: Oxford University Press, 1957), 101. On the development of apocalyptic view, see Lobkowitz, *Theory and Practice*, 194.
18. Hegel, *Logic, Part 1 of the Philosophical Encyclopedia* (Oxford: Clarendon Press, 1975), 121.
19. Feuerbach, *Philosophy of the Future*, 5.
20. Hess, *Philosophy of the Deed*, 6.
21. Karl Marx, and Friedrich Engels, *The Economic and Philosophic Manuscripts of 1844*, trans. Martin Milligan (Amherst, NY: Prometheus, 1988).

22. See Kojève text, Introduction 7.

23. viz. Norman Cohn, *The Pursuit of the Millennium* (New York: Oxford University Press, 1970).

24. See Lauth, "Einflusse slawischer Denker auf die Genesis der Marxschen Weltanschauung," 419, and Jiirgen Gebhardt, *Politik und Eschatologie: Studien zur Geschichte der Hegelschen Schule in den Jahren 1830–1840* (Munich: Beck, 1963), 130, for references to Cieszkowski's influence upon Slavic thought.

25. See Moller van der Bruck, *Das dritte Reich*, ed. H. Schwartz (Hamburg: Hanseatische Verlagsanstalt, 1931), 67f., on the special mission of Germany to pursue a "third way."

26. Koyre, *Etudes sur l'histoire de la pense'e philosoplzique en Russie*, 189.

27. In Hess's view, Cieszkowski was the only Young Hegelian with enough intelligence to understand how a "Philosophie der Tat" could be derived from Hegelianism. See Edmund Silberner, *Moses Hess: Geschichte seines Lebens* (Leiden: E.J. Brill, 1966), 73. It would seem possible, without reflection, to argue further for the inclusion of Ruge and Vatke among those inclined to seek a solution to history in praxis

28. Karl Löwith, *Die Hegelsche Linke: Texte aus den Werken von Heinrich Heine, Arnold Ruge, Moses Hess, Max Stirner, Bruno Bauer, Ludwig Feuerbach, Karl Marx und Sören Kierkegaard* (Stuttgart-Bad Cannstatt: F. Frommann, 1962), ii.

29. Karl Marx, *Early Writings*, trans. and ed. T. B. Bottomore (New York: McGraw-Hill, 1964), 59.

30. Ego, p. 74.

Chapter 4

The First Step

DAVID FREDERICH STRAUSS, 1808–1874

From the beginning, my critique of the life of Jesus was closely tied to the Hegelian philosophy.

In 1835, a brilliant theological study was published, with the rather innocent title of *The Life of Jesus Critically Examined*. Give full reference to *Life of Jesus*, it was written by a young and little known theologian, David Friedrich Strauss, a recent graduate of the Protestant Seminary in Tübingen. Today it is difficult to even imagine the wave of public and political excitement, which erupted upon the appearance of Strauss's work.

> Thrown like a fire-bomb into the tinder-dry pietistic forest of Wüttemberg, it was indeed not surprising that the Life of Jesus ignited a conflagration which quickly spread through the whole of Germany. What is fact roused the anger of the orthodox was not the Hegelian conclusion . . . but the fact that Strauss' book – if its conclusions be accepted—would demolish the whole historical foundation of the Christian faith. The bastion of which the Reformation had been built now seemed to have been completely undermined, and the mighty fortress about to collapse. Those who had set their faith on the biblical Christ now learnt that practically nothing could be known about the historical Jesus. God, Christ, the Bible—all appeared to have been overthrown by the intensity of the daring frontal assault, so that like the temple of Jerusalem, not one stone remained upon another"[1]

More than one biblical scholar would agree that the work was "to cleave nineteenth century theology into two eras—before and after 1835."[2] It was a "work of such epoch-making significance that to this day theological writers acknowledge 1835 as "the year of the revolution of modern theology"[3] From the moment it was published, the work provoked a heated and invariably negative reaction from orthodox biblical scholars. The theological revolution came just four years after the death of Hegel. The publication of Strauss's *Life of Jesus* confirmed what the leading Pietist, Hegenstenburg, had earlier predicted: "The Hegelian philosophy will in the near future develop into a much more diabolical force than the declining rationalism . . . it is our holy duty to watch out and to attack immediately.[4]—and the counter-attack began almost immediately after the appearance of the *Life*.

There had been a number of critical studies directed against Hegel's philosophy well before Strauss's work appeared as well as a number of sympathetic studies (e.g., Goschel's Aphorismen of 1829), but whereas the former took a stance against Hegel and the latter more or less repeated Hegel, Strauss was the first to attempt to apply the critical logic of Hegel toward a rational reading of the gospel narratives.[5]

It was Hegel's revolutionary logic which elevated Strauss's reading of the gospels into a "revolution of modern theology" for without the dialectical thrust which reached beyond the mere criticism, as with the *philosophes* of the Enlightenment the dialectic drove toward a higher synthesis. Without this press to a conclusion, the work would not have been a "revolution" but simply another Enlightenment gathering of negative readings without resolution or meaning. Strauss's criticism went beyond the criticism of a Voltaire, or a Bayle, or a Lessing as it was more than a mere criticism, but a speculative, dialectical criticism which led to a conclusion, a "true positive." "Criticism" became, along with "Praxis," a term that was particularly significant among the Young Hegelians, as it was not taken as simple negativity, but rather a negativity which had a positive conclusion. The term had one of final echoes in 1845, with the first work of Marx and Engels, ironically titled *The Holy Family or Critique of Critical Criticism: Against Bruno Bauer and Company.*

Strauss's work marked the end of the "Accomodationalists," and as Marheineke, who led them, correctly, if grimly, noted "We will never recover."[6] He was correct. Never again were the conservative Hegelians to regain the official approval which they had enjoyed during Hegel's tenure, and once being identified as "rationalists" by the "Christian-German" followers of the new king they became academic pariah.

Not unexpectedly, even if Strauss had not declared it to be the case, *The Life of Jesus* had all of the markings of a Hegelian treatise for he had been a devoted admirer and student of Hegel's philosophy from almost the beginning of his academic career. In 1825, just as Hegel before him, he began his studies in theology at the University of Tübingen. After graduation, in 1830, he went on to become an assistant to a country preacher and the professor of

Latin, history, at two Evangelical seminaries. His efforts to adjust his weakening hold on Christian dogmas as well as his own desire to study philosophy, led him travel to Berlin, where he could study philosophy with Hegel as his teacher, but he arrived only a few days prior to Hegel's death, Returning to Tübingen in the summer of 1832, Strauss accepted a position as an assistant lecturer in the theological college when he lectured on logic and metaphysics, ethics, and philosophy since Kant. All of his lectures, set out from a Hegelian standpoint, were fully appreciated by his students—less so by the philosophy faculty who viewed the young theologian as an unwelcome guest. His religious orthodoxy, just as Hegel's, was suspect—with good reason. As early as 1828, he had cast aside a central Christian dogma. He wrote, after writing an essay submitted in a student prize-contest on the "Resurrection of the Dead," that "as I made the last full stop, it was clear to me that there was nothing in the whole idea of the resurrection."[7] By 1830 "any active faith which he might have had in the traditional Christian beliefs had been completely destroyed."[8]

By the fall of 1833, weary of the academic squabbles and desiring to have the time to write something he had long wanted to write, a life of Jesus, he resigned from his teaching post. It is hard to believe that this major work was ready for publication by the fall of 1834. Strauss was then only twenty-seven years old.

It was published on June 1, and by June 11, the Director of Studies at Tübingen petitioned that the work of the young tutor be officially questioned as to its compatibility with Christian doctrine. Needless to say, it was not, and so began the ending of Strauss's academic and clerical career.

This first work is a brilliantly lucid study, and as Albert Schweitzer wrote:

Considered as a literary work, Strauss' first Life of Jesus is one of the most perfect things in the whole range of learned literature. In over fourteen hundred pages he has not a superfluous phrase; his analysis descends to the minutest details, but he does not lose his way among them; the style is simple and picturesque, sometimes ironical. But always dignified and distinguished.[9]

The work itself, insofar as it treated the biblical narratives regarding the life of Jesus as largely mythic, was not particularly original. That had been done well before Strauss, in Enlightenment France by C. Francois de Volney (1742–1820) and Charles-Francois Dupuis (1742–1809). However, it made Strauss's work not only more original but it was firmly cast within the frame of Hegel's dialectical logic. This gave the work a coherency and a compelling power that could never be obtained by any mere eclectic gathering of biblical events set under the category of "myths."

For Strauss, philosophic critique, taken as antithetical to common belief, was the only antidote to dogmatic religious stagnation. It was again a matter of taking "healthy human understanding," in this case common faith under philosophic analysis so as to elevate the latent Idea, or Begriff of Christianity into full consciousness, into the "true positive." Strauss, just as all of the revolutionaries seeking to bring about a new and more rational world, had first to criticize the old, and this meant that the total traditional acceptance of the Gospel stories had to be recast—and this required a complete criticism of what had previously been taken as the authentic life of Jesus, and so, as the subtitle of his work indicates the life of Jesus was to be "Critically examined." The orthodox "given" was to be rendered into a coherent and complete philosophic concept—a conceptual synthesis, which fused the myriad contradictions found in the historical life of Jesus. This was nothing less than a revolution, but however unpleasant such a purging of comforting traditions might be, it was intended to remove the illusions that clouded the minds of dogmatic Christians. In short, it was, as all Young Hegelian programs, set upon the goal of redeeming Humanity.

Strauss accepted Hegel's treatment of the natural religious conscious as set out in the *Phenomenology* (which he had twice read in its entirety), which took that consciousness as finding satisfaction in the form of imaginative images, of "miraculous visions," which served as the content of a mythic narrative. The ordinary and natural religious mind could not, of itself, ascend to a higher form of spiritual life, for it could only look upon philosophic questioning as the feared antithesis to the security of common belief.

In accord with the principles of dialectical logic, the total work was planned to have three major sections, set out in three distinct, separate volumes. In 1832, he set out his proposal in a letter to his friend Christian Märklin (1807–1849): "The whole thing would fall reasonably into three parts . . . , a traditional, a critical, and dogmatic part, or, into a directly positive, a negative, and a part which would recover the true positive." This "true positive" is always the desired result of dialectical logic, but it is always a vague and elusive conclusion, as it was with Struass's final identification of Mankind with Christ. Only the negative moment held Strauss's interest, that same negative, antithetical, and revolutionary moment which held the interests of all revolutionary reformers—among them being the Young Hegelians. Strauss never examined either the "traditional" life or the "true positive" life of Jesus but found his interests satisfied in the life of Jesus "critically examined." As he noted in the same letter, "But the dance really gets started in the second critical part." Needless to say, all revolutionary reformers, and Strauss was of them, have good intentions. Strauss intended his criticism as a beneficial medication:

Strauss's aim was to uncover the basic truth, not to demonstrate the falseness, of Christianity. He preferred not to lead men away from Christianity but to lead them up to the next stage of spiritual development from Christianity.[10]

A case in point was the debate between the Evangelical reading and the rationalist reading of the conception of Jesus—a critical or reflective reading of the events surrounding the virgin birth of the Christ. For the supernaturalists the story is, or at least must be, taken as an authentic account of what actually occurred. But for Strauss, neither faith (which was in itself no rational explication) nor strained attempts to explain putative miracles as merely the effect of natural causes were satisfactory. The key to his Hegelian reconciliation of the two antithetical views was found by taking each of the "miraculous" episodes in turn and demonstrating that in every instance they were ultimately the products of a fusion between a real natural event and the subjective religious inspiration of the one who took the event as a miracle. The product, the miracle, Strauss termed a "Myth." Myths were not falsehoods, but merely a form of religious perception. Naturalistic attempts to explain miracles, as with Paulus, had been encouraged by the success of empirical science since the Enlightenment, which took "objectivity" as its normative stance. However, this very objectivity had led to the discounting of the important role that religious subjectivity played in creating the miracle stories. Strauss, who proceeded to critically examine every episode in the life of Jesus concluded that the whole of the gospel narratives were fundamentally mythic creations grounded in the messianic expectations of the Old Testament authors and generated under the press of religious enthusiasm. The basic stories were fictional, but "without evil design"—the reference here being to the notorious life of Jesus composed by the theologian Herman S. Reimarus (1694–1768). His work, *Apologie oder Schutzschrift für die vernünftigen Verehrer Gottes* ("Apologia or Defense for the Rational Believers of God"), discovered in fragmentary form by Gotthold Ephraim Lessing (1729–1781), presented a shocking reading of the life of Jesus, whom he viewed as simply one suffering under the delusion that he was the expected Messiah. After his crucifixion, his followers concealed his body and then declared his Resurrection—which, once believed, ensured their own honor and financial security.[11] In 1862, Strauss published a biography of Reimarus.[12] By then he had completely abandoned Christianity, and not unexpectedly was quite sympathetic to Reimarus—as the first sentence of the *Forward* to the biography reads: "Almost thirty years ago, when I first became acquainted with the so-called 'Wolfenbüttel Frangmantist,' this writer has remained a special object of my love and reverence."

In setting his work from that of Reimarus, Strauss allowed that, given the times when the biblical accounts of the life of Jesus were being composed, there was no simple and enlightened distinction between fact and faction. As Strauss had it:

> In ancient times, and especially amongst the Hebrews, and yet more when this people was stirred up by religious excitement, the line of distinction between history and fiction, prose and poetry, was not drawn so clearly as with us. (5)

In proposing the ancient confusion of history and fiction, Strauss found the rationalization for own mythic theory: Strauss was then enabled, as one of his biographers has it, to hold that "those who had invented the miraculous stories were neither frauds nor fools, but sincere and intelligent men, deeply immersed, however, in the thought patterns of their time and culture."[13] This opened a clear, if narrow, path to being able to discard the historical truth of the miracle stories without declaring them to be false. Neither the natural nor the supernatural explications of the miraculous events of the gospels could be separately taken as true, as both were, under Strauss's criticism, proven to be inadequate, as they were only explicable in terms of mythic impositions upon the recorded events. These myths found their source in the messianic expectations of the Jewish community, which were drawn from the Old Testament. The person of Jesus became the incarnation of these myths.

On one side stood the "naturalists" or "rationalists," such as Heinrich Paulus (1761–1851), who maintained that the miracles could be explained by recourse to purely natural causes. On the other side stood the "supernaturalists," orthodox believers who took the miracle stories as literally true. However, again and again throughout his work, Strauss points out the inherent contradictions, errors, and simple absurdities, which make them unacceptable to anyone reasonable. This was the conclusion of those who set enlightened reason against unreflective acceptance. A case in point was presented by Strauss, who questioned the few appearances of Jesus after the Resurrection. There was no disagreement among them as to his Resurrection, but full disagreement as to when he first appeared, where he first appeared, and to whom he first appeared. On these issues, all of the Gospels differ. Strauss devoted a lengthy criticism concerning the accounts of the Resurrection, but he was clear that Jesus had actually died; it was not, as the rationalistic readers had it, an "apparent" death. Strauss does not concern himself, as Reimarus did, with the disappearance of the body, and as to the disparate stories of the appearance of the risen Christ, they are but mystical visions or hallucinations provoked by the shock of the crucifixion. As for the final appearance of Jesus, when he ascended into Heaven, all that is but a mythical recasting of the taking up of Enoch (Gen. 5, 24). Enoch walked with God; then he was no more because God took him, and Elijah in the fiery chariot (2 Kings 2, 11). As they were walking along and talking together, suddenly a chariot of fire and horses of fire appeared and separated the two of them, and Elijah went up to Heaven in a whirlwind.

At the very conclusion of his work, Strauss promised that there would be a positive result following his negative criticism, what might be taken as an antithetical moment leading to a positive synthesis:

> Through the results of our investigation, everything that the Christian believes concerning his Jesus now seems to have been annihilated .. . . Piety turns away in horror from such a monstrous act of desecration, and from its impregnable self-assurance of its faith makes the authoritative pronouncement: an insolent criticism may attempt what it will—everything which the Scriptures declare and the Church believes in Christ, will still remain eternally true, and not one iota of it needs to be discarded.

In this case, criticism has again offended the "self-assurance of its faith"—which can be taken as the religious expression of "healthy common sense"—which is always orthodox and dogmatically fixed in its "given." But, given the triadic logic, a synthesis will follow upon the antithetical negation of the given thesis. Simple and dogmatic belief, if it can bear up under criticism, will rise up into a "true positive": "Thus, at the conclusion of the criticism of the history of Jesus, the task presents itself: to re-establish dogmatically what has been destroyed critically."[14]

> Thus, when we know the incarnation, death and resurrection, the duplex negatio affirmat as the eternal circulation, the infinitely repeated pulsation of the divine life, what special importance can attach to a single fact [that of the historical Jesus], which merely represents the process in a perceptible way. Our age demands to be led in Christology to the idea in the fact, to the race in the individual: a dogmatics which, in its doctrines of Christ, stops short at him as an individual, is no dogmatics, but a devotional talk.[15]

The *duplex negatio affirmat* is a purely dialectical idea, the "double negation," the "negation of negation" leading to the synthesis of two antithetical statements. It is a common principle in Hegelian explanations of any form of development, as with Marx's explanation of the "re-establishment' of individual property, which is similar to Strauss's "re-establishment" of Christology:

> It is the negation of negation. This re-establishes individual property, but on the basis of the acquisitions of the capitalist era, i.e., on co-operation of free workers and their possession in common of the land and of the means of production produced by labour. The transformation of scattered private property, arising

from individual labour, into capitalist private property is, naturally, a process, incomparably more protracted, arduous, and difficult, than the transformation of capitalistic private property, already practically resting on socialized production, into socialized property.[16]

Strauss's employment of the formula, the "negation of the negation," which, in his case, is Christianity, finds expression in all of Young Hegelian criticism of what is the "given." With Strauss it has to do with the very nature of God, which followed upon his attempt to reconcile, to find a synthesis between the finite and the infinite, between the infinite God and the finite Jesus, which led him directly to taking "Mankind" as the union between God and Man:

> Humanity is the union of the two natures—God become man, the infinite manifesting itself in the finite, and finite spirit remembering its infinitude. . . . It is Humanity that dies, rises, and ascends to heaven; from the suppression of its spirit o the heavens.[17]

As to Jesus of history, he was in large measure a product of the "false consciousness" of the times, a creation made up, as the Frankenstein monster, of bits and pieces of Jewish messianic mythic fantasies.

In Strauss's case the "fixity" that Hegel had criticized was the dogmatic belief in the life of Jesus as given in the orthodox gospel narratives. He entered on the "Path of Doubt" and paid a heavy price. As all of the Young Hegelians, he took it as his calling to be more than simply a spectator who merely revealed the dirty truths under the aging veil cast by "healthy human understanding" but rather argued that a new religious belief would be that the present Humanity, not the Christ of faith, could save itself. This proposal, once accepted, became the fundamental rationale for atheistic humanism, a conclusion that could not but undermine, if not finally destroy, the established political and religious forms of his day. The impact of the *Life* was not limited to the religious sphere, but because the Prussian state rested upon the authority of pietistic Christianity, the work threatened the basis of the Monarchy itself, so it was not long before Strauss became as much a political pariah as a theological anarchist.[18]

Soon after the work of Strauss, despite the many attempts to discredit it, the "Quest for the historical Jesus" began in earnest. From the early works of Ferdinand Christian Baur (1792–1860) to the present day, the issue of determining the relationship between a shadowy historical figure and Christian dogma "is still an open question."[19]

Strauss's benign intention, through criticism, to elevate the "common sense" and unquestioning view of the gospel narratives to a higher philosophic level, fitted well with the overall intention of all of the Young Hegelians. They all shared the same project—with the exception of Stirner—which was the "freeing of determinate thoughts from their fixity so as to give actuality to the universal." It can be argued that, given one's view of history, the long-term influence of *The Life of Jesus* has played as great a role in essentially changing the character of Western culture as Marx's *Communist Manifesto*. The present world has, with the exception of the literal-minded Evangelical Christians, accepted Strauss's disjunction between *The Christ of Faith, and the Jesus of History*.[20] Today's media commonly takes a purely humanistic view of Jesus, as is evidenced in the mass of books, movies, and television presentations in which he has been reduced to a rather mild and more or less successful moralist. A clear example of how Strauss's work displaced the view that Jesus as inseparable from the Christ of faith is found in the half century following its initial appearance in England. The immediate orthodox reaction was expected damnation: it was "the most pestilential book ever vomited out of the jaws of hell" [149]. However, although its arrival was piecemeal, with only partial translations and scholarly rumors as to its destructive character, it rapidly displaced all of then widely read Lives of Jesus—and seriously damaged the credibility of all prior gospel studies. Its ascendency was assured with the excellent translation by George Eliot (Marian Evans).[21]

Both clearly contributed to the rise of the modern world. Just as with Marxism, in which the given economic world was to be actually destroyed before a "classless society" could be realized, so with the given religion of Strauss's world: the given idea of Jesus must be critically destroyed before the idea of Humanity as the Christ can come into being.

In Strauss's identification of Christ as Humanity, Stirner joined Nietzsche in contempt of this equation. As to the person of Jesus, who was a real, and not a "mythic figure," the persistent attempts to view him as but a liberal reformer were simply wrong. In an extended statement regarding the political and social teachings of Jesus, Stirner wrote:

> While, to get greater clearness, I am thinking up a comparison, the founding of Christianity comes unexpectedly into my mind. On the liberal side it is noted as a bad point in the first Christians that they preached obedience to the established heathen civil order, enjoined recognition of the heathen authorities, and confidently delivered a command, "Give to the emperor that which is the emperor's." Yet how much disturbance arose at the same time against the Roman supremacy, how mutinous did the Jews and even the Romans show themselves against their own temporal government! In short, how popular was "political discontent!" Those Christians would hear nothing of it; would not side with the "liberal tendencies." The time was politically so agitated that, as is said in the gospels,

people thought they could not accuse the founder of Christianity more successfully than if they arraigned him for "political intrigue," and yet the same gospels report that he was precisely the one who took least part in these political doings. But why was he not a revolutionist, not a demagogue, as the Jews would gladly have seen him? Why was he not a liberal? Because he expected no salvation from a change of conditions, and this whole business was indifferent to him. He was not a revolutionist, like Caesar, but an insurgent; not a state-overturner, but one who straightened himself up. That was why it was for him only a matter of "Be ye wise as serpents," which expresses the same sense as, in the special case, that "Give to the emperor that which is the emperor's"; for he was not carrying on any liberal or political fight against the established authorities, but wanted to walk his own way, untroubled about, and undisturbed by, these authorities. Not less indifferent to him than the government were its enemies, for neither understood what he wanted, and he had only to keep them off from him with the wisdom of the serpent. But, even though not a ringleader of popular mutiny, not a demagogue or revolutionist, he (and every one of the ancient Christians) was so much the more an insurgent, who lifted himself above everything that seemed sublime to the government and its opponents, and absolved himself from everything that they remained bound to, and who at the same time cut off the sources of life of the whole heathen world, with which the established state must wither away as a matter of course; precisely because he put from him the upsetting of the established, he was its deadly enemy and real annihilator; for he walled it in, confidently and recklessly carrying up the building of his temple over it, without heeding the pains of the immured. (Ego, 187 leopold)

Stirner's Jesus stands out in history as the "deadly enemy" of the established order but not as a "revolutionary" seeking an ideal cause but as an actual "insurgent," who stands up only for himself. He would seem to be a role-model for Stirner.

NOTES

1. Horton Harris, *David Friedrich Strauss and His Theology* (Cambridge: Cambridge University Press, 1973), 2.
2. Ibid., 20.
3. Richard S. Cromwell, *David Friedrich Strauss and His Place in Modern Thought* (New Jersey: Burdick Publishers, 1974), 51.
4. Bigler, *The Politics of German Protestantism*, 108.
5. See Karl Rosenkranz's *G.W.F. Hegels Leben* (1844; reprinted, Berlin: 1944), 422ff.
6. Bigler, *The Politics of German Protestantism*, 117.

7. Harris, *David Friedrich Strauss and His Theology,* 119.

8. Ibid., 20.

9. Albert Schweitzer, *The Quest of the Historical Jesus* (New York: Macmillan Publishing Co., 1968), 78.

10. Brazill, *The Young Hegelians,* 102.

11. Hermann Samuel Reimarus, *Fragments,* trans. Ralph S. Fraser (Philadelphia: Fortress Press, 1970).

12. Herman Samuel Reimarus und Seine Schützschrift für vernuftigen Verehrer.

13. Harris, *David Friedrich Strauss and His Theology,* 45.

14. Strauss, *LJ,* 757.

15. Strauss, *LJ,* 11, 738; Harris, *David Friedrich Strauss and His Theology,* 56.

16. [K. Marx, *Das Kapital,* 793.] [*Capital,* volume I, Chapter 33, page 384 in the MIA pdf file.]

17. *.7 find reference in Nenon? Find in LJ.*

18. On the political ramifications of the *Life,* see Marilyn Chapin Masey, *Christ Unmasked: The Meaning of the Life of Jesus in German Politics* (Chapel Hill: University of North Carolina Press, 1983).

19. Harris, *David Friedrich Strauss and His Theology,* 277.

20. *The Christ of Faith and Jesus of History,* Intro. and trans. Leander Keck (Philadelphia: Sigler Press, 1976).

21. On the major impact of Strauss's work upon English Evangelicals, see Daniel L. Pals, *The Victorian "Lives" of Jesus* (San Antonia: Trinity University Press, 1982).

Chapter 5

An Atheistic Turn: Bruno Bauer

> Thus in Christianity the alienation had become total, and it was this total alienation that was the biggest obstacle to the progress of self-consciousness.
>
> —Bruno Bauer

BRUNO BAUER, 1809–1882

Bauer entered the University of Berlin as a Theological student in 1828, just one year after Stirner had enrolled. He soon became a devoted Hegelian, and his early career was largely concerned with the task of clearly reconciling the unorthodox tendencies of Hegelianism with the dogmatic Christianity of his age.

Unlike Stirner, Bauer was a prolific and inexhaustible writer,[1] and in his first years as a lecturer, at Berlin, he published forty-three articles and reviews. Bauer was a prolific writer, but nevertheless, despite having seen dozens of his books and articles published, there is no critical edition of these works. And again, unlike Stirner, his works are almost completely forgotten, and, as one scholar pointed, most of Bauer's works "remain inaccessible,"[2] and almost all left untranslated.

During his years at the University, Bauer's theological talents were recognized by the "Old Hegelians," who, under increasing pressure from both orthodox pietists and conservative monarchists, were desperately trying to distance themselves from Strauss's radical reading of Hegel. They decided to choose Bruno Bauer to rebut Strauss. But as it turned out, the Hegelians had made a very bad choice in selecting him, for he developed into a much more radical atheist than Strauss had ever been.

In 1837, Strauss reacted to the criticisms of the *Life of Jesus* with a small but focused work, *Streitschriften zur Vertheidigung meiner Schrift uber das Leben Jesu zur Charakteristik der gegenwartigen Theologie.*[3] Some of the major "Accomodationalists," most of what are now-termed "The Old Hegelians," were subjected to Strauss's defense of his major thesis in the *Life*, who well knew what the dire consequences that work would have upon their already-threatened hold-upon academic and political status. Strauss had clearly understood that "the many opponents of the Hegelian philosophy used its conclusions to demonstrate the destructive consequences of the Hegelian philosophy" and "so as to protect itself from being identified with it" (7). It was in this work that Strauss set up a schema which would thereafter classify the followers of Hegel:

> To the question of whether and to what extent the gospel history is proven as history by the idea of the unity of the divine and human natures, there are three possible answers: either the entirely of the history is proven by this concept, or merely a part of it, or finally, that neither as a whole nor in part is it to be confirmed as historical by the idea. If each of these answers and directions were indeed represented by a branch of the Hegelian school, then using the traditional analogy, the first direction as standing closest to the long-established system, could be named the right, the third direction named the left, and the second named the center. (Defense, 38)

As to the "traditional analogy," although for Strauss it merely characterized theological stances, it soon was transformed, and has remained, political positions. For Strauss, the categorizations were not a matter of politics but rather how the life of the historical Jesus might be taken in the light of Hegel's absolute reason: as either fully in accord with it, or partially in accord, or not at all. In time, the ambiguous "Center" was discarded, and the classifications were simply reduced to either "Right," which was identified with the conservative "Old Hegelians," or the more radical "Left," which, in time, became the "Old" and "Young" Hegelian schools.

Strauss placed Bruno Bauer as one of the "Right," who, at twenty-six years of age, had been chosen to be the young champion of the "Old Hegelians." Bauer took up the challenge of refuting the mythic theory of Strauss's *Life of Jesus* and immediately embarked upon a series of articles in the *Jahrbücher fur wissenschaftliche Kritik*—sometimes humorously referred to as the "Hegel Gazette." Bauer attempted the extraordinary task of proving the logical inexorability of the Virgin Birth. The extremely complex and abstruse argument that Bauer presented had little consequence, and it was not long before Strauss responded to Bauer, and Strauss publicly dismissed his argument as "nothing but a trite and childish play"[4] and privately ridiculed as a "foolish piece of pen-pushing."[5] Bauer abandoned the debate and shortly came to the conclusion that the historical Jesus was largely a literary creation rather than a concrete individual—a conclusion in fundamental agreement with the thesis of Strauss.

In 1838, Bauer had formulated his initial view of the relationship between philosophy and religion in a two-volume work: *Die Religion des Alten Testaments in der geschichtlichen Entwicklung ihrer Principien dargestellt* (*The Religion of the Old Testament Presented in its Historical Development and Principles*). This work established his conception of the Gospel narratives as but the unconscious expressions of the religious mind, and to trace their full expression in the traditional history of Christianity. In 1839, the Privat-Docent Bauer, becoming somewhat notorious among conservative theologians, was assigned to teach at the University of Bonn, where he might be less noticeable. This thesis was first set further forth in his *Kritik der evangelischen Geschichte des Johannes* (*Critique of the Gospel of John*). From this point on, Bauer labeled himself the "Kritik."

Proceeding with his studies of the Gospel narratives, Bauer went well beyond a simple Enlightenment critique of accepted religious belief and set about establishing the theoretical foundation of total atheism as the ground for human freedom. In time, his logic led him to the denial of the very existence of the historical Jesus, reducing this most sacred object into a fictional entity created by the Gospel writers. For him it was "The Terrorism of Pure Theory,"[6] which was a totally unimpeded and irreverent critical dismissal of all that which had been considered "holy"—and that implied the authority of the Church as a support of the State. Human freedom was only to be gained by the exercise of unrestrained thinking, "without preconditions [*Vorassetzunglos*]."

Not unexpectedly, on March 1842, and after some debate, Bauer's teaching certificate, his *venia docendi*, was revoked.[7] His angry reaction to this theological censorship led him directly to write a bitter critique of the whole of Christianity, with the title *Christianity Exposed*.[8] It was censored and left unpublished until a copy was recently recovered.

By the end of June 1840, Bauer began another major study of the gospels, the three-volume *Kritik der evangelischen Geschichte der Synoptiker* (*Critique of the Synoptic Gospels*), which presented the final statements of Bauer regarding the actual existence of the historical Jesus. In this work the problem of whether or not Jesus was in fact a historical figure was finally resolved:

In the autumn of 1840, Bauer concluded the writing of *Die Posaune des jüngsten Gerichts über Hegel den Atheisten und Antichristen: Ein Ultimatum*

(*The Trumpet of the Last Judgement against Hegel the Atheist and Antichrist: An Ultimatum*). This anonymous work was to rally all the various interpreters of Hegel into one camp from which they could enter into what he termed "The Campaign of Pure Criticism." It asserted that the prudent "Old Hegelians" associated with German academic life had consciously concealed the total incompatibility of Hegelian philosophy with traditional Christian belief and conservative political order.[9] This was, for Bauer, an untenable policy, for "Hegel's theory is praxis, and for that very reason most dangerous, far-reaching and destructive. It is the revolution itself."[10] Whether or not Hegel's teaching is in accord with traditional Christian belief is still a matter of debate.[11]

Albert Schweitzer concisely traced Bauer's steady turn from a defense of the traditional accounts of the life of Jesus into a total rejection of them:

> The task which Bauer had set himself at the beginning of his criticism of the Gospel history, turned, before he had finished, into something different. When he began, he thought to save the honor of Jesus and to restore His Person from the state of inanition to which the apologists had reduced it, and hoped by furnishing a proof that the historical Jesus could not have been the Jesus Christ of the Gospels, to bring Him into a living relation with history. This task, however, was given up in favor of the larger one of freeing the world from the domination of the Judaeo-Roman idol, Jesus the Messiah, and in carrying out this endeavor the thesis that Jesus Christ is a product of the imagination of the early Church is formulated in such a way that the existence of a historic Jesus becomes problematical, or, at any rate, quite indifferent.

Schweitzer also added his insight into Bauer's character after his expulsion from the academy:

> One has the impression of walking alongside a man who is reasoning quite intelligently, but who talks to himself as though [145] possessed by a fixed idea.... (205) Bauer hated the theologians for still holding fast to the barbarous conception that a great man had forced himself into a stereotyped and unspiritual system, and in that way had set in motion great ideas, whereas he held that that would have signified the death of both the personality and the ideas; but this hatred is only the surface symptom of another hatred, which goes deeper than theology, going down, indeed, to the very depths of the Christian conception of the world. Bruno Bauer hates not only the theologians, but Christianity, and hates it because it expresses a truth in a wrong way. It is a religion which has become petrified in a transitional form. A religion which ought to have led on to the true religion has usurped the place of the true religion, and in this petrified form it holds prisoner all the real forces of religion. Religion is the victory

over the world of the self-conscious ego. It is only when the ego grasps itself in its antithesis to the world as a whole, and is no longer content to play the part of a mere talking gentleman in the world-drama, but faces the world with independence and reserve, that the necessary conditions of universal religion are present. (218)

By the late 1830s he had become the "leader of the Young Hegelians in Berlin."[12] By 1840, he had written a number of multi-volume studies devoted to explaining that biblical history was fundamentally an imaginative exercise having little or no actual basis in historical fact—"The Free Ones." The focal point of the radical "Young Hegelians"—it was the favorite forum for the discussion of atheism and radical politics. Among the regular participants were his own brother Edgar and Max Stirner—who became his lifelong friend. On the depth of this friendship, it can be noted that, Ludwig Pietsch, the well-known Berlin artist, wrote a touching account of the scene on the day of Stirner's death. He was asked by Bauer if he would sketch a portrait of Stirner. Bauer offered what money he had, but Pietch, knowing Bauer's poverty, did not accept it and finished the portrait.[13]

Their friendship endured despite Stirner's criticism of Bauer in the *Ego*, and it did not seem to suffer in the face of their contrary views as to the "Jewish Question"[14] nor to Stirner's unwillingness to join Bauer in the composition of his radical critique of Christianity expressed in Bauer's suppressed book, *Das entdeckte Christentum im Vormärz*.[15] Indeed, Stirner went on to a criticism of that work, seeing it merely as ironic support of Christianity itself:

> Christianity is not annihilated, but the faithful are right in having hitherto trustfully assumed of every combat against it that this could serve only for the purgation and confirmation of Christianity; for it has really only been glorified, and "Christianity exposed" is the—human Christianity. We are still living entirely in the Christian age, and the very ones who feel worst about it are the most zealously contributing to "complete" it. The more human, the dearer has feudalism become to us; for we the less believe that it still is feudalism, we take it the more confidently for ownness and think we have found what is "most absolutely our own" when we discover "the human."[16]

And so, Bauer, within a decade after attempting to defend the traditional readings of the Gospel narrative, arrived at the conclusion that Christians had created a history of God from out of its own unconsciousness, they could only rid themselves of that distant and alien Christian God by embarking upon a "ruthless" self-criticism which would reveal its own unconscious fantasies.[17] In short, in order to free the world from being forever crushed, the religious mind itself would have to engage in a radical purgation of its fantastic beliefs so as to come into full self-consciousness, which to Hegel would be the realization of freedom—the goal of world history. The illusion of God would have to be critically erased from the religious mind in order that "Man" could come into being—and so "Man has been discovered" through the "terrorism of pure theory."

The whole illusion of Christianity would have to end—and only a radical self-criticism could affect the task. It was not long before Bauer placed "Man" in the vacancy left by the purgation of God, and so "Man has been discovered." This same "Man" was the "supreme being" of Feuerbach. Stirner's response to the elevation of "Man" into the level of being "the supreme being" is clear:

> Haven't we the priest again there? Who is his God? Man with a great M! What is the divine? The human! Then the predicate has indeed only been changed into the subject, and, instead of the sentence "God is love," they say "love is divine"; instead of "God has become man," "Man has become God," etc. It is nothing more or less than a new—religion.[18]

This new God, "Man," is an ideal which cannot be obtained by a real individual, and this impossibility is a central principle in Stirner,

> The ideal "Man" is realized when the Christian apprehension turns about and becomes the proposition, "I, this unique one, am man." The conceptual question, "what is man?"—has then changed into the personal question, "who is man?" With "what" the concept was sought for, in order to realize it; with "who" it is no longer any question at all, but the answer is personally on hand at once in the asker: the question answers itself.[19]

But although their friendship endured, by the mid-forties, Bauer's theoretical and theological concerns were becoming less and less of interest among the radical Hegelians, who were more concerned with applying their theory toward the practical overthrow of the reactionary forces controlling German political life. The admiration of the revolutionary actions of France compared to the speculative passivity of Germany took hold among such Young Hegelians as Moses Hess, expressed in his 1843 work "The Philosophy of the Deed," and is to be found as the basis of the 1844 *Deutsch-Französische Jahrbücher* (*The German French Yearbooks*), edited by Arnold Ruge and Karl Marx. For these radical reformers, set upon a revolutionary path, the "Terrorism of Pure Theory" became but a play of ideas, without practical substance. In 1844, Marx, turned materialist by Feuerbach, had ended his dealings with the idealistic Young Hegelians with a book bearing the satiric title: *The Holy Family or Critique of Critical Criticism: Against Bruno Bauer and Company.* Stirner was not named among the "Company"—but the *Ego* would shortly appear, and the Marx-Engels team would once again re-think their thinking.

Unlike Feuerbach, who had immediately and publicly responded to Stirner's criticism, Bauer remained silent. Only one follower of Bauer, writing under the pseudonym "Szeliga,"[20] responded publicly. Stirner refused to take this response as even coming from Bauer himself and dismissed it as merely coming from "out of the masses [aus der Masse]."[21] Stirner has ironically recalled Bauer's own term *"Masse"* which he employed to label an easily lead and deceived mob.[22] As to Szeliga, he had

> in all seriousness . . . identified it [Der Einzige] with a "man" then proceeded with a rather vague middle term, an "individual in world history" to draw the conclusion, "after a definition of spooks (from which it emerges that "a spirit lacking thought is a body, and that the pure and simple body is the absence of thought"), that the unique is "the spook of spooks."[23]

But, nevertheless, Szeliga did have a "sense" that the Einzige is an "empty phrase":

> Szeliga takes the pain to show that the unique "measured by its own principle of seeing spooks everywhere becomes the spook of all spooks." He senses that the unique is an empty phrase, but he overlooks the fact that he himself, Szeliga, is the content of the phrase.[24]

In a significant passage, Stirner supplied the "empty phrase," the meaning of the term *"Einziger"*:

> The unique is an expression with which, in all frankness and honesty, one recognizes that he is expressing nothing. Human being, spirit, the true individual, personality, etc. are expressions or attributes that are full to overflowing with content, phrases with the greatest wealth of ideas; compared with these sacred and noble phrases, the unique is the empty, unassuming and completely common phrase.[25]

In short, "Szeliga hasn't in the least entered into the innermost depths of Stirner's book, as we've shown, and so we would like to consider him here not as the pure critic, but simply as one of the mass who wrote a review of the book.[26]

Later in 1845, an anonymous article, *"Characteristik Ludwig Feuerbach,"* appeared in the young Hegelian quarterly journal, *Wiegands Vierteljahrschrift.*[27]

It was published in the same issue that Stirner had responded to his critics.[28] The *Characteristik* has been taken as written by Bauer. As its title indicates, it is directed against Feuerbach, with only two of its sixty pages dealing with Stirner. The criticism of Stirner is similar to what others had directed against Stirner, criticisms based upon how they decided to define Stirner's "Ego." In the article attributed to Bauer, Stirner's "Ego" is "substance at its hardest, 'the spook of all spooks [*ist die Substanz in ihrer härtesten Härte,' 'das Gespenst aller Gespenster*]'" This "spook of all spooks" phrase had also appeared earlier in Szeliga's response to Stirner. The polemics of Szeliga, as well as in the bitter criticism of Moses Hess, also found an echo in the pages attributed to Bauer. Here, Stirner's "Ego" is but an "I that needs hypocrisy, deceit, external force, and petty persuasion to support its egoism." This rather insulting response, if indeed coming from Bauer, does not easily accord itself to the fact of their deep and continuing friendship.

Be this as it may, Stirner did not reply to Bauer's [?] brief criticism found in the *Characteristik*.

For Stirner, all of his critics seemed unable or unwilling to accept that the "*Einziger*," the "Unique One" was simply beyond definition—being neither a "substance" nor an "idea." The unique concrete individual simply eludes a generic definition.

In continuing his response to Szeliga, Stirner then turns to a clarification of a term that is commonly taken to signify sociopathic tendencies: "egoism." In his rebuttal, Stirner proposes and supports through some examples, the thesis that self-interest, which suffers under the pejorative label of "egoism," actually generates more actual love and communality than the self-denying performances of the weak and unassertive ego which has fallen under the dominating ideals of another.

In looking over the extensive bibliography of Bauer's works as compiled by Professor Hans-Martin Sass, I could not help noticing that the last work that Bauer dedicated to the project of the "*reinen Kritik*" was published in early 1845.[29]

It will be recalled that Stirner's work appeared in November of 1844. Bauer's sudden cessation of activity was noted by Professor Sass, who wrote:

> Bruno Bauer's campaign of pure criticism, which had begun in 1838, reached its highpoint in 1844, and its strategy of increasing the intensity of its criticism had broken through on all fronts. The campaign ended shortly thereafter. It ended, not because one side had defeated the other, but because Bauer's criticism had left the field peacefully [die Kritik kampflos das Feld räumt]. It had simply faded away. As Ernest Barnikol writes, "All of its intellectual strength faded into an empty and impotent criticism."[30]

Even Bauer, in 1853, admitted that insofar as his criticism was absolute, it had "negated itself in its critical process."[31]

Now, a question: Might it be possible that Bauer, just as Feuerbach and the Young Marx, also found a reason to conclude his "Campaign of Pure Criticism [*Feldzüge der reinen Kritik*],"[32] after reading *Der Einzige und sein Eigentum*?

Certainly, something had made Bauer, and only himself, but his brother Edgar and his follower, Szeliga, to suddenly take leave of their "Campaign" and then, unexpectedly, join forces with their opponents. Bruno, turning to historical studies, would later serve as the editor of a conservative Prussian journal, the *Wagener'schen Staats-und Gesellschaftslexikon*. He then went on to edit the "Kreuzzeitung."[33] His loudly atheistic brother Edgar, whom Engels had earlier described as "blood-thirsty,"[34] converted to Catholicism and became the editor of a Catholic journal, the "Kirchlichen Blätter." Szeliga abandoned his pseudonym and went by his full name "Franz Szeliga Zychlin von Zychlinsky" when he went on to become a Prussian General. He ended up writing military studies, among them being the two-volume history of the Prussian twenty-fourth Infantry Regiment.[35]

No doubt there were practical grounds for these unexpected, antithetical turns, but there might well be theoretical grounds as well—such as Bauer's own realization that he had witnessed "the end of philosophy."[36] Stirner agreed that with Hegelianism philosophy had come to an end: it is "the Triumph of Philosophy. Philosophy cannot hereafter achieve anything higher [und mit ihm der Triumph der Philosophie. Höheres kann die Philosophie nicht mehr leisten]."[37]

It cannot be denied that Bauer also knew Hegel and appreciated him: "Hegel was the only German of recent times who knew where to find men, and to learn something from them.[38] However, he mainly employed Hegel to support his own passionate atheistic agenda. It is not necessary here to debate whether or not Bauer's reading of Hegel as an atheist is correct. There has always been a constant argument among Hegelians as to his "orthodoxy," a debate which continues to this day.[39] Stirner seldom mentioned atheism, only four times in the Ego, as it was, for him, merely a label to cover a new "theism." He was Hegelian enough not to accept the "either/or" logic which would set theism against atheism:

> The fear of God in the proper sense was shaken long ago, and a more or less conscious "atheism," externally recognizable by a wide-spread "unchurchliness," has involuntarily become the mode. But what was taken from God has been superadded to Man, and the power of humanity grew greater in just the degree that that of piety lost weight: "Man" is the God of today, and fear of Man has taken the place of the old fear of God.

But, because Man represents only another Supreme Being, nothing in fact has taken place but a metamorphosis in the Supreme Being, and the fear of Man is merely an altered form of the fear of God.

Our atheists are pious people.[40]

In any case, Bauer seems to have had no doubt that Hegel was an atheist. Bauer's rationale for his atheistic reading of Hegel is fully expressed in *The Trumpet of the Last Judgment against Hegel the Atheist and Antichrist: An Ultimatum* [*Die Posaune des jüngsten Gerichts über Hegel den Atheisten und Antichristen: Ein Ultimatum*].[41] However, amid the many supporting citations drawn from Hegel's writings, he never cites from what might be taken as a fundamental work: the *Phänomenologie des Geistes*. For the purposes of his argument, it was not an important matter. However, this absence of reference might be of some importance for Hegelians interested in Bauer, those who would reflect upon whether or not Bauer had perceived, in the *Phenomenology*, that there was indeed a dialectical passage from his critical consciousness to Stirner's uncritical "egoism." I would maintain that there is such a passage. If Bauer understood this to be the case, he might well have sensed that Stirner had gone beyond him and so had put an end to criticism, which would mean not only the abandonment of the missionary "Campaign" but a turn to his own self-interests—a right turn that was also taken by Szeliga and his brother Edgar.

Seen in the perspective of the *Phenomenology*, Bauer is an exemplar of the Enlightenment [A*ufklärung*] consciousness. He took Voltaire as a "Propheten"[42] of the new age and passionately adopted his demand to Écrasez l'infâme. He became, as Ruge had it, "des Messiah des Atheismus,"[43] and he took upon himself the mission of saving Germany from the curse of Christianity. Bauer's atheistic mission, his *Feldzüge der reinen Kritik*, is anticipated and clearly discerned in Hegel's own lengthy discussion, found in the *Phänomenologie*, of "The struggle of the Enlightenment with Superstition [*Der Kampf der Aufklärung mit dem Aberglauben.*]"[44]

Indeed, Hegel's description of what was involved in that *Kampf* reads as if Bauer might have written it:

The masses are the victims of the deception of a priesthood which, in its envious conceit, holds itself to be the sole possessor of insight and pursues its other selfish ends as well. At the same time it conspires with despotism, which, as the synthetic, non-notational unity of the real and this ideal realm . . . stands above the bad insight of the multitude and the bad intentions of the priests, and yet unites both within itself. From the stupidity and confusion of the people brought about by the trickery of priestcraft, despotism, which despises both, draws for itself the advantage of undisturbed domination and the fulfillment of its desires and caprices, but is itself at the same time this same dullness of insight, the same superstition and error.[45]

But as one might expect from Hegel, this bitter *Kampf* of the *Aufklärung Kritik*, between, as Bauer has it, the "Mob of theological worshippers [*Schar der theologischen Anbeter*]"[46] and the Enlightenment critic, is finally resolved in an armistice. Both come to realize that "both sides are essentially the same" [daß beide wesentlich dasselbe sind].[47] Both are the antithetical aspects of the religious consciousness—faith and skepticism. In the final section of his description this struggle between the twin poles of faith, Hegel comes to "The Truth of the Enlightenment [*Die Wahrheit der Aufklärung*"]. The truth, in this case, is that both sides emerge from a shared religious consciousness; at that time, in the course of the development of self-consciousness, both find themselves in fundamental agreement: "The two worlds are reconciled, and heaven is transplanted to earth below [*Beide Welten sind versöhnt, und der Himmel auf die Erde herunter verpflanzt*]."[48]

The unconscious tendency of Bauer and the other "critics" of religion was, in the last analysis, nothing more than the final religious effort to transplant Heaven to Earth—to simply turn Man into a new God. The truth of the *Aufklärung*, found behind its blustering cover, was nothing more than a "time of dependence on thoughts, the *Christian* time." The "*heaven-storming actions*"—[*Himmelstürmende* Tätigkeit][49] of the *Aufklärung* were but a superficial "clearing off," which ultimately restored, in a new guise, the old domination of heaven of over the earth—if albeit a modern "humanistic" heaven. The atheistic humanists had merely set about

> to wreck all customs in order to put new and—better customs in their place—their act is limited to this. It [this "heaven-storming"] storms heaven only to make a heaven again, it overthrows an old power only to legitimate a new power, it only—improves.[50]

Stirner, in following Hegel, understood the incomplete character of the humanistic atheism of such as Bauer, or those "beautiful souls" who, after their critical "Campaign" had finally ended, had yet to obtain that final shape of consciousness: Absolute Knowing.

> At the entrance of the modern time stands the "God-man." At its exit will only the God in the God-man evaporate? And can the God-man really die if only the God in him dies? They did not think of this question, and thought they were through when in our days they brought to a victorious end the work of the Illumination, the vanquishing of God: they did not notice that Man has killed God in order to become now—"sole God on high." The other world outside us is

indeed brushed away, and the great undertaking of the Illuminators completed; but the other world in us has become a new heaven and calls us forth to renewed heaven-storming: God has had to give place, yet not to us, but to—Man. How can you believe that the God-man is dead before the Man in him, besides the God, is dead?[51]

And so, Bauer's radical atheistic criticism, as understood by the Hegelian Stirner was nothing more than a mere *Schein*, an illusory revolution, in which the content of the Religious Consciousness was not only retained but now would be the total content of consciousness. Arnold Ruge, then friend of Marx, had sighted the surfacing of this religious consciousness in Bauer:

> Certainly, Bauer is the completed and thus the final Heretic, but he also, as such, the last Theologian. He denies all Theology, and hates nameless Theologians, and persecutes them terribly; but also, on the other hand, he does this with theological fanaticism; he is fanatic for Atheism, he is superstitious of disbelief [er is fanatisch fur den Atheismus, er ist abergläubisch für den Unglauben].[52]

In tracing the path of Hegel's treatment of that resolved consciousness, its next move would be to advance itself into the realm of "Absolute Freedom and Terror [*Die absolute Freiheit und der Schrecken*]." This later section of the *Phenomenology* suggests Bauer's own "*Terrorismus reiner Theorie*."[53] For Engels, Bauer was indeed a "Robespierre."[54] Stirner simply dismissed these revolutionary atheists as but a recrudesce of the old order: "Robespierre and St. Just were priests through and through [*Robespierre z.B., St. Just usw, waren durch und durch Pfaffen*],"[55] and as the "servants of a highest essence are one and all—pious people, the most raging atheist not less that he most faith-filled Christian [*Diener eines höchsten Wesens insgesamt—fromme Leute: der wütendste Atheist nicht weniger als der gläubigste Christ*]." Terror and oppression would always to be visited upon any particular individual, any "Einziger," who resisted the domination of the "higher essence" be it either the idea of a distant God or Bauer's newly discovered "Man."

The final chapter of the *Phenomenology* is entitled "Absolute Knowing [*Das Absolute Wissen*]." In the very first sentence of this concluding chapter, Hegel prepares the dialectical ground for the appearance of Absolute Knowing by briefly describing that penultimate, that *vorletze* shape of consciousness. Here, "The Spirit of the revealed religion [*der Geist der offenbaren Religion*]" dominates. It has yet to supersede itself and obtain to Absolute Knowing:

> The Spirit of the revealed religion has not yet surmounted its consciousness as such, or what is the same, its actual self-consciousness is not the object of

its consciousness; Spirit itself as a whole, and the self-differentiated moments within it, fall within the sphere of picture-thinking and in the form of objectivity. The content of this picture-thinking is absolute Spirit; and all that now remains to be done is to supersede this mere form].[56]

For Stirner, this was the case with Bauer. The *Feldzüge* was but the negative reflection of positive religion, and as such still dialectically linked to and dependent upon the religious consciousness. This dependency upon the "*Geist der offenbaren Religion*" rendered him incapable of going beyond atheism, beyond religion. In short, what now had to be done, as Hegel had it, was to supersede the whole of religious consciousness. This is what Stirner intended.

If the end of Hegel's *Phenomenology* can only be reached by overcoming its penultimate form, by going beyond the fixed religious consciousness of the "pious atheists," then Stirner might be said to have advanced to "*Absolute Wissen*." I would propose that Stirner's thought is congruent with and reflective of Hegel's "*Absolute Wissen*," and that he has indeed reached that final state of consciousness which, following Hegel, has overcome the fixed thoughts and definitions of previous "*Geistesgestalten*." At this point Stirner's thought would reflect this final state by setting itself beyond definition and fixed ideas.

Stirner took himself at standing "at the boundary of a period,"[57] and followed Hegel's request that "The task nowadays consists . . . in freeing determinate thoughts from their fixity so as to give actuality to the universal . . . [*Jetzt besteht darum die Arbeit . . . das Aufheben der festen bestimmten Gedanken des Allgemeine zu verwirklichen und zu begeisten*]."[58] In taking up this task, Stirner would press beyond the revolutionary liberalism of such as Feuerbach and Bauer, beyond those whom Hegel described as "*beautiful souls [die schöne Seele]*." These souls are fixed in the painful shape of a consciousness unable to reconcile its inward ideals to the objective world. For Hegel, "this 'beautiful soul' . . . being conscious of this contradiction in its unreconciled immediacy, is disordered to the point of madness [zur Verruüktheit zeerrüttet]."[59]

In short, it is the mind of the frustrated revolutionary idealist and reformer, who, driven to seek an ideal "better world," must nevertheless live in the actual world. It might begin in a benign idealism but if pursued, will lead to revolutionary terror and final madness. It is a mind of the adolescent grown old, unable to surmount its infatuation with "Ideals."[60] For Stirner the mind of the violent revolutionary and the mild humanist are one and the same, a mind which presents itself in the grandiloquent declaration of Heinrich Heine, who "did not consider himself a disciple at all [of the Saint-Simonian Félicien David] but rather the servant of an idea: "We seize upon no idea, rather the idea seizes us, and enslaves us, and drives us into the Arena, that we, as forced Gladiators, struggle for it [*Wir ergreifen keine Idee, sondern die Idee ergreift uns, und knechtet uns, und peitscht uns in die Arena hinein, dass wir, wie gezwungene Gladiatoren, für sie kämpfen*]."[61] Heine would clearly fall into Stirner's category of the "possessed"—as well as all of the "The Young Hegelians."

Bruno Bauer, who had not abandoned his "Critique" in the face of Marx's lengthy polemics found in the *Holy Family*, was less sure of his position after reading Stirner. In any case, Schweitzer remarked that

> After 1843, with the confiscation of Christianity Exposed, [Bauer] then turned his attention to secular history and wrote on the French Revolution, on Napoleon, on the Illuminism of the Eighteenth Century, and on the party struggles in Germany during the years 1842-1846. At the beginning of the 'fifties he returned to theological subjects, but failed to exercise any influence. His work was simply ignored. (196)

It is not impossible that Stirner's criticism of this specific work had helped Bauer to turn his attention from biblical to secular history.

However, Bauer might have defended himself from Stirner, as in 1845, in an anonymous article, "Characteristiks Ludwig Feuerbachs," appeared in the young Hegelian quarterly journal, Wiegands *Vierteljahrschrift*. The Characteristik has been taken as written by Bauer, but as its title indicates, it is directed against Feuerbach, with only two of its sixty pages dealing with Stirner. In short, Bauer never directly responded to Stirner's criticism.

In looking over the extensive bibliography of Bauer's works, I could not help noticing that the last work that Bauer dedicated to the project of the "*reinen Kritik*" was published in early 1845. It will be recalled that Stirner's work appeared in November 1844. Bauer's sudden cessation of activity was noted by Hans-Martin Sass, who wrote:

> Bruno Bauer's campaign of pure criticism, which had begun in 1838, reached its highpoint in 1844, and its strategy of increasing the intensity of its criticism had broken through on all fronts. The campaign ended shortly thereafter. It ended, not because one side had defeated the other, but because Bauer's criticism had left the field peacefully [die Kritik kampflos das Feld räumt]. It had simply faded away. As Ernest Barnikol writes, "All of its intellectual strength faded into an empty and impotent criticism."[62]

The same absence of any further citations of works by Bruno Bauer after 1844 is to be found in the *Literaturverzeichnis* of Godwin Lämmerman's work, *Kritische Theologie und Theologiekritik: Die Genese der Religion-un Selbstbewusstseinstheorie: Bruno Bauers*[63]

Even Bauer, in 1853, admitted that insofar as his criticism was absolute, it had "negated itself in its critical process." Now, a question: Might it be possible that Bauer, just as Feuerbach and others had renounced their "pious atheism" after reading Stirner? It can be argued that Bauer seems not the only Young Hegelian to change his "campaign" after the appearance of the *Ego*.

NOTES

1. See Stepelevich, Lawrence S. Bibliography. Bauer, Bruno (1809–1882), 1998, *Routledge Encyclopedia of Philosophy*, Taylor and Francis; also https://www.rep.routledge.com/articles/biographical/bauer-bruno-1809-82/v1/bibliography/bauer-bruno-1809-82-bib. Copyright © 1998-2019 Routledge.
2. Douglas Moggach, *The Philosophy and Politics of Bruno Bauer* (Cambridge: University Press, 2003), 1.
3. Translated and edited with Introduction by Marilyn Chapin Massey, *In Defense of My Life of Jesus: Against the Hegelians* (Archon Books, 1983).
4. Strauss, *In Defense of My Life of Jesus*, 49.
5. Harris, *Strauss*, 80.
6. Letter of Bauer to Marx, March 28, 1841.
7. Edgar Bauer, Streitschriften gegen cite.
8. Give details of Christianity Exposed.
9. Stirner's review of this work is to be found in the *Addenda*.
10. Bruno Bauer, *The Trumpet of the Last Judgment against Hegel: The Atheist and Antichrist*, trans. Lawrence S. Stepelevich (Lewiston: Edwin Mellen Press, 1989), 127.
11. A recent extended debate over this issue occurred in the Hegelian journal, *The Owl of Minerva* (spring/summer 2005) over William Desmond's book, *Hegel's God*.
12. Harris, *Strauss*, 80; Mehring, *Karl Marx*, 21.
13. Barnikol, *Das entdeckte Christentum*, 141.
14. On the difference between Stirner and Bauer on the matter of Judaism, see author's "Stirner and the Jewish Question"; also David Leopold, "The Hegelian Antisemitism of Bruno Bauer," *Hist of European Ideas* 25 (1999): 179–206.
15. Barnikol, *Das entdeckte Christentum im Vormärz*.
16. Ego, 278 leo.
17. A concise and lucid study of Bauer's course from being a defender of Christian doctrine to that of being one of its greatest critics is to be found in Albert Schweitzer's *The Quest of the Historical Jesus*.
18. Ego, 34.
19. *Ego*, 323, Leopold.
20. Franz Szeliga Zychlin von Zychlinski, "Der Einzige und sein Eigenthum." *Norddeutschen Blätter fur Kritik, Litteratur und Unterhaltung*," March 1845.

21. Max Stirner, *Stirner's Critics*, trans. Wolfi Landstreicher (Berkeley: LCB Books, 2012), 20; Max Stirner, *Kleinere Schriften* (Stuttgart: Frommann-holzboog, 1976), 376.
22. See Bauer's 1844 essay, "*Die Gattung und die Masse.*"
23. Stirner, *Critics*, 4.
24. Ibid., 7.
25. Ibid., 5–6.
26. Ibid., 20.
27. *Wiegand's Vierteljarhschrift*, III 124–25.
28. *Kleinere Schriften*, "Recensenten Stirners," 343–96.
29. Bruno Bauer, *Feldzüge der reinen Kritik*, ed. Hans-Martin Sass (Frankfurt am Main: Suhrkamp, 1968), 69–278. The same absence of any further citations of works by Bruno Bauer after 1844 is to be found in the *Literaturverzeichnis* of Godwin Lämmerman's work, *Kritische Theologie und Theologiekritik: Die Genese der Relligion-un Selbstbewusstseinstheorie: Bruno Bauers* (München: chr. Kaiser Verlag, 1979).
30. *Feldzüge*, 263. [Bruno Bauers Feldzüge der reinen Kritik, die 1838 begonnen hatten, erreichten ihren Höhepunkt and die strategisch von der Kritik, wie sie meinte, vorbereitete letzte Zuspitzung der Fronten im Jarhe 1844;—bald danach is der Feldzüge beendet, nicht etwa weil der beiden Seiten die andere besiegt hättte, sondern weil die Kritik kampflos das Feld räumt, sie is plötzlich weg—verpufft. 'Alle geistige Kraft verpufft in leerer wirkungsloser Kritik' schreibt Ernst Barnikol.].
31. Karl Löwith, *From Hegel to Nietzsche*, trans. David E. Green (New York: Doubleday, 1964), 108; *Von Hegel zu Nietzsche* (Stuttgart: Kolhammer, 1958), 125.
32. Bruno Bauer, *Feldzüge der reinen Kritik*, ed. Hans-Martin Sass (Frankfurt am Main: Suhrkamp, 1968).
33. Issued from Berlin 1848–1939. Known as the Kreuzzeitung or Kreuz-Zeitung, its emblem being the Iron Cross. It was established during the 1848 German revolution by Herrmann Wagener, and was a leading advocate of Prussian conservatism.
34. MEW, *Ergänzungsband, Zweiter Teil* (Berlin: Dietz, 1967), 300.
35. Bruno Bauer, *Feldzüge der reinen Kritik* (Frankfurt am Main: Suhrkamp, 1968), 264.
36. Bruno Bauer, *Russland und das Germantum* (1853), 44. See Karl Löwith, *From Hegel to Nietzsche*, 105; *Von Hegel zu Nietzsche*, 122.
37. Ego, 69; Einzige, 80.
38. *Feldzüge der reinen Kritik*, 255 [Hegel war der einzige deutsche Mann der neuern Zeit der da wußte, wo man Männer findet and von Männern etwas lernen kann].
39. For an example of the present state of debate see *The Owl of Minerva: Journal of The Hegel Society of America* (Spring/Summer 2005), which devoted a full issue to William Desmond's critical work, *Hegel's God: A Counterfeit Double* (Aldershot: Ashgate Publishing, 2003
40. Ego, 166.
41. Bruno Bauer, Die Posaune des Jüngsten Gerichts Über Hegel, den Atheisten und Antichristen: Ein Ultimatum (Leipzig: Otto Wiegand, 1841); *The Trumpet of the Last Judgment against Hegel the Atheist and Antichrist: An Ultimatum.* Translated,

introduced, and annotated by Lawrence S. Stepelevich (Lewiston: Edwin Mellen Press, 1989).
42. Barnikol, *Das entdeckte Christentum im Vormärz*, 44ff.
43. Ibid., 78.
44. *Phenomenology of Spirit*, 329–49; *Phänomenologie des Geistes* (Hamburg: Meiner Verlag, 1952), 385–407. Hereafter: *Phenomenology*; *Phänomenologie*.
45. *Phenomenology*, 330; *Phänomenologie*, 386.
46. Bauer, *Feldzüge der reinen Kritik*, 173.
47. *Phenomenology*, 330; *Phänomenologie*, 387.
48. *Phenomenology*, 355; *Phänomenologie*, 413.
49. A German idiom for destructive radicalism.
50. Ego, 65; Einzige, 82.
51. 58 *An dem Eingange der neuen Zeit steht der "Gottmensch." Wird sich an ihrem Ausgange nur der Gott am Gottmenschen verflüchtigen, und kann der Gottmensch wirklich sterben, wenn nur der Gott an ihm stirbt? Man hat an diese Frage nicht gedacht und fertig zu sein gemeint, als man das Werk der Aufklärung, die Überwindung des Gottes, in unsern Tagen zu einem siegreichen Ende führte; man hat nicht gemerkt, daß der Mensch den Gott getötet hat, um nun – „alleiniger Gott in der Höhe" zu werden. Das Jenseits außer Uns ist allerdings weggefegt, und das große Unternehmen der Aufklärer vollbracht; allein das Jenseits in Uns ist ein neuer Himmel geworden und ruft Uns zu erneutem Himrnelsstürmen auf: der Gott hat Platz machen müssen, aber nicht Uns, sondern—dem Menschen. Wie mögt Ihr glauben, daß der Gottmensch gestorben sei, ehe an ihm außer dem Gott auch der Mensch gestorben ist?* Einzige, 170; Ego, 139.
52. Barnikol, *Das entdeckte Christentum im Vormärz*, 78–79.
53. MEW (Bauer to Marx, March 28, 1841) XXVII, 13.
54. Barnikol, *Das entdeckte Christentum im Vormärz*, 45.
55. Ego, 71; Einzige, 83.
56. Pheno, 479. [*Religion hat sein Bewußtsein als solches noch nicht überwunden, oder, was dasselbe ist, sein wirkliches Selbstbewußtsein ist nicht der Gegenstand seines Bewußtseins; er selbst überhaupt und die in ihm sich unterscheidenden Momente fallen in das Vorstellen und in die Form der Gegenständlichkeit. Der Inhalt des Vorstellens ist der absolute Geist; und es ist alien noch um das Aufheben dieser blossen Form zu tun...* Phänomenologie, 549
57. Ego, 282; Der Einzige, 358.
58. *Phenomenology*, 20; *Phänomenologie*, 30.
59. *Phenomenology*, 407; *Phänomenologie*, 470.
60. On the madness of "The Beautiful Soul" see Daniel Berthold-Bond, *Hegel's Theory of Madness* (Albany: SUNY Press, 1995). The parallel views of Hegel and Stirner on the adolescent and reforming mind see the author's article, "Ein Menschenleben," in *The New Hegelians* (Cambridge: University Press, 1995).
61. E. M. Butler, *The Saint-Simonian Religion in Germany: A Study of the Young German Movement* (Cambridge: University Press, 1926), 153.
62. Bruno Bauer, *Feldzüge der reinen Kritik*, ed. Hans-Martin Sass (Frankfurt am Main: Suhrkamp, 1968), 263, 269–78.
63. (München: chr. Kaiser Verlag, 1979).

Chapter 6

From the God-Man to the Man-God: Ludwig Feuerbach

The task of the modern era was the realization and humanization of God—the transformation and dissolution of theology into anthropology.

—Ludwig Feuerbach

LUDWIG FEUERBACH, 1804–1872

In the long series of studies directed to either Stirner or Feuerbach, it has always been a matter of debate as to where they stand in relation to Hegelianism after Hegel. For some, Feuerbach was Hegel's fate "Feuerbach belongs to Hegel as much as the beaker of hemlock to Socrates,"[1] and others have agreed with this claim that Feuerbach concluded the Hegelian project, such as Manfred Vogel:

> The line of the development leading to and culminating in Feuerbach is the theme of man's apotheosis which is being proclaimed with ever-increasing consistency and clarity. It reaches new heights in Hegel and culminates in Feuerbach.[2]

But to others, Stirner appears as "the last link of the Hegelian chain,"[3] or as "an ultimate logical consequence of Hegel's historical system,"[4] Other commentators, such as the historian and Hegelian, Johann Erdmann, support this contention:

> Quotations from the work of Marx and from Feuerbach's Principles of the Philosophy of the Future, make it appear that Max Stirner is the one who really represents the culminating point of the tendency begun by Hegel.[5]

A recent article continues the debate, and sides with Feuerbach, proposing that Stirner is but the later follower of Feuerbach and that "Stirner's aim is to bring to completion the critique of Hegelian idealism begun by Feuerbach himself."[6] However, if Stirner had, as maintained in this article, a "misconception of Feuerbach's notion of the Gattungswesen or species-essence," it cannot be denied that their debate immediately and simply silenced Feuerbach—who evidently thought that Stirner had not any misconception—nor did Marx, who suddenly disowned Feuerbach after reading Stirner. Perhaps Feuerbach did conclude that Hegelianism terminated in "man's apotheosis," but Stirner went beyond Feuerbach and obliterated the meaning of Feuerbach's understanding of Hegel. The conclusion that Hegelianism termed in the concept that "Man" is really "God" is to Stirner but a pious tautology, a terminological play, and the debate as to the termination of Hegelianism after Hegel is finally between Stirner's concrete individualism, egoism, or Feuerbach's universal altruism—between concrete realism or abstract idealism.

It appears certain that Stirner and Feuerbach were not personally acquainted. At the same time, it also appears improbable that they should not have met. Born in 1804, Feuerbach was Stirner's senior by two years, but both were, by at least a decade, senior to many of the more well-known of the Young Hegelians, such as Marx and Engels, or the lesser-known, such as Cieszkowski and Edgar Bauer. Their seniority gained both the opportunity of learning their Hegel directly from Hegel, an almost rare occurrence among the Young Hegelians. In particular, it is known that they at least shared the experience of hearing Hegel's lectures on religion, Feuerbach attending the Summer series of 1824, and Stirner those of the Summer of 1827. Nevertheless, they could not have met in Berlin, as Feuerbach left in the Summer of 1826, shortly before Stirner arrived to begin his studies. In time, both transferred from Berlin to the University of Erlangen, but again, by the space of a few months, they lost their last likely opportunity for a personal encounter. However, even if they had met, it seems certain that they would not have become close enough to influence one another personally. Stirner's improvident bonhommie, among Berlin's noisy and notorious "Free Ones," would hardly be expected to attract the retiring and studious Feuerbach.

As they grew older, they shared a fate common to most Young Hegelians—they were forced to abandon their academic careers by reason of their unorthodox views. Unlike Stirner, who, at the time was quite unknown, Feuerbach was known, as he came from a large and famous family, being the brother of the famous painter Anselm Feuerbach, and the son of a powerful Jurist, known for his reforming of Bavaria penal codes, Paul Johann Anselm Ritter von Feuerbach. In 1837, Feuerbach entered into a lifelong marriage with the daughter of a wealthy porcelain manufacturer and at least, before the factory failed, had a relatively better life than Stirner, who married his first wife in that same year; however, she died a year after their marriage. Feuerbach had the usual share of human unhappiness, but he lived longer and suffered less than Stirner.

Feuerbach's fame among the radical Hegelians, or notoriety among the conservatives, was early and immediately assured upon the publication, in 1830, of his work, *Gedanken über Tod und Unsterblichkeitt aus den Papieren eines Denkers* [*Thoughts on Death and Immortality from the Papers of a Thinker*].[7] As its thesis denied the immortality of the soul, it marked an irreparable break with his orthodox Hegelian past, as well as destroying his opportunity for any future academic career. This first declaration of his freedom from orthodox Hegelianism developed into ever more complete and positive forms. Before 1844, the year that Stirner's *Ego* appeared, Feuerbach had written over a dozen influential studies, including two major essays, *Vorlaufige Thesen zur Reform der Philosophie* (1842) and its more comprehensive successor, the *Grundsätze der Philosophie der Zukunft* [*Principles of the Philosophy of the Future*].[8] And so, while Stirner remained almost silent and without influence, Feuerbach displayed his talent in a proliferation of popular essays and books, all setting forth his "new philosophy."

In 1841 his major work, *The Essence of Christianity* [*Das Wesen des Christentums*][9] appeared. It was the culmination of what he termed the "genetico-critical examination" of past thought. It is not surprising that Feuerbach's work drew an enthusiastic response from Germany's liberal intellectuals, for his vision was both simple in form and excitingly unique in content. It represented a radical turn from Hegelianism, which seemed, nevertheless, not to collapse into the expected pietism or pessimism of previous departures. By June 1842, a youthful Marx, who had been Feuerbach's disciple since 1839, was heatedly proclaiming the pun that "there is no other road for you to truth and freedom except that leading through the stream of fire [the Feuer-bach]. Feuerbach is the purgatory of the present time."[10] Almost a half-century later, in 1888, Engels still recalled the effect that *The Essence of Christianity* had exercised:

> Then came Feuerbach's Essence of Christianity. With one blow, it pulverized the contradiction, in that without circumlocutions it placed materialism on the throne again. Nature exists independently of all philosophy. It is the foundation upon which we human beings, ourselves products of nature, have grown up. Nothing exists outside nature and man, and the higher beings our religious fantasies have created are only the fantastic reflection of our own essence. The spell was broken; the "system" was exploded and ast aside, and the contradiction, shown to exist only in our imagination, was dissolved. One must himself have experienced the liberating effect of this book to get an idea of it. Enthusiasm was general; we all became at once Feuerbachians.[11]

This enthusiasm was shared by the political theorist Arnold Ruge, the theologian David F. Strauss, the poet Herwegh, the novelists Gottfried Keller and George Eliot, and the young revolutionary and composer Richard Wagner.[12] Stirner was soon engaged upon composing his reply to the "new philosophy"—and Feuerbach's *Essence of Christianity* found an early reference in the *Ego*.

Stirner addressed himself to a doctrine which held, in sum, that the traditional notion of God was nothing more than the abstract and therefore alienated essence or idea of man set over and against man as an object of worship. In Feuerbach's words:

> Man—and this is the mystery of religion—projects his being into objectivity, and then again makes himself an object to this projected image of himself thus converted into a subject; he thinks of himself as an object to himself, but as the object of an object, of another being than himself.[13]

It was Feuerbach's therapeutic intention to see to it that human consciousness developed to the point where it immediately understood the principle that *Homo homini deus est*, that "Man [*Mensch*] is the true God and Savior of Man."[14] The knowledge of this alienation, between actual "Man" from its true essence, God, is based upon the feeling rather than any abstract intellectual idea. The resolution of Man's self-alienation can only come about when the real feeling of self comes into focus when the finite Man of the present feels himself to be what he has concealed from himself, that he is indeed the present God, the new God. He envisioned his philosophy would carry forth the work of the new age, "the realization and humanization of God—the transformation and dissolution of theology into anthropology."[15] This was indeed the "new philosophy" appropriate to a new age which would be marked by mankind becoming aware of itself as the true God.

But at this point a question emerges. If, to Feuerbach, "Man" is the true object of religious feeling, the basis of all notions of divinity, is this "Man" the concrete and particular conscious subject, the personal ego, or, is "He" a universal essence, an abstract idea, participated in by individuals? Feuerbach left the issue unresolved. Manfred Vogel, in his fine introduction to his translation of Feuerbach's Principles of the *Philosophy of the Future*,[16] has clearly expressed this fundamental ambiguity and incompleteness found at the core of Feuerbach's religious anthropology:

> Eliminating God and concretizing man were for Feuerbach, two sides of the same coin. The less real God is, the more real man is, and conversely. Feuerbach's reduction, however, remains in the end ambiguous. On the one

hand, God is radically eliminated. But, at the same time, man is not completely concretized. Feuerbach stops short of fully and completely concretizing man. Sometimes he speaks of man as indeed fully concretized—as the earthly, finite human individual—but at other times lie is speaking of generic man, of man in general, of the human species.[17]

It is Feuerbach's failure to resolve this issue in favor of concrete individuality, a resolution in accord with his sensuous epistemology, which leaves him open to Stirner's charge of presenting nothing more original than another form of theism. Marx, incidentally, soon shared Stirner's rejection of Feuerbachian abstractions,' but Marx treated Feuerbach rather mildly, and his criticisms contained in *The German Ideology*, as well as his *Theses on Feuerbach*, were unpublished and so unknown to Feuerbach. The same restraint cannot be said of Stirner's criticism. Not unexpectedly, Feuerbach was soon aware of Stirner's critical work. In early December 1844, a month after its premature appearance in press copies, Feuerbach had read *The Ego and His Own* and had set about establishing a defense. At this time, he wrote to his brother that Stirner had written:

A highly intelligent and ingenious work, and it contains the truth of egoism itself—but established eccentrically, one-sidedly, and incorrectly. I give him his due—up to one point: he essentially doesn't touch me at all. Nevertheless, he is the most talented and most natural writer I know.[18]

A short time later, Feuerbach again wrote to his brother, but this time, with an acidity uncharacteristic of him, he complained that Stirner's "attack betrays a certain vanity, as if he would make a name for himself at the cost of my name. But one must allow people the childish joy of a momentary triumph."[19]

Feuerbach's first impulse was to publish an open letter in response to Stirner, but this idea was abandoned in favor of placing an anonymous reply in Wiegand's *Vierteljahrsschrift*.[20] Along with Feuerbach, representatives of the whole spectrum of post-Hegelians rose up to refute Stirner—and they were not the last. Leading the Berlin Young Hegelians, Bruno Bauer published an anonymous response to Stirner's attack, Moses Hess defended the socialists with an angry essay, and the hectic reply of Marx and Engels was contained in their unpublishable polemic, *The German Ideology*. From the "left-wing" radicals such as Arnold Ruge to the right with Karl Rosenkranz, and passing through less easily categorized figures as Kuno Fischer and Bettina von Arnim, a line was formed against a common enemy—Max Stirner. Only one of these major figures was able to credit Stirner as being "right in rejecting Feuerbach's 'man', or at least the 'man' of *Das Wesen des Christentums*"—and this from Engels![21]

In the main, it is Feuerbach, that "pious atheist," who bears the brunt of Stirner's criticism, and Bauer is left relatively un-abused. One reason for this, philosophically, is that Bauer's "pure criticism" bears a closer relation to Stirner's individualism than Feuerbach's altruistic anthropology. Another reason, less philosophical, is that Bauer and Stirner were close friends both before and after the publication of *The Ego*. Knowing the circumstances and iconoclastic attitudes of the *Freien*, one can even imagine Bauer enjoying Stirner's criticism, although within a year after the *Ego* was published, he turned his attention from philosophy and theology to the subject of political history.

The philosophic content of *The Ego* is focused upon revealing the actual dependency of all normative and regulative concepts, such as God, man, mankind, state, society, or law, upon the willful determinations of the singular ego. This concrete ego, *der Enzige*, which in its concreteness and uniqueness, transcends all classifications, is the real source of all values that its creations. The religious mind, the mind of the believer, has been terrorized and awed, like Frankenstein, by monsters of its own creation. It is this mind which Feuerbach would comfort by discarding and replacing the old and alien God with "Man."

As Stirner would have it, Feuerbach is merely another preacher of pathological obsessions and fixed ideas. In this instance, the "spook" now being presented as the "higher essence" is named "Man." The "new philosophy" is but the old theology. Far from actually freeing individuals and permitting them to take pleasure in themselves, Feuerbach is but another false prophet leading them into a new servitude, a new self-denial. The "epochal new method of transformational criticism"[22] was merely a linguistic sleight-of-hand, which intensified human alienation rather than relieving it. *Feuerbach thinks that if he humanizes the divine, he has found the truth. No, if God has given us pain, "Man" is capable of pinching us still more torturingly.*[23] In two brief paragraphs, Stirner has stated his position as well as his understanding of Feuerbach:

> Let us, in brief, set Feuerbach's theological view and our contradiction over against each other: "The essence of man is man's supreme being; now by religion, to be sure, the supreme being is called God and regarded as an objective essence, but in truth it is only man's own essence; and therefore the turning-point of the world's history is that henceforth no longer God, but man, is to appear to man as God."
>
> To this we reply: The supreme being is indeed the essence of man, but, just because it is his essence and not he himself, it remains quite immaterial whether

we see it outside him and view it as "God," or find it in him and call it "Essence of Man" or "Man." I am neither God nor Man, neither the supreme essence nor my essence, and therefore it is all one in the main whether I think of the essence as in me or outside me. Nay, we really do always think of the supreme being as in both kinds of otherworldliness, the inward and outward, at once; for the "Spirit of God" is, accord-to Christian view, also "our spirit," and "dwells in us." It dwells in heaven and dwells in us; we poor things are just its "dwelling," and if Feuerbach goes on to destroy its heavenly dwelling and forces it to move to us bag and baggage, then we, its earthly apartments, will be badly overcrowded.[24]

Stirner is the first to declare, from arguments as above, that "Our atheists are pious people," a line echoed later by Engels, whose criticism of Feuerbach traced the path first opened by Stirner. Engels is merely repeating Stirner when he says of Feuerbach, "He by no means wishes to abolish religion: he wants to perfect it."[25]

And so, just as Feuerbach's "genetico-critical examination" had earlier revealed Hegelian philosophy to be a covert theology, so Stirner revealed Feuerbach's humanism as a covert religion. If, to Feuerbach, "Speculative philosophy is the true, consistent, and rational theology,"[26] so then, to Stirner, "The HUMAN religion is only the last metamorphosis of the Christian religion."[27] Neither the esoteric formulas of Hegel's doubtful theism nor the bravest declarations of his most atheistic students had served to free any of them from the iron grip of Christianity's "magic circle." It is Stirner's desire to break out of this obsessive circle which leads him to develop a radical egoism, an individualism which must stand in direct contrast to Feuerbach's altruistic humanism.

Feuerbach's public response to Stirner was only a dozen pages in length. It was, not uncommon for the time, left unsigned. A year later it reappeared, slightly expanded, in the first volume of Feuerbach's own edition of his *Sämtlichen Werke*.[28] It is of interest to note that this brief reply was Feuerbach's only publication for that year. This stands in marked contrast to his previously high level of productivity. The tenor of Feuerbach's essay has been best described by his contemporary, the historian Johann Erdmann: "Feuerbach seems to have been somewhat taken by surprise—at least he never replied with such moderation and humility as on that occasion—when the work of Max Stirner . . . Appeared."[29]

His reply, delivered as if by a third party, is, in the main, intended as a *reductio ad absurdum*, to show that taking Stirner's principles leads to manifest contradictions. This same logical technique, delivered with greater skill, was later employed by Moses Hess in his reply to Stirner. Each of the fourteen paragraphs comprising Feuerbach's response contains an argument, sometimes little more than a positional restatement. The first argument suggests the strength of those to follow, and its concluding lines deserve to be cited in entirety:

> "I have set my cause upon nothing" sings the Unique One [der Einzige]. But is not Nothing a predicate of God? is not the statement "God is nothing," a religious expression as well? So, the "Egoist" also sets his cause upon God! So he also belongs to the "pious atheists!"

At this point, the reader is surely reminded of what Engels once said in reply to one of Feuerbach's arguments: "Such etymological tricks are the last resort of idealist philosophy."[30]

Feuerbach's third argument begins with a citation from Stirner:

> Even Feuerbach himself says that he is concerned only with annihilating an illusion; yes, but an illusion upon which all illusions, all prejudices, all—unnatural—limits of Man depend, but not, however, immediately; because the fundamental illusion [Grundillusion], the fundamental prejudice, the fundamental limit of Man is God as Subject. Who turns his time and energy to undoing the fundamental illusion and fundamental limit, cannot be expected, at the same time, to set about solving the peripheral illusions and limits.

Here, somewhat peevishly, Feuerbach is simply ignoring Stirner's objection—touched upon in the opening citation 44—that he is engaged in a quixotic struggle with the "spooks" and "fixed ideas" of the idealists. But at this point it is best to turn directly to Stirner's rejoinder to his critics, where he takes each of Feuerbach's arguments in turn, and where his response to the third argument is as brief as that argument.

It was cryptically signed "M. St.," with Stirner referring to himself throughout in the third person—following Feuerbach's conceit. His specific reply was brief, with only seven pages set aside to answer Feuerbach's fourteen defensive arguments. Just as in the case of Feuerbach, the temper of these counter-arguments are best illustrated by citing Stirner's full answer to Feuerbach's first charge that to say "God is Nothing" is to say something religious.

> Feuerbach has removed the "nothing" from Stirner's "I have set my cause upon nothing" and so concludes that the Egoist is a pious atheist. Nothing is certainly a definition of God. But Feuerbach is playing with a word. Besides, it is said, in The Essence of Christianity "Hence he alone is the true atheist to whom the predicates of the Divine Being—for example, love, wisdom, justice—are nothing; not he to whom merely the subject of these predicates is nothing." [p. 21] Isn't this the same with Stirner, especially since, to him, Nothing cannot be attributed to Anything? [wenn ihm nicht das Nichts für Nichts aufgeburdet wird?]

This brief and slightly flippant rejoinder to Feuerbach's first argument is followed closely by an even briefer retort to Feuerbach's third contention—that he is applying his "time and energy" to solving the *Grundillusion.*

Feuerbach says that "the fundamental illusion is God as subject." But Stirner has shown the fundamental illusion to be the thought of the "Perfect Essence." Hence, Feuerbach, who defends this "fundamental prejudice" with all his energy, is exactly, in this respect, a true Christian. As to the matter of altruistic love, Stirner argues that a disinterested, an unselfish interest or love, is actually no interest or love, for these sentiments are rooted in one's personal evaluation of the loved object. To love altruistically out of "sacred duty" is not to love but to obey, and obedience is the quintessential expression of self-denial, the opposite of egoism.

And so the debate proceeds, with Stirner—throughout the serial of his responses to Feuerbach's defensive arguments—conceding absolutely nothing.

Their debate continued and, by mid-century, was politically radicalized by Russian revolutionaries, in this case the struggle for power between the Nihilists and the Narodniks, between individualists and collectivists. At the time, "Nihilism" was not, as it now generally understood, another form of "terrorism," but rather, as with Bazarov, in Turgenev's *Fathers and Sons,* more iconoclastic and egoistic than programmatic and political.[31] The Nihilistic movement, after the assassination of Alexander II, in 1881, was, with little foundation, prosecuted as a terroristic political movement. Dmitry Ivanovich Pisarev (1840–1868) took Stirner's thought as supportive of his own "nihilistic" program, which was mainly intended to encourage independent and unconventional thinking. He had a strong influence upon Lenin, who wrote favorably about him in his influential 1902 essay, *What Is to be Done?* The Feuerbachian objections to Stirnerian "solipsism" attracted such revolutionaries as Alexander Herzen (1812–1870) and Nikolay Chernyshevsky (1828–1889). Chernyshevsky founded the "Narodnik" party, which worked toward a socialist society based upon the structure of the Russian peasant commune, which might be compared to the contemporary "Kibbutz." Lenin was critical of this movement, which he perceived as having little substance, which would explain its "disintegration" after reaching a high point in 1870.[32]. It does seem, from the point of view of the Feuerbachian scholar, Simon Rawidowicz, who carefully examined the Russian debate, that Stirner often appeared to be the victor "machmal scheinst er the Sieg uber Feuerbach."[33]

After reading Stirner, and perhaps because of this reading, just as Bauer before him, Feuerbach abandoned his original philosophy. In 1845, shortly after the first appearance of the *Ego,* the usually prolific Feuerbach only wrote one short item—a weak reply to Stirner's work, which later appeared in his *Collected Works*.

Certainly, more than one Feuerbachian scholar, such as Eugene Kamenka,[34] has agreed with the judgment of Simon Rawidowitz that "Max Stirner's critique . . . appears to have impelled him [Feuerbach] to take a further step, to advance from anthropology to naturalism." It is generally agreed that "something" happened after 1845 to Feuerbach's view of "Man," and this could not have been other than the shock of Stirner's critique. It would seem that Feuerbach's career unexpectedly ran into the same radical "epistemological break" that would later turn Marx into a "Marxist." Certainly, it has been a problem for commentators. Ted Gooch in his article on Feuerbach's *Essence of Christianity* even managed to avoid mentioning Stirner.[35]

Actually, Stirner's critique might have impelled Feuerbach to advance from humanism to materialism, as he approved of Feuerbach's epistemological sensualism since it brought "sensuousness to honor."[36] After a period of silence, Feuerbach conceded that his book (*The Essence of Christianity*) was "still haunted by the abstract Rational Being . . . as distinct from the actual sensuous being of nature and humanity."[37] He then went on to engage in a disappointing political career, which ended in 1848. Then, a few years later, he resurfaced in a celebrated review of Jacob Moleschott's *Theory of Nutrition* (1850), and, dispensing with his earlier predilections to present the "Perfect Essence" to agree with Moleschott's materialistic presuppositions. It was at the end of the review that the famous phrase "man is what he eats" makes its appearance.[38] Still of a revolutionary cast of mind, he looked to the physical sciences for an answer to the question of what would be the material preconditions for social revolution, and he found it answered by the newly discovered science of food chemistry. He was certain that this science had proved that diet determined human culture, and therefore, insofar as protein-lacking potatoes were the major nutritional source which ensured the passivity of the working class, a revolution could only be provoked by a change to a more protein-rich died, for example, beans—hardly a romantic vision.

In 1851, in the *Forward* to his Lectures on the *Essence of Religion*, which were to be included in his *Collected Works*, Feuerbach declared that this would be his "last work," his "last Will and Testament" [letzten Willen und Gedanken][39]—and so it was.

The unwillingness of the Feuerbachians to accept this last will has not been lost upon the followers of Stirner, who, such as Hubert Kennedy, observed:

> The old disciples and friends of Feuerbach—Rau, Bolin, Duboc—are still making efforts from time to time to rescue their beloved master from Stirner and to cover up the ignorance that he himself has shown. It is useless effort, the Feuerbachian man has long since passed away.[40]

NOTES

1. 'Hermann Glockner, Die Voraussetzungen der Hegelschen Philosophie, quoted in Sidney Hook, *From Hegel to Marx*, 220.
2. Translator's introduction to *Feuerbach's Principles of the Philosophy of the Future* (Indianapolis, 1966), xliv.
3. Avron, *Aux Sources de l'existentialisme*, 177.
4. Löwith, *From Hegel to Nietzsche*, 103.
5. Erdmann, *A History of Philosophy*, trans. W. C. Hough (London, 1890), 100.
6. Ted Gooch, "Max Stirner and the Apotheosis of the Corporeal Ego," The Owl of Minerva 37, no. 2 (Spring/Summer 2006): 159–190.
7. Trans. with intro and notes by J. A. Massey (Berkeley: University of California Press, 1980).
8. Trans. M. Vogel with an intro by T. E. Wartenberg (Indianapolis: Hackett, 1986).
9. Trans. G. Eliot with an intro by K. Barth and a foreword by H.R. Niebuhr (New York: Harper Torchbooks, 1957).
10. Marx-Engels, *Werke*, I, 27.
11. Friedrich Engels, *Outcome*, 6.
12. In particular, Feuerbach's early essay, "Thoughts on Death and Immortality, See.
13. *Feuerbach, Essence*, 30.
14. Ibid., 387. This Young Hegelian premise would find its immediate source in Strauss's Life of Jesus, in which "Mankind" rather than "Man" was taken as its own Savior.
15. "Principles of the Philosophy of the Future"
16. (Bobbs-Merrill, Indianapolis, 1966), 5.
17. Future, xxv.
18. Quoted in Mackay, 166. Also in L. Bolin, Ludwig Feuerbach und sein Werke und sein Zeitgenossen (Stuttgart, 1891), 107.
19. John Henry Mackay, *Max Stirner: His Life and His Work*, trans. Hubert Kennedy (Concord, CA: Peremptory Publications, 2005), 167; Wilhelm Bolin, *Ludwig Feuerbach, Sein Wirken Und Seine Zeitgenossen. Mit Benutzung Ungedruckten Materials* (Stuttgart: J.G. Cotta, 1891), 108.
20. The publishing house of Otto Wiegand, of censor free Leipzig, was the favorite of the Young Hegeliaas and published the major works of Stirner, Feuerbach, Bauer, Marx, and Engels, among others.
21. Letter of Engels to Marx, November 19, 1844.
22. Robert Tucker, *Philosophy and Myth in Karl Marx* (Cambridge: Cambridge University Press, 1961), 103. It is interesting to note that Tucker does not even mention Stirner, despite citing from Feuerbach's reply to Stirner.
23. Stirner, *Ego and His Own*, 156.
24. Stirner, *Ego and His Own*, 34–35.
25. Engels, *Outcome*, 33.
26. Feuerbach, *Principles of the Philosophy of the Future*, 6
27. Stirner, *Ego and His Own*, 158.

28. Feuerbach's reply *"Ober das Wesen des Christentums 'in Beziehungs auf den Einzigen und scin Eigentum'"* can be read in a critical reissue in *Ludwig Feuerbach: Kleinere Schriften I*, ed. Werner Schuffenhauer (Berlin, 1970), 427–41.

29. *A History of Philosophy*, trans. W. S. Hough (London, 1890–92), III.

30. Engels, *Ludwig Feuerbach*, 34.

31. As the *Encyclopaedia Britannian* has it, "Nihilism" (from Latin nihil, "nothing"), originally a philosophy of moral and epistemological skepticism that arose in nineteenth-century Russia during the early years of the reign of Tsar Alexander II. The term was famously used by Friedrich Nietzsche to describe the disintegration of traditional morality in Western society. "It is of interest to note that Nietzsche found some basis for his own thought in Stirner."

32. On Narodism, in Lenin *Collected Works*, Progress Publishers (1975), Moscow, Volume 18, pp. 524–28.

33. Simon Rawidowicz, *Ludwig Feuerbachs Philosophie: Ursprung und Schicksal* (Berlin: Walterde Gruyter, 1964), 478

34. Eugène Kamenka, *The Philosophy of Ludwig Feuerbach* (New York: Routledge & K. Paul, 1970), 156.

35. Entry under "Feuerbach," in *Stanford Encyclopedia of Philosophy*.

36. Ego, 340.

37. G.W. X.: 188.

38. See Melvin Cherno, "Feuerbach's 'Man Is What He Eats': A Rectification," *Journal of the History of Ideas* 24, no. 3 (July–September, 1963): 397–406 (10 pages).

39. Simon Rawidowicz, *Ludwig Feuerbachs Philosophie: Ursprung und Schicksal* (Berlin: Walter De Gruyter, 1964), 187.

40. Kennedy, *Max Stirner*, 19.

Chapter 7

The New World as the New Jerusalem: Moses Hess

The task of the philosophy of spirit now consists in becoming a philosophy of action.

MOSES HESS, 1812–1875

By the early 1840s the proposal that *praxis* must supplant theory was a ritual maxim among Young Hegelian circles, but it fell to one thinker—Moses Hess—to press Cieszkowski's millennial Hegelianism into an even more radical religious formulation, a formulation that—although its triads and language sometimes resembled Hegelianism—had little to do with it either in its origin or intention. Just as Cieszkowski had revised Hegel, so Hess would revise Cieszkowski, and the resulting doctrine would be passed on to inspire Marx.

From his earliest years, Hess was infused with the despairing sentiments that arose from being of an oppressed people. In a telling anecdote of his youth, he recalled the evenings spent with his beloved grandfather, and of hearing the tales of the long sufferings of the Jewish people. While the grandfather read of the expulsion of the Jews from their home in Israel, "the snow-white beard of this strong old man was covered with tears in the telling of this story, and we children ourselves could not hold back from weeping and sobbing."[1] It seems fitting to remark here that in 1840—the year in which Hess revised the work of Cieszkowski—the Jewish community celebrated the year as 5600, a year that many thought would herald anew, and better age for all Jews.[2] Would not Hess have shared in this hope? It is not hard to imagine that the Rhineland Jews, and Hess was one, had felt their new sufferings under Prussian rule all the more acutely after they had enjoyed a brief moment of right under the Napoleonic code. He was of the same generation of Heine, Lasalle, Borne, and Disraeli, and he suffered the same confused pains of a liberal Jew in a cruel and conservative age, but—even when most in doubt about the role of his faith in the modem world—he never turned against it or its people with the repellent bitterness of a Marx. However, at twenty-three, Hess despaired of Judaism, and declared that since the destruction of the Temple there had been no religion, but only a longing after a lost and never-to-be recovered good, and yet even with this powerful longing every trace of that early and authentic Judaism would—and should—vanish[3]

In Hess, the sentiment was one of longing—but not for "a lost and never-to-be recovered good"—but for a future of reasoned peace and social harmony in which the angry and competing tensions of this contrary present age would be resolved and forgotten. The resolution of these present conflicts could not be gained by the passivity of traditional philosophy, but by an active "Philosophy of Action."[4]

But if young Hess lost his first religion, he soon gained another—Spinozism. To Hess, Spinoza was what Hegel had been to Cieszkowski - not merely a personal inspiration, but a crucial Christ-like turning point in history. In 1837, Hess published *The Sacred History of Mankind (Die heilige Geschichte derMenschheit)*. He signed it only as "a disciple of Spinoza." It was his first book, badly written and bearing all the flaws of the autodidact, the work was hardly noticed, yet it can claim to be the first original socialist work to appear in German directed to Germans. Both in form and content it indicated the course that both Hess and German Socialism were to follow in the years to come. It was, as the *Prolegomena*, fixed into the familiar triadic form.

Later, looking back upon its composition, Hess remarked that "Spinoza had elevated my consciousness of God to a height where I—with the bible in one hand and the *Ethics* in the other—wrote *The Sacred History of Mankind*."[5] There was, he asserted, no further influences working upon him other than these two revered sources; there was "no Swedenborg, no Saint-Simon, no Bentham, no Lamennais, no Hegel, no Heine, no so-called Young Germany." (24) Historical evidence would support the contention that young Hess knew little of Hegel or Hegelianism at the time he wrote *The Sacred History*. In sum, the triad, which he will henceforth employ—at least in its origins—is not either a conscious or unconscious reflection of Hegel's dialectical form, but is rather grounded in the prophetic tradition of biblical literature. As it will be seen, if it does resemble a Hegelian form, it resembles the developmental form of nature, in which "the second term is a difference, and appears . . . as a duality." This ignorance of and Manichean divergence from the Hegelian mode of development merits notice, for it means that Hess's socialistic dialectic does not originate in Hegel, and to attribute explicit Hegelian influences upon Hess's first and fundamental expression of Communist theory—as Isaiah Berlin has done[6]—is to allow socialist doctrine, at least in this instance, to draw sustenance from the authority of Hegel.

The Sacred History—"sacred" because human history is the manifestation of the divine will—is an unstable amalgam of Enlightenment epistemology and biblical enthusiasm—or inspiration—that traces mankind's historical *via delarosa* to what Hess terms the "New Jerusalem."[7]

The first age is, not unexpectedly, the age of the Father—one of innocence, unity, and passivity. In this period, knowledge of God is found in the imagination alone, which picture Him set beyond human reach. This childhood of mankind, reaching from Adam to Christ, was one of implicit equality and freedom—as yet untouched by the evils of private property. The second age, that of the Son, now recognizes the holy as an inward disposition of the soul. Christ was the first to know God in this exclusive manner, privately, in his heart. Quite naturally, this inward feeling of a loving presence led to the evils of egoism. God, as known by the Christian, will be so identified with the private sentiments of the individual that social division must result. The sin of the present is grounded in the Christian's myopic concern with the disposition of his soul, and this egoism readily translates into economic selfishness, Capitalism. To Hess, Christian exclusiveness not only generated the opposing poles of clergy and laity, the poles of medieval aristocracy and peasantry, but—in its final perfection—an aristocracy of wealth set over and against the impoverished mass. Monetary egoism is the final expression of Christianity. All this opposition will pass, however, in the third and final age of man. This age was initiated by Spinoza, who first understood God with an intellectual love unknown to his predecessors, a love which transcended all distinctions and oppositions. This love, a new form of knowledge, will reveal God to all men with a yet unimagined intellectual clarity. This enlightenment, which transcends and synthesizes the shared imagination of the past and the deep private feelings of the present, will enable all men to order their lives according to the recognized precepts of universal reason. To use a Marxian expression, it will be the end of ideology, that false consciousness generated by the alien world of private property. As Adam was but the man of Nature, and Christ the man of God, so—to Hess—is Spinoza, He is the pure man, the prototype of the future, the discoverer of God in reason. Henceforth, in the light of this reason, man will come to know "how to order his views and deeds according to the all-comprehending Law, and, with the clear consciousness of his eternal life in God, proceed with firm, steady, and manly strides upon the path of under-standing."[8] And, in this beatific future, *the whole country will be a great garden. In it everybody will be diligent and happy. Everybody will enjoy life as befits man. One will look for misery in order to remedy it. Yet one will find little of it. Distress will have left man.*[9]

In time, Hess' vision of a "sacred history" would lose all of its explicit religious content, but the religious or mythic form of his thought would remain in his later works, and—if anything—take on even stronger apocalyptic overtones. Hess' secularized content, abstracted and set into its familiar Marxian expression is but the standard socialistic triad: primitive communism, the fallen world of private property, and communism regained through the saving sacrifices of messianic socialism. As in Marx's words,

> Communism therefore as the complete return of man to himself as a *social* (i.e., human) being—a return accomplished consciously and embracing the entire wealth of previous development. This communism, as fully developed naturalism, equals humanism, and as fully developed humanism equals naturalism; it is the genuine resolution of the conflict between man and nature and between man and man—the true resolution of the strife between existence and essence, between objectification and self-confirmation, between freedom and necessity, between the individual and the species. Communism is the riddle of history solved, and it knows itself to be this solution.[10]

But yet, through this romantic veil of economics and new understandings, the ancient mythic shape is easily glimpsed: Israel founded, Israel suffering—the diaspora—and Israel regained. This is the fundamental mythical dialectic inspiring Marxism. It is far from being derived from Hegel. In this regard, attention must be drawn to Hess's lifelong interest in what has come to be known as "Zionism." His longing for a Jewish homeland, which was first evidenced in a letter written by Hess when he was but nineteen years old,[11] found its fullest expression over thirty years later, in his final work, *Rom und Jerusalem,* which was published in 1862. This impassioned call for the Jews to return to their ancient land, was, as Isaiah Berlin notes, Hess' "real life work."[12] Hess' continuing work in the cause of Zionism led Theodor Herzl to say that "all of what we sought had already been understood by him—but suffering under Hegelian terminology—Judaism since Spinoza has brought forth no greater spirit than the now forgotten and dimmed figure of Moses Hess!"[13] This obscuring Hegelian terminology was, of course, originally derived from Hess's reading of Cieszkowski.

Early in 1841, just as he personally encountered Marx for the first time, Hess' second work appeared. It was *The European Triarchy (Die europaische Triarchie)*—written in response to a now totally forgotten work, *The European Pentarchy (Die europaische Pentarchie).* The Triarchy was initially to have been entitled "Europe's Rebirth"—just as *Rom und Jerusalem* would later be tentatively entitled "Israel Reborn."[14] This second work continued along much the same lines as his first, although the *Triarchy* stressed the importance of conscious human action in the construction of the New Jerusalem, whereas the Sacred History had cast man principally in the role of an unconscious agent of the divine will. The welcome apocalypse had grown ever more immanent, and industrial England was now seen as the Armageddon field in which the inequalities of wealth were to be obliterated.

> The antagonism between poverty and wealth and the aristocracy of money will reach a revolutionary level only in England, just as that opposition between spiritualism and materialism could reach its culmination in France and the antagonism between state and church could reach its apex only in Germany.

Hess conveyed this vision directly and convincingly to Marx and Engels.

In the *Triarchy*, Hess fully agreed with the "geistvolle Cieszkowski" in seeing Hegel's philosophy of history as the weakest point of the whole speculative system, but unlike Cieszkowski, he did not charge this to an inexplicable misstep on the part of Hegel. To Hess, Hegel simply lacked the "intellectual love" that inspired Spinoza, a love that would have enabled Hegel to elevate his theory into a philosophy of action. Without this love Hegel could only sink into a despairing reflection upon the "slaughter—bench of history." For this reason, Hess declared that he "could not consider himself a participant in the Hegelian school."[15]

In the course of the *Triarchy*, Hess rather immodestly, if not incorrectly, declared that his first work, the *Sacred History* was, along with Cieszkowski's *Prolegomena*, a fundamental work in the needed transformation of abstract German theory into a program of effective and concrete action. However, as one historian noted,

> Hess's stature as a leading socialist thinker was due to the influence of his second book, The European Triarchy. In that work Hess criticized Hegel's philosophy as a history of spirit that denied the equally spiritual characteristics of matter and activity. Hegel's was also a philosophy of the past. The left Hegelian movement was a transition, Hess argued, to the philosophy of action and represented the philosophy of the future. Socialist historians narrowly focused upon Hess's critique of Hegel and its relation to dialectical materialism.[16]

Here, it is noteworthy that Hess does not consider his more popular later work, the *Triarchy*, to be as important as the *Sacred History*, which did contain some signs of Hegel. But even these signs were drawn mainly—if not exclusively—from Cieszkowski,

Shortly after the publication of the *Triarchy*, Hess confided to his friend Auerbach that he was yet intending to make a fundamental (grundlich) study of "German philosophy, namely Fichte and Hegel."[17] In short, whatever Marx acquired from Hess it could not have had much to do with the actual doctrines of Hegel.

Hess, always sensitive to present sufferings and humiliations—which he, as an individual, had sadly encountered—could only see in Cieszkowski's optimistic triad a blindness to the divisive forces rending the present world. The modem age, as antithetical to the past, was not a compliment to that past—as Cieszkowski had thought—but was an age of radical self-opposition. The triad of history presented by Cieszkowski had understood the antithetical period as but the negative compliment of the first period, but Hess took the antithetical period itself as internally antithetical—as set over and against itself in the form of class oppositions, of "*der Gegensatz der Pauperismus und der Geldaristokratie*" (38). The evils of the present world, with its ever "increasing misery," could only be overcome by a political apocalypse

As earlier noted, Hess, by all evidence and his own admissions, was never a Hegelian. But he was, in the words of Engels, "The first Communist in the Party."[18] Among other titles Hess was said to be "The Father of German Socialism,"[19] and was recalled as "The Herald of Socialist Zionism" at the First Zionist Congress held at Basel in 1897.[20] Even the subtitle of Avineri's book on Hess, the *Prophet of Communism and Zionism*[21] echoes his prescience. But with all of this, it was not Hegel but Hess—Arnold Ruge's "Communist Rabbi"[22]—who first introduced Marx to compose a political ideology which found its fruition in biblical mythology and the "One Substance" of Spinoza—the Classless Society.

Shlomo Avineri, in his study of Moses Hess writes that

> Hess, in his 1845 article, The Last Philosophers (die letzen philosophers), gets into a detailed critique of Stirner's The Individual and His Property (Der Einzige und sein Eigentum), ii which he sees as the most extreme philosophical expression of egoistic individualism. This criticism should not concern us here in its details.[23]

Given the concise nature of his book, (226 pages) Aveneri's lack of concern over the details of Hess's criticism is understandable. However, not to consider the details of Hess's criticism of Stirner, as well as to ignore Stirner's rebuttal, is to lose sight of a most important philosophical confrontation between two antithetical and radical social thinkers: Stirner and Hess. As a survey of the literature indicates, Avineri is not alone in this avoidance of the confrontation. But nevertheless, the debate between Stirner and Hess is not only the first, but perhaps the most profound confrontation occurring between a powerful advocate of social communism and equally powerful advocate of capitalistic individualism.

Stirner's work was mainly directed against the radical humanistic doctrines of Ludwig Feuerbach and Bruno Bauer, and evoked an extraordinary response—not only from those named, but by those unnamed, such as Moses Hess.

Unlike Stirner, who still attracts attention, Hess has been, in the main, forgotten, with almost all of his writings left untranslated and difficult to obtain. Nevertheless, along with being "The First Communist in the Party," Hess might also claim to be "The First Communist to read the *Ego*," as he and Engels read the proof copies of the work while both were in Cologne in late 1844. Their copy was set along to Marx. Although Hess was unmentioned in *The Ego*, a quotation taken from Hess's 1843 essay "Socialismus und Communismus" did appear in it.

> With the ideal of "absolute liberty," the same turmoil is made as with everything absolute [and according to Hess,] it is said to "be realizable in absolute human society." Indeed, this realization is immediately afterward styled a "vocation"; just so he then defines liberty as "morality": the kingdom of "justice" (equality) and "morality" (liberty) is to begin, etc. . . . Ridiculous is he who, while fellows of his tribe, family, nation, rank high, is - nothing but "puffed up" over the merit of his fellows; but blinded too is he who wants only to be "man." Neither of them puts his worth in exclusiveness, but in connectedness, or in the "tie" that conjoins him with others, in the ties of blood, of nationality, of humanity.[24]

It is likely that Hess, upon reading this, decided to respond to the charge of being "ridiculous," and in 1845, wrote his reply, which ran to about thirty pages, which Stirner termed a "Brochure," *Die letzten Philosophen [The Recent Philosophers]*.[25]

Unlike Marx, who was determined not to be identified with Judaism, Hess never disowned his Jewish ancestry, and indeed saw in the history of Judaism the very center of European history itself. In his first work, *The Holy History of Mankind*, which appeared in 1837, he systematically divided world history into three periods: the first being that of Adam, the second that of Jesus, and the third by Benedict Spinoza. As one scholar noted, this "fantasy of a third and most glorious dispensation had . . . , over the centuries, entered into the common stock of European social mythology." (xix)

In his tripartite division of history, Hess had not only inherited, as so many of his contemporaries, the mystical "dritter Reich" of Joachaim de Fiori, which forms the ground of Cieszkowski's *Die Prolegomena zur Historiosophie*. This feudal schema also finds reflection in the three historical stages of Communism, in which social history begins in primitive communism, passing through the anti-communism of private property, of Capitalism, and then terminates in final Communism—a "Classless Society."

Marx's final Communism and Hess's final "community of love" are similar visions.

Stimulated by the revolutionary expectations of his age, such as Feuerbach, Hess also determined that the future age, the third and final age of mankind, would be one in which a universal community founded upon mutual love would prevail. Humanity would then live under the inspiration of Spinoza's "amor intellectus dei," and live under a "law of love" in which "freedom and order do not collide with each other." Hess, in his 1843 work, *The Philosophy of the Deed" [Die Philosophie der Tat]*[26] encouraged Hegelian philosophers to turn from their impotent theorizing to a "praxis" (a term devised by Cieszkowski), to action which would bring forth the future society in which "The majesty and sovereignty of the One has transformed itself into the majesty and sovereignty of Everyman." xxi A new international union of national cultures would press beyond the petty interests of nationalism and proceed to establish a new world order based upon the shared principles of German philosophy, French politics, and English economics. In time, Hess' vision of a future world unhampered by competitive nationalism would find political reflection in the international aspirations of Marxism.

However, Hess was disturbed by certain "recent philosophers," such as Bauer and Stirner, who persisted in theorizing rather than enlisting in revolutionary praxis. They were unconscious that they were defending the ancient Christian "unhappy consciousness [unglückliche Bewußtsein]" so well described by Hegel. This self-contradicted consciousness was of the essence of Christianity, it had generated a false world-view that envisioned social reality as torn between two contradictory elements: a future theoretical heaven of communal happiness, confronting the present world dominated by the conflict of self-interest. This self-interest, this Egoism, was but the covert expression of the divided reality of Christianity, and it first had to be banished before the practice of the future, a unifying love, could come into being. To this end, "The Recent Philosophers" focused upon refuting the misguided and unconscious Christian Egoism of Bauer and Stirner.

Hess' essay runs to about 7,000 words. It evidences all of the usual virtues and vices of a work written by an autodidact—often quite creative, but sometimes marked by an imaginative excess which tended to an excited polemics. But this polemical "excitement" was not uncommon among the Young Hegelians of the pre-revolutionary vormärz. The impending revolution of 1848 seemed confirmation of Hegel's own view, that *our epoch is a birth-time, and a period of transition.*

Although he was no Marx when it came to vitriolic debating, Hess did well enough. However, considering the widespread anti-Semitic attitudes of his age, Stirner might have found some non sequitur support for his argument by simply echoing Arnold Ruge—who dismissed Hess as "the Communist

Rabbi." But he did not. There is no anti-Semitism to be found in any of his writings, and he did not join the majority of his colleagues who were antisemitic.[27] However, if Stirner was silent about Judaism, Hess did have something to say about Christianity.

> Neither Bauer nor Stirner ever allowed themselves to be influenced from without. It is rather the case that this "insanity" emerged directly from the inner living development of this philosophy and so it is that exactly in this manner, and no other, must the progeny of the Christian ascetics take their departure from the world.[28]

This remark contains the essence of Hess' critique, and if Bauer had introduced "The Jewish Question,"[29] the Hess had introduced "The Christian Question," For him it was this religion which had set a chasm between the real and the ideal, the world and a heaven, the soul and the body. It was their covert Christianity which drove such as Bauer and Stirner, these "progeny of the Christian ascetics" to "take their departure from the world." Their Egoism reflected their contempt for the world, leading them to retreat into the "insanity" of Egoism. Early in his essay, Hess briefly presents the problem of "recent philosophy" and his solution:

> Since the rise of Christianity men have worked to resolve the difference between the Father and the Son, the Divine and Human—in a word, between the "Species-Man [Gattungsmenschen]"and the "bodily" man. But as little has become of this effort as has come to Protestantism in its annulment [Aufhebung] of the visible Church—for the invisible Church (Heaven) and the invisible Priest (Christ) endure—and so a new clergy is permitted to rise up. The recent philosophers will gain just as little by casting off [aufhoben] this invisible Church and establishing the "Absolute Spirit," "Self-Consciousness," and "Species-Being [Gattungswessen]" in the place of Heaven. All of these attempts to theoretically resolve the difference between the particular man and the human species must miscarry, for even if the singular man does comprehend the world and mankind, nature and history, he yet in actuality remains only a sundered man [Vereinzelung] as long as the division of man is not practically overcome. But this separation of man will only be practically resolved through Socialism—that is, if men unite themselves in community life and activity, and surrender private gain.[30]

With this, Hegel's "Absolute Spirit," Feuerbach's "Species-Being" and Bauer's "Self-Consciousness" are drawn into Hess's circle of theoretical solutions which failed to resolve the divided reality inherited from "Christian dualism." Hess's own attempt to "resolve the difference between the particular man and the human species" called for the "surrender of private gain." This solution could hardly be expected to find Stirner in agreement, as his "Egoism" was expressed in "private gain" only to be surrendered at the cost of private destruction. For Stirner, Socialism was in the last analysis nothing less than the demand that the individual commit suicide. It was a radical and unacceptable resolution to the Christian problem of being "a sundered man [*Vereinzelung*]."[31] As Stirner had looked to a fully conscious Egoism as a remedy to resist the oppressive demands for communal enslavement, so Hess took it as the principle source of all past and present oppression. The curse of Egoism was, in religious form, nothing less than the "Original Sin" which had alienated man from both his world and himself. For Hess, the curse was now fulfilled by the creation of a fallen "mercenary world":

> The "free competition" of our modern mercenary world is not only the perfected form of rapacious robbery, but it is also the perfected consciousness of the complete diversity of human estrangement. The pre-historical world, classical slavery, Roman bondage, were all more or less unfitted to the essence of this estrangement. They still had limited perspectives, and so had not attained to the universality and general justification of rapacity now found in our commercial world The present mercenary world is the developed, essentially befitting, "conscious" and "principle" form of Egoism.

And further, even the most liberal politics are but the expression of the "modern mercenary world" (which Marx simply termed "Capitalism"):

Not only is the beast of prey [*das Raubtier*] perfected in our mercenary world, but the consciousness of this highest expression of the animal world is perfected as well. . . . Privileged plundering comes to an end; the arbitrary exercise of power is now universal human right. . . . The celebrated declaration of "The Rights of Man" is celebrated in that henceforth all preying bests are equally justified . . . because they are autonomous and free beings, justified because they, as Egoists, as "independent individuals" are now recognized and legally acknowledged.[32]

Clearly, Hess has expressed the central moments of Marx's "materialist conception of history," from the fundamental role economics exercised upon ideology, from the progress of egoistic doctrine from its initial support of slavery, to its historical termination in Capitalism. However, despite these major contributions to Communist theory, Hess was badly treated—as any competitor to Karl Marx might expect.

For Hess, Stirner was the only one who proposed a practical (but for him an absurd) solution to the issue of human self-alienation—a *Verein von Egoisten* (Union of Egoists).[33] The idea of such a *Verein* was touched upon only a few times in the *Ego*, but it drew Hess' attention in that it was, however it might appear as an oxymoron, given as an alternative to the desired Socialist society, in which "Everyone can cultivate, exercise and perfect their human qualities."

Considering the relative length and emotional energy that both invested in the debate over the nature of this "Union," it seems that both understood it to be a matter of considerable importance. It can be argued that the essential moral opposition between free- market Capitalism and a regulated Communistic society is present in the debate between the Stirner's idea of a "Union of Egoists" and Hess's "social union with our neighboring men."[34]

However, what Hess might define as a "social union" is never fully presented in any clear and positive idea, and what might be understood of it is found by only by reversing his unsparing criticism of Stirner's "Union." However, here is one of the rare, more or less clear, statement of Hess's own "solution" to the divisive state of human society:

> A Socialist establishes the proposal that we should become real species-being [wirkliche Gattungswesen], and thereby proposes a society in which everyone can cultivate, exercise and perfect their human qualities. Stirner wants to know nothing of.[35]

Hess's notion as to the actual specifics, either of the political character or the legal structure of his proposed future Communist xxxii society is left unstated. This silence is not unexpected, as all world-reformers, from before Christ to beyond Marx, all those who call for a "better world"—a future world usually without either sin or money—leave its necessary details to the imagination of their followers. xxxiii Nevertheless, what is absolutely necessary in all visionary calls for the future which "ought to be," is the specific enumeration of present evils—which are always clearly in evidence in the eyes of the reformers. In the case of Christ, it was "sinners," in the case of Marx "Capitalists"—and their followers were given the task to purge the world of evil and remake it into what it "out to be." On this matter, and surely to Hess's chagrin, Stirner seems to have taken Hegel's advice when he cautioned philosophers not to teach "what the world ought to be [wie die Welt sein soll], to be, since "Philosophy always arrives too late to do any such teaching."[36] Certainly, considering Stirner's whole passivity, if not irritated rejection of all social reformers it is likely that he did indeed take Hegel seriously. Hess would have read the very first lines of the *Ego and Its Own*, which clearly sets him and Stirner at odds:

> What is not supposed to be my concern! [Was soll nicht alles Meine Sache sein!] First and foremost, the good cause [Sache], then God's cause, the cause of mankind, of truth, of freedom, of humanity, of justice; further, the cause of

my people, my prince, my fatherland; finally, even the cause of Mind, and a thousand other causes. Only my cause is never to be my concern. "Shame on the egoist who thinks only of himself!"[37]

By late 1845, Stirner was prepared to defend himself against his critics[38]
In his defense, Stirner, (who throughout refers to himself in the in the third-person), takes on three "notable writings": Szeliga's critique in the March edition of the "Northern German Gazette" xxxvii; Feuerbach's "On The Essence of Christianity in Relation to The Ego and Its Own," which had appeared in Wigand's Vierteljahrsshrift, and the "brochure" of Moses Hess, "The Recent Philosophers." Stirner's response to his three critics ran to about fifty pages, with his rebuttal taking on each of his opponents, and dealing with a clarification of what he meant by his Einzigkeit ["uniqueness"], as well as his understanding of Egoism. Although Hess had joined Bauer and Feuerbach in their questioning of what Stirner had meant by "Einzigen" and "Egoismus," only Hess questioned Stirner's contribution to social theory, the "Union of Egoists."

Hess never directly engages in any effort, which to Stirner would be futile, to define the indefinable, but

> only alludes to the unique. He first identifies Stirner with the unique, and then says of the Unique: "He is the headless, heartless trunk, i.e., he has the illusion of being so, because in reality he doesn't just lack spirit, but body as well; he is nothing other than his illusions." And finally he pronounces his judgment on Stirner, "the unique": "He is boasting." From this, the unique appears as "the spook of all spooks," as "the sacred individual, which one must chase from the head" and as the "pale boaster."[39]

It seems to Stirner that all of his critics failed to comprehend that he, as a unique individual, cannot be comprehended, and so could not be gathered up into a generic collective—moral or otherwise. To understand what lead Stirner to define the individual as a being without definition, to be "beyond" all definition, beyond absolute thought, is to also understanding the rationale of his Egoistic philosophy. If nothing can be predicated of the *"Einziger"* then nothing can be said of any generic normative thought or behavior— even what it is to act or think as a "human being [*Mensch*]." The *"Einziger,"* being beyond definition, can be termed just as much an "Unmensch" as "Mensch"—just as much an inhuman as a human.[40] Stirner takes this confusion of labels as the fundamental ground which directly leads to the universal humanistic condemnation of Egoism:

> It is necessary to say a further word about the human being. As it seems, Stirner's book is written against the human being. He has drawn the harshest

judgments for this, as for the word "egoist," and has aroused the most stubborn prejudices. Yes, the book actually is written against the human being, and yet Stirner could have gone after the same target without offending people so severely if he had reversed the subject and said that he wrote against the inhuman monster [Unmenschen]. But then he would have been at fault if someone misunderstood him in the opposite, i.e., the emotional way, and placed him on the list of those who raise their voice for the "true human being." But Stirner says: the human being is the inhuman monster [Unmensch]; what the one is, the other is; what is said against the one, is said against the other.[41]

Stirner's effort to clarify what he meant by the "Einziger" being just as much inhuman as human by setting the two antithetical terms into a synthetic union, in which "what the one is, the other is" was certainly "misunderstood" by such as Hess. It was in this very misunderstanding that lead humanists to fear Egoism as simply an inhuman display:

The human being, which our saints agonize so much to recognize, insofar as they always preach that one should recognize the human being in the human being, gets recognized completely and actually only when it is recognized as the inhuman monster.[42]

It would come as no surprise to Stirner that Hess would see in him an advocate of an inhuman Egoism which would directly lead to a Hobbesian world, wherein "the war of all against all is sanctioned." Hess, as an ethical idealist, would naturally chose another world—one in which "men unite themselves in community life and activity, and surrender private gain." However, there was an option which neither Hess, nor any of the others who raise their voices for "the true human being" seem unable to recognize: individual competition.

When what Hegel terms the "logic of the understanding," the either/or logic that characterizes "common sense," there seems only two exclusive alternatives when it comes to choosing a socio-economic model: either communistic cooperation, in which there are no individual decisions or actions to be made other than the decision and action benefitting the whole (the One), or, on the other hand, the free and unrestrained decisions and actions of each and every individual seeking their own "selfish" good. Hess chose the former.

It is important to note that in his defense of competitive human relations, Stirner implicitly defends what might now be termed "free-market Capitalism":

Hess calls free competition the complete form of murder with robbery and also the complete consciousness of the mutual human alienation (i.e., Egoism). Here again, Egoism should still be guilty. Why then did one decide on competition?

Because it seemed useful to each and all. And why do socialists now want to abolish it? Because it doesn't provide the hoped-for usefulness, because the majority do badly from it, because everyone wants to improve his position and because the abolition of competition seems advisable for this purpose.

Is Egoism the "basic principle" of competition, or, on the contrary, haven't egoists just miscalculated about this? Don't they have precisely because it doesn't satisfy their Egoism?

People introduced competition because they saw it as well-being for all; they agreed upon it and experimented collectively with it. This thing, this isolation and separation, is itself a product of association, agreement, shared convictions, and it didn't just isolate people, but also connected them. It was a legal status, but this law was a common tie, a social federation. In competition, people come to agreement perhaps in the way that hunters on a hunt may find it good for the hunt and for each of their respective purposes to scatter throughout the forest and hunt "in isolation." But what is most useful is open to argument. And now, sure enough, it turns out—and, by the way, socialists weren't the first ones to discover it—that in competition, not everyone finds his profit, his desired "private advantage," his value, his actual interest. But this comes out only through egoistic or selfish calculations.[43]

The desire to correct "private advantage" is the moral ground for socialism, and it follows from the fact that in a competitive economy "the majority do badly." However, it is not only Stirner who sees this lack of universal reward, the "to each according to his need," lacking in the Capitalist (competitive) world, but also Hegel. It is presented as a simple expectation that there will be "losers." Competitive economic life is the compromise resting between individual "egoistic" struggle and "communal" agreements. The failure to successfully compete, in any arena of human relationships, cannot be denied. As Jesus had it, "The poor are with you always." Both Hegel and Stirner agree that although competition is the only "useful" relationship, nevertheless, one of its necessitated results is failure. As in the case of any competition, including writing articles for journals, not all can be "successful" and so publishable. In his excellent study of the issue, Michael Hardimon briefly summarized Hegel's view on the issue of poverty:

> Hegel maintains that the modern social world is a home despite the fact that it contains poverty. In his view, poverty is not an accidental or contingent feature of modern society but is instead systematic and structural: the fact that people in modern society tend to fall into poverty and form an underclass is the result of the normal operation of the economy (Ph. of Right, ¶ 241). Even though Hegel is acutely aware of the horrors of poverty, he still maintains that the modern social world is a home.[44]

What Hegel means by the "world is a home" is evident, that is, it is not a "home" to be displaced by an ideal, a future "home." Neither Hegel nor Stirner were revolutionary reformers. As to the matter of a synthesis between self-interest and communal life, Stirner also followed Hegel's view:

> As everything is useful for man, man is likewise useful too, and his characteristic function consists in making himself a member of the human herd, of use for the common good, and serviceable to all. The extent to which he looks after his own interests is the measure with which he must also serve the purpose of others, and so far as he serves their turn, be is taking care of himself: the one hand washes the other. But wherever he finds himself there he is in his right place: he makes use of others and is himself made use of.[45]

In this, both Hegel and Stirner reflected the economic theory of Adam Smith. In 1845, shortly after concluding the Ego. Stirner became both the editor and translator of Adam Smith's *Wealth of Nations*, and Jean-Baptiste Say's *Traite d'Economie Politique*. His translations, contained in multi-volume series commissioned by Otto Wigand,[46] It is interesting to note that Smith's well-known example of the "pin factory" appears in the *Ego*: *He who is in a pin factory only puts on the heads, only draws the wire, works, as it were, mechanically, like a machine.*[47]

As to what is "useful," the egoist concludes that

> I, the egoist, have not at heart the welfare of this "human society," I sacrifice nothing to it, I only utilize it; but to be able to utilize it completely I transform it rather into my property and my creature; that is, I annihilate it, and form in its place the Union of Egoists [Verein von Egoisten][48]

A contemporary analogue to the *"Verein,"* and possibly inspired by it, can be found in the popular work of Ayn Rand, *Atlas Shrugged*. In this novel, a group of conscious individualists, similar to Stirner's "conscious egoists," have taken refuge in a hidden camp to escape the restrictions upon their freedom by the over-regulatory Socialistic society of bureaucratic "looters and moochers" which had, in a slow revolution, replaced the free-market Capitalism of the United States. They hold that

> No matter whose welfare he professes to serve, be it the welfare of God or of that disembodied gargoyle he describes as "The People," no matter what ideal he proclaims in terms of some supernatural dimension—in fact, in reality, on earth, his ideal is death, his craving is to kill, his only satisfaction is to torture.

Stirner would agree with this, and wrote that those such as Hess, say that *You love man, therefore you torture the individual man, the egoist; your philanthropy (love of men) is the tormenting of men.*[49]

For Stirner, as with Hegel, dialectical logic was not the same as the common logic "either/or" of the understanding, and was the basis of Spinoza's work. It forced an absolute choice between contradictory terms, but rather the case that both could be obtained only if neither of the alternatives was taken as the fixed and exclusively "true" element. In the "Verein von Egoisten" the antithetical terms, "*Verein*" and "*Egoisten*" find their dialectical unity. Although at first it might not seem at all the case, there is nevertheless a deep similarity between Hegel's conception of the State and Stirner's "*Verein.*" For Hegel,

> The state is the actuality of concrete freedom. But concrete freedom consists in this, that personal individuality and its particular interest not only achieve their complete development and gain explicit recognition for the right . . . they also pass over of their own accord into the interest of the universal.[50]

Hess, as the "True Communist," always maintained that an irreconcilable contradiction, an unbridgeable chasm, divided the abstract universal of the "Community" and the concrete "particular interest" of the individual. Taken in their fixity, as simple irreconcilable contradictories, the individual "of its own accord" could not pass over "into the interest of the universal"—and it is this passage which would have to be forced upon individuals. The power of the state would force the passage. Individuals as such, "egoists," would have to be subordinated to that universal (be that universal either God or the State). And so, for Hess, there were only two antithetical options: either one must live in world of alienated (sinful) individuals engaged in "rapacious robbery" or to live an ideal universal (a Heaven on Earth) in which that savage individuality was annihilated (Hell). For Hess, the very conception of a "Verein von Egoisten" was an oxymoron. However, Stirner is prepared to defend the conception by an appeal to common experience:

> Hess reprimands Stirner like this: "Oh, unique, you are great, original, brilliant!" But I would have been glad to see your 'union of egoists', even if only on paper. . . . It would be another thing indeed, if Hess wanted to see egoistic unions not on paper, but in life. Faust finds himself in the midst of such a union when he cries: "Here I am human, here I can be human"—Goethe says it in black and white. If Hess attentively observed real life, to which he holds so much, he will see hundreds of such egoistic unions, some passing quickly, others lasting. Perhaps at this very moment, some children have come together just outside his window in a friendly game. If he looks at them, he will see a playful egoistic union. Perhaps Hess has a friend or a beloved; then he knows how one heart finds another, as their two hearts unite egoistically to delight (enjoy) each other, and how no one "comes up short" in this. Perhaps he meets a few good

friends on the street and they ask him to accompany them to a tavern for wine; does he go along as a favor to them, or does he "unite" with them because it promises pleasure? Should they thank him heartily for the "sacrifice," or do they know that all together they form an "egoistic union" for a little while?

To be sure, Hess wouldn't pay attention to these trivial examples, they are so utterly physical and vastly distinct from sacred society, or rather from the "fraternal, human society" of sacred socialists."[51]

However, it is upon these "trivial examples" that Stirner's argument is based. The "Verein" is justified by an inductive logic which rests upon empirical evidence; Hess' argument for the "Community" rests upon an a priori argument that finds its premise in the generic definition of "human being," of "Man," as a "Species-Being [*Gattungswesen*]." Stirner bases his case on the resent reality of social life in which egoists gather together for their own pleasure. Hess looks to a future communal state in which the definition of "Man" as "Species-Being" is fulfilled; and he understood the present reality, justified by Stirner, as stifling human aspirations. It should be noted that Hess was not at all a dreamy idealist, and later corrected his more youthful "Messianic" ideals into a more realistic program of reform. Still, his idealism endured. In his first major work, the 1837 Heilige Geschichte der Menschheit [The Holy History of Mankind], a young Hess, in what Avineri described as a "messianic style," proclaimed a "New Jerusalem" in which

> The politics of future society will be based on altruism, solidarity, and harmony. Peace will reign is society, both internally and externally; with the disappearance of class differences between the poor and the rich, the distinction between town and country will also disappear: "Villages will adorn themselves with stately buildings and towns with stately gardens."[52]

A quarter of a century later, in his major work, *Rome and Jerusalem*, Hess still held to his vision of a redeemed humanity, this time cast as the fulfillment of the Jewish dream of returning to Zion:

> We see already from afar the Blessed Land of organized humanity; we can already reach out with our own eyes to the Promised Land, toward which all human history has been directed, despite the fact that we cannot yet cross over into it.[53]

It was left to such as Theodor Herzl to "cross over into it," and to transform the ancient dream into a practical reality, and so Hess received recognition as the "The Herald of Socialist Zionism." Perhaps, in this turn from an idealized economic socialism to socialist Zionism, Hess also reflected the "unnerving" effect of Stirner's *Ego.*

It is significant that the subtitle of Hess's *The Holy History of Mankind* is "von einem jünger Spinozas," as Stirner is considered as "Junghegelianer." It might be well argued that both Spinoza and Hegel have found their ideological representatives in Hess and Stirner. Hess, who called Spinoza "The Master" throughout *The Holy History of Mankind,* a work "bristling with a messianic message,"[54] fully accepted Spinoza's doctrine that the "Absolute" rendered individuality metaphysically unjustified.[55]

And as to Hegelianism itself, it was but another recrudesce of dualistic Christianity, which simply "preserved Christian dualism, and . . . In this way Hess saw Hegelian philosophy as legitimizing social oppression, as did the philosophy of the Enlightenment."[56] On the other hand, Stirner, well-versed and committed to Hegel's dialectical logic, was not about to surrender his real individuality for the sake of an abstract ideal consistency (an "Absolute") that could only satisfy a mind unable to transcend the "either/or" logic of understanding. To surrender to that common logic would insure "legitimizing social oppression."

In the dense metaphysical thickets which separated the two opponents, what one had taken as obvious, that an undivided Community must encompass and absorb the "egoistic" many, was taken by the other as merely a conceptual reduction based upon the false logic that antithetical terms could never be reconciled. It was Hess who proposed a communality in which "men unite themselves in community life and activity, and surrender private gain." It was Stirner who defended the individual need for private gain. In retrospect, their debate reflected the difference between the philosophies of Hegel and Spinoza, which were themselves but the later reflection of the absolute opposition which held between the philosophies of Heraclitus and Parmenides. Hegel candidly asserted that "there is no proposition of Heraclitus which I have not adopted in my logic."[57] Since "the reasoning of Parmenides and Zeno is abstract understanding"—and not speculative dialectic, so the Eleatics were unable to comprehend the contradictory nature of reality. The same Eleatic philosophy repeated itself in Spinoza:

> The simple thought of Spinoza's idealism is this: The true is simply and solely the one substance, whose attributes are thought and extension or nature: and only this absolute unity is reality, it alone is God. . . . Taken as a whole, this constitutes the Idea of Spinoza and is just what τό ον (the One Being) was to the Eleatics.[58]

In 1827, Stirner had attended Hegel's *Lectures on the History of Philosophy,* and he well knew, as with Hegel, that it was only with the advent of the dialectical philosophy of Heraclitus that the dead abstraction of the "One" had been displaced by the concrete and given reality of the "unity of opposites." Stirner follows Hegel in understanding Spinoza's philosophy simply being one in which "all particularity and individuality pass away in the one substance."[59]

But Hess followed the Eleatic Spinoza, and so it was that he proclaimed that in the future Communal society "The majesty and sovereignty of the One has transformed itself into the majesty and sovereignty of Everyman." This "One," was as with the Eleatics, absolute, and the particulars, the individuals, were mere expression of this "One," Marx fully agreed with the Eleatic view, and so stated in his *Grundrissse*, that "Society does not consist of individuals, but expresses the sum of interrelations, the relations within which these individuals stand." But Stirner held to Hegel and Heraclitus, and justified the present social world as formed by real individuals engaged within a competitive "Union of Egoists." In this world actual individuals existed before they entered into relations with others—and that social "relations" were grounded upon distinct and concrete individuals. The singular individual was not a mere function of the "One" or "Society" and Stirner's doctrine rests upon this ontological base. The debate between the "jünger Spinozas" and the "Junghegelianer" is as ancient as philosophy itself,

NOTES

1. Found in Hess's unpublished *Tagebuch*, September 30, 1835. Cited from Edmund Silberner, *Moses Hess: Geschichte Seines Lebens*, 4.

2. A Messiah was expected who would gather into one community the scattered Jewish communities of the world. Silberner, *Moses Hess: Geschichte Seines Lebens*, 63ff.

3. Silberner, *Moses Hess: Geschichte Seines Lebens*, 24. Found in Hess's unpublished *Tagebuch*, September 30, 1835.

4. The term "Philosophie der Tat" was first used as a title in one of Hess's articles published in Herweg's *Einundzwanzig Bogen aus der Schweiz* (Zurich, 1843).

5. *The Sacred History of Mankind (Stuttgart, 1837) Die heilige Geschichte der Menschheit: Von einem Junger Spinozas* (Rpt. Gerstenberg Verlag, Hildesheim 1980). See Silberner for details of the composition of this work, pp. 49ff.

6. Isaiah Berlin, *The Life and Opinions of Moses Hess* (Cambridge: Cambridge University Press, 1959), 6.

7. The closing chapter of The Sacred History was entitled "D neue Jerusalem und die letzten Zeiten."

8. *Sacred History*, 176.

9. For a full description of the "New Jerusalem," see Silberner, *Moses Hess: Geschichte Seines Lebens*, 42ff.

10. *Economic and Philosophical Manuscripts 1844*, "Private Property and Communism," Pt. 3.

11. *Letter* to M. Levy, April 1831 in *Briefivechsel*, hrsg. E. Silberner, *Moses Hess: Geschichte Seines Lebens,* 45.

12. Berlin, *Life and Opinions*, 29.

13. *Tagebücher* (manuscript found in International Instituut voor Sociale Geschiedenis, Amsterdam), 2:599.

14. Moses Hess, *Briefivechsel,* hrsg. E. Silberner Letter of March 10, 1841.

15. Moses Hess, *The European Triarchy* (Die europäische Triarchie) (Leipzig: Otto Wiegand, 1841), 38.

16. Ken Koltum-Fromm, *Conceptions of Self and Identity in Hess's Early Works and Rome and Jerusalem* (Bloomington: Indiana University Press, 2001), 14–15.

17. Letter of March 10, 1841 in Silberner, *Moses Hess.*

18. *Werke* (Dietz, 1964), 1, p. 494.

19. Lobkowicz, *Theory and Practice: History of a Concept from Aristotle to Marx,* 231.

20. Edmund Silberner, *Moses Hess: Geschichte seines Lebens* (Leiden: E. J. Brill, 1966), 73.

21. Shlomo Avineri, *Moses Hess: Prophet of Communism and Zionism* (New York University Press, 1985).

22. Arnold Ruge, *Zwei jahre in Paris: Studien und erinnerungen.* Vol. 1 (Leipzig: W. Jurany, 1946), 31.

23. Schlomo Aveneri, *Moses Hess: Prophet of Communism and Zionism* (New York and London: NYU Press, 1987), 138.

24. The phrase "according to Hess," was not in the original text, but was inserted by the Editor of the recent Cambridge edition of The Ego *and His Own, David Leopold.*

25. Moses Hess, *Die letzten Philosophen.* Darmstadt: C. W. Leske [Juni] 1845, IV+28 S. Found also in Kurt W. Fleming (Hg.), *Recensenten Stirners. Kritik und Anti-Kritik* (Leipzig: Verlag Max-Stirner-Archiv, 2003), S. 27–43. Translated by the author as Although the "letzten" in the title lends itself to being translated as "The Last Philosophers," a reading of Hess' work indicates that it was directed against "recent" philosophers," such as Bauer and Stirner.

26. "Such as Bauer and Stirner," *in Einundzwanzig Bogen aus der Schweiz* (Zurich: Literarischen Comptoirs, 1842), 309–31; rpt. Topus Verlag:Vaduz, 1977; See Avineri, *Moses Hess*, 95.

27. Stepelevich, "Max Stirner and the Jewish Question," 34–1.

28. Hess, *Die Letzten Philosophen.* Essay translated by author, in *The Young Hegelians*, Intro. and edited by Lawrence Stepelevich (Cambridge: University Press, 1983), 360.

29. Bruno Bauer, was the first to employ the term *"The Jewish Question [Die Judenfrage]"* within German intellectual circles.

30. Hess, *Recent Philosophers,* 360.

31. In the 1840 *German-English Dictionary* (Philadelphia: Mentz and Son) the term Vereinzelung" not only connotes "dismembering" but also "retailing, selling in single portions, an economic usage undoubtedly known and appreciated by Hess.

32. Hess, *Recent Philosophers*, 369.

33. *"Verein von Egoisten"* has commonly been translated as a "Union of Egoists." However, the term "Verein" can also mean an "Association," "Club" or a "Society"—suggesting a more informal gathering, and seems more in accord to what Stirner had in mind

34. Hess, *Recent Philosophers*, 360.

35. *Recent Philosophers*, 373. Hess, as most of the "Young Hegelians" is prone to italicize terms to suggest that they have a deeper meaning, but obscure term "Gattungswesen" [Species-Essence] is not clarified by being italicized.

36. Preface, *Philosophy of Right*.

37. *Ego*, 5.

38. "Recensenten Stirners," in Max Stirner: Kleinere Schriften (Stuttgart: Bad Cannstatt, 1976). The English translation of Wolf Landstreicher, *Stirnernstatt, 19* (Berkeley: LBC Books, 2012) will be used when citing from Stirner's text.

39. Stirner, *Critics*, 54.

40. In the "Translator's Preface" to *Stirner's Critics*, Wolfi Landstreicher notes that "In Byington's translation of *Der Einzige und Sein Eigentum*, he usually chose to simply translate the latter word as "unman." But in German, the word refers to a "monster," and knowing Stirner's enjoyment of playing with words and ideas in ways that are likely to get the goat of his opponents, I think that he most likely meant just that. To further emphasize Stirner's intent of contrasting this with the abstract, conceptual human being, I chose to translate the term as "inhuman monster." This leads to such delightful statements as: "You are an inhuman monster, and this is why you are completely human, a real and actual human being, a complete human being." Delightful, perhaps, but Byington's translation is *exactly* what Stirner intended by the term "Unmensch"—an "unman," or as the recent Editor of the Ego has it, "non-man"

41. Stirner, *Critics,* 73.

42. Ibid., 79.

43. Ibid.

44. Michael O. Hardimon, *Hegel's Social Philosophy: The Project of Reconciliation* (Cambridge: University Press, 1994), 32.

45. *Phenomenology,* para. 550.

46. Stirner's German translations appeared in 1846-47, and remained the standard translation for some years.

47. Ego, 108.

48. Stirner, *Critics,* 161.

49. Ego, 258.

50. Hegel, *Philosophy of Right*, 160.

51. Stirner, *Critics*, 100.

52. Cited by Avineri, *Moses Hess*, 39–40.

53. Ibid.

54. Ibid., 22.

55. Yitzhak Melamed's "Acomism or Weak Individuals? Hegel, Spinoza, and the Reality of the Finite," *Journal of the History of Philosophy* 48 (2010): 77–92.

56. Aveneri, *Moses Hess,* 125.

57. *History of Philosophy*, trans. E. S. Haldane (Routledge & Kegan Paul, 1955), I, 279.

58. *History of Philosophy*, III, 156–57.

59. *Lectures on the History of Philosophy*, III, 254.

Chapter 8

A Sudden Turn to Scientific Socialism: Marx and Engels

Bauer and Stirner are the only important philosophical opponents of Socialism—or rather Communism. *The New Moral World* (No. 46, May 10, 1845).

—Frederich Engels

KARL MARX, 1818–1883 AND FREDERICH ENGELS, 1820–1895

Among others who shared the "new discovery" of Man would have been Karl Marx. At the time that time that the *Ego* appeared was considered a devoted follower of Feuerbach, and had even set about writing a work based upon Feuerbach's *Philosophy of the Future*. It is not insignificant that Bruno Bauer, the "Messiah of Atheism"[1] was Marx's friend and teacher during Marx's brief student days in Berlin. They had not only planned a *Journal of Atheism*, but both had studied the *Book of Isaiah*. This Old Testament work is a gathering of oracles, prophecies, and reports with one common theme: the coming of a Messiah to save the oppressed. It is not unimaginable that Marx, who had descended from a long line of Rabbis, might well have considered himself the new Messiah, one bent upon the salvation of the poor downtrodden Proletariat and leading them into a heavenly, if earthly, "Classless Society." The idea that Marxism was in essence a religion was first presented by Stirner, and it later developed into an accepted view. On this, at a later time, Bertrand Russell found himself in agreement with Stirner when it came to taking Communism as a theological doctrine:

> The Jewish pattern of history, past and future, is such as to make a powerful appeal to the oppressed and unfortunate at all times. St. Augustine adapted this pattern to Christianity, Marx to Socialism. To understand Marx psychologically, one should use the following dictionary: Yahweh = Dialectical Materialism; The Messiah = Marx; The Elect = The Proletariat; The Church = The Communist Party; The Second Coming = The Revolution; Hell = Punishment of the Capitalists; The Millennium = The Communist *Commonwealth*[2]

Other than not casting the role of the Lumpenproletariat as the "unelected," Russell is onto something. Indeed, his comparison of Marx to St. Augustine is well taken. The ideological line from St. Augustine to the horrors of the Inquisition has been repeatedly traced, most recently by Peter Zagorin.[3] The line from Marx to the eradication of political heretics can be just as clearly laid out.

In a theological formulation of Marxism, Stirner would be dismissed as an apostate. As it happened, even he admitted that he was an "apostate" if by that is what is meant being an egoist:

> In short, the party [Socialist] cannot bear non-partisanship, and it is in this that egoism appears. What matters the party to me? I shall find enough anyhow who unite with me without swearing allegiance to my flag. He who passes over from one party to another is at once abused as a "turncoat." Certainly, morality demands that one stand by his party, and to become apostate from it is to spot oneself with the stain of "faithlessness"; but ownness knows no commandment of "faithlessness"; adhesion, and the like, ownness permits everything, even apostasy, defection.[4]

For even Hess, once praised by Engels as "the first communist of the party," and credited with converting Engels to Communism,[5] nevertheless fell into the error of "True Socialism." The "True Socialism" of Moses Hess is simply heresy.[6] Within three years, Hess, who had contributed to *The German Ideology*, was excommunicated in the *Communist Manifesto*. As Sidney Hook long ago noted, the *Manifesto* "unmistakably concentrates its fire on Hess, making allowances neither for the actual development of Hess' views nor for his revolutionary integrity."[7] Karl Marx, in the *Manifesto*, and in one of his poetic moods, considered his former follower had merely spun

> a robe of speculative cobwebs, embroidered with flowers of rhetoric, steeped in the dew of sickly sentiment, this transcendental robe in which the German

Socialists wrapped their sorry "eternal truths," all skin and bone, severed to wonderfully increase the sale of their goods among such a public.

Needless to say, in any religious doctrine, heresies—being nothing less than various differing opinions regarding the declared "Truth"—need to be quickly detected and condemned (so as not to mislead the true believers). True Socialism was not the last Communist heresy, and more were soon detected and condemned—such as "Trotskyism" or "defeatism" or the pernicious Menshevik heresy. Stirner would not have been surprised at the revelation of the inquisitorial core of Marxian "pious atheists," who, just as pious Christians, are committed to the "continuations and consistent carryings-out of the Christian principle, the principle of love, of sacrifice for something general, something alien."[8]

In the late fall of 1844, shortly after their first joint work, *The Holy Family*, in which Stirner's name had not appeared, was sent off to its publisher, Engels and Hess had obtained an early press copy of Stirner's work. Shortly thereafter, Engels sent a letter to Marx, then in Paris, a in which Engels suggested that the work was of value in promoting the Communist cause. Engels had just returned from England, where Jeremy Bentham was a popular social reformer, and known as the founder of "Utilitarianism," and an advocate of egoism. Engels also would have known that Stirner, just as Bentham, had proposed a form of "Utilitarianism."[9] A comparison would be expected, and so it was—Stirner, "takes for his principle Bentham's egoism." Of course, for Engels, no matter how favorably he might view Stirner, insofar as *der Einzige* was fundamentally critical of Communism, his work could only be awarded the Communist label, so often employed, as being "absurd." Still, as a friend and admirer of Stirner (having noted that "Stirner is the most talented, independent and hard-working of the Free"), Engels must have thought a bit about just how he could favorably introduce Stirner to his new friend. He managed to find something positive to write about Stirner's work—"after all we must not just cast it aside." And so, this positive side of Stirner's work found expression in two strained arguments: The first was of a practical nature (which might appeal to Marx), that is, that it was right for Communists to become egoists, as it gave them a personal impetus to promoting Communism. The second, more recondite, was based upon Engel's reading of Hegelian logic, for with it, the "one-sidedness" of Stirner's egoism was but a penultimate stage of self-consciousness. It must pass over, by its own dialectical self-negation, into terminal Communism. As Engels had it,

> This [Stirner's] egoism is taken to such a pitch, it is so absurd and at the same time so self-aware, that it cannot maintain itself even for an instant in its one-sidedness, but must immediately change into communism. In the first place it's

a simple matter to prove to Stirner that his egoistic man is bound to become communist out of sheer egoism. That's the way to answer the fellow. . . . But we must also adopt such truth as there is in the principle. And it is certainly true that we must first make a cause our own, egoistic cause, before we can do anything to further it—and hence that in this sense, irrespective of any eventual material aspirations, we are communists out of egoism also, and it is out of egoism that we wish to be human beings, not mere individual.[10]

Marx's reply has been lost, but that he replied is certain. His recent follower must have been forcefully reminded that Stirner was not welcome among Communists. Engels, in his next letter, was apologetic and almost immediately set about explaining his favorable remarks over Stirner: "As regards Stirner, I entirely agree with you. When I wrote to you, I was still too much under the immediate impression made upon me by the book. Since I laid it aside and had time to think it over, I feel the same as you."[11]—it was a close call for the "second fiddle." It is quite possible that Engels had ignored Stirner's criticism of Marx's Feuerbachian declarations.[12]

And so, a somewhat unenthusiastic Engels then went along with Marx, and both began writing a heavy-handed and lengthy polemic mainly directed against Stirner. Marx had simply dismissed Engel's unhappy complaint about directing another work against the Berlin Hegelians. Engels had found "all this theoretical twaddle daily more tedious and am irritated by every word that has to be expended on the subject of 'man', by every line that has to be read or written against theology and abstraction no less than against crude materialism." Finally, by the summer of 1845, the second joint effort was finally finished and bears the English title *The German Ideology: a Criticism of Recent German Philosophy and its representative Feuerbach, Bruno Bauer and Stirner, and a criticism of German Socialism and its Various Proponents.*[13]

Here, it is of interest to note that 1845 was a critical year in the formation of the early Socialism, with both Marx and Engels leaving Brussels for England to visit the leaders of the Chartists, a British socialist movement. It does seem remarkable that Marx had turned from organizational activity to embarking upon another lengthy criticism of the Berlin Hegelians—unless Stirner had to be dealt with. The manuscript was not accepted for publication and remained so until 1932 when Stalin ordered its publication.

In 1886, years after it had been written, Engels recalled the circumstances which lead to its composition:

> In the preface to *A Contribution to the Critique of Political Economy*, published in Berlin, 1859, Karl Marx relates how the two of us in Brussels in the year 1845 set about: "to work out in common the opposition of our view"—the materialist

conception of history which was elaborated mainly by Marx—to the ideological view of German philosophy, in fact, to settle accounts with our erstwhile philosophical conscience. The resolve was carried out in the form of a criticism of post-Hegelian philosophy. The manuscript, two large octavo volumes, had long reached its place of publication in Westphalia when we received the news that altered circumstances did not allow of its being printed. We abandoned the manuscript to the gnawing criticism of the mice all the more willingly as we had achieved our main purpose—self-clarification![14]

That "We abandoned the manuscript to the gnawing criticism of the mice" speaks to their willingness to turn from any further consideration of the manuscript, and subsequent disciples of Marx were of the same opinion, and with this, for all practical purposes, the case of Stirner was closed.[15] However, as the hundreds of writings, critical and otherwise, given over to Stirner since the publication of the Ego attest, he was not easily dismissed.

The Marxian tendency to dismiss Stirner as unworthy of consideration, as absurd—although, sadly enough, he had to be taken into some account—has found recent echoes in such Marxian restorations as found in such Lukacs, Derrida, and Habermas.[16] On this, an interesting confirmation that Marx's judgment remains "unchallenged" can be found on the internet when one seeks to read the stated "full text" of *The German Ideology* in the PDF publication of the "Marxist.org": Here the reader is advised that "If you would like to read their critique of Saint Max and Saint Bruno then read the book. . . . While a critique of Saint Max and Saint Bruno would be useful to read if the ideas they expressed were of any relevance or importance, this is not the case. The ideas they supported are long since forgotten."—That is, in the Marxian Memory Hole.[17] Checking recent English language editions of the *German Ideology*, the lengthy chapter on Stirner is simply dismissed: "Part II consisted of many satirically written polemics against Bruno Bauer, other Young Hegelians, and Max Stirner. These polemical and highly partisan sections of the 'German Ideology' have not been reproduced in this edition."[18] Evidently although the "satirically written polemics" of Marx and Engels are acceptable, the "polemical and highly partisan" writings of Bauer and Marx are not. Marx's rejection of Stirner remains, as always among Marxists, unspoken and unchallenged. Robert J. Hellman's in his study of the Berlin "Free Ones" noted:

> The Berlin Young Hegelians were not ignored by Marx. Rather it was their even greater, if ironic, misfortune, to be discussed, contemptuously, at great length, in a book of his so clumsy that Marxist scholars have ignored it whenever possible. Die deutsche Ideologie (The German Ideology) is not Marx at his best—it is a petty, snide, wordy, sometimes-funny, but woefully disorganized book. It has been the fate of this book, as a consequence, to be little read and half-known

and the individuals who make up its subject matter equally so. Marx's contempt has been duly recorded but the merit of his critique has simply been assumed, leaving his judgment unchallenged.[19]

In the 1960s, that flowery period of "hippie" subculture, a loving "Young" Marx was suddenly discovered, one quite unlike the dour old Marx of *Das Kapital*. Reflecting the times, Eric Fromm, in 1961, gathered up a collection of Marx's early writings under the title of *Marx's Concept of Man* (Marx's 1844 essay, on the *Judenfrage*, is noticeable by its absence.) Sitrner is also among the missing, even with Fromm's inclusion of a section of *The German Ideology*.[20]

Fromm, among others, was intent upon presenting Marx as a Guru of the counter-culture, an early advocate of the "Make love not war" generation. It was easy enough to find confirmation of a "loving Marx" among the many vapid Feuerbachian observations found in the *Economic and Philosophic Manuscripts*:

> Let us assume man to be man, and his relation to the world to be a human one. Then love can only be exchanged for love, trust for trust, etc. If you wish to enjoy art you must be an artistically cultivated person; if you wish to influence other people you must be a person who really has a stimulating and encouraging effect upon others. Every one of your relations to man and to nature must be a specific expression, corresponding to the object of your will, of your real individual life. If you love with-out evoking love in return, i.e., if you are not able, by the manifestation of yourself as a loving person, to make yourself a beloved person, then your love is impotent and a misfortune.[21]

But the sentimental followers of the "Young Marx," had forgotten the "Old Marx," who had, in the spring of 1845, suddenly ceased being a Feuerbachian. The first signs of a new and scientific "Marxian" Marx appeared in early 1845, in his critical "Theses on Feuerbach." It was a sudden transformation, for just a year earlier, in the *Holy Family*, Marx had clearly rejected Bauer's "infinite self-consciousness" in favor of Feuerbach:

> But who, then, revealed the mystery of the "system"? Feuerbach Who annihilated the dialectics of concepts, the war of the gods that was known to the philosophers alone? Feuerbach. Who substituted for the old lumber and for "infinite self-consciousness," if not, indeed, "the significance of man"—as though man had another significance than that of being man!—at any rate "Man"? Feuerbach, and only Feuerbach.[22]

Fromm carefully avoided Marx's sudden and rather blunt turn from Fuerbach to "Scientific Socialism" after he had encountered the *Ego*. As

Louis Althusser saw it, in 1845, there was a sudden "epistemological break" in Marx's philosophy.[23] It was more than "epistemological," it was a radical break with his idealism, and thereafter he became the realistic and hard-hitting thinker of *Das Kapital*. The peaceful "path to truth and freedom through the Fiery Brook [*Feuer-Bach*]" had to be abandoned,[24] and a more stringent path had now to be taken to "truth and freedom."

After reading Stirner, Marx and Engels faced a crucial problem. If Stirner were correct, then they should discard Feuerbachian idealism and along with it the temptation to issue heated and quasi-religious calls for revolutionary action. However, this might meant to also turn away from being a leader of a Socialist revolt, and "Communism" would be reduced to a mere philosophy of history. Since Stirner was not easy to reject, as the cases of both Feuerbach and Bauer suggested, a compromise was needed. It found expression in the doctrine of "Historical Materialism," a.k.a. "Materialist Conception of History." The conception first appeared in *The German Ideology,* and has, ever since, remained a fundamental, if contentious, Marxian doctrine.

The doctrine of Historical Materialism insured that Communist reform adhered to "scientific," "realistic," and "materialistic" laws to predict the course of economic history from primitive communism to pure communism, and therefore was in no way an "idealism." However, although the course of history was scientifically necessitated to reach its goal in "pure Communism," the movement would still require underlying revolutionary ideals and deeds. The necessitated laws of Historical materialism give secure promise to the revolutionary movement, that "What the bourgeoisie therefore produces, above all, are its own grave-diggers. Its fall and the victory of the proletariat are equally inevitable."[25]

But nevertheless, this "inevitable victory" still requires revolutionary action. It is no more difficult to believe in this paradoxical doctrine than the Christian doctrine which holds that the Omnipotence of God's Providence yet allows for human free will.

Walter Benjamin compared Marxian doctrine to an eighteenth-century mechanized chess-playing automation, a puppet, the "Turk." The seemingly complex mechanical device actually concealed within it a dwarf, who actually played the chess game. As Walter Benjamin has it, "[t]he puppet called 'historical materialism' is always supposed to win. It can do this with no further ado against any opponent, so long as it employs the services of theology, which as everyone knows is small and ugly and must be kept out of sight."[26] Marx concealed the hidden "small and ugly" theological side of Marxism under the complex "scientific" automaton of "Historical Materialism," and under the many levers and gears, the complex mechanism of "productive forces" and "ideological superstructures," the actual prime mover of

Marxism, theological idealism, would be hidden. But Stirner had already seen the concealed religious thought underlying and driving Communism:

> Communism, which assumes that men "have equal rights by nature," . . . Altogether, this entire revolutionary or Babouvist principle rests on a religious, that is, false, view of things. Who can ask after "right" if he does not occupy the religious stand-point himself? Is not "right" a religious concept, something sacred? Why, "equality of rights," as the Revolution propounded it, is only another name for "Christian equality," the "equality of the brethren," "of God's children," "of Christians"; in short, *fraternité*.[27]

The *German Ideology* falls into two parts, later framed as two volumes. The first volume contains three chapters; the first (originally entitled "Feuerbach") discusses the views of Marx and Engels. The second chapter is an analysis of Bauer's reply to charges against him in *The Holy Family*, and the third chapter deals with Stirner's *Ego*. Moses Hess has been credited as the author of the second volume, entitled "True Socialism." For present purposes, only that section dealing with Stirner is of interest. It happens to be, by far, the longest and most important section of the work, and indeed filled more pages of relentless criticism against the *Ego* than found in the *Ego* itself.[28]

Chapter 3 is modeled upon Stirner's *The Ego and His Own*, which has two major divisions: "*Der Mensch*" ("Man") and "*Ich*" ("Ego"). Both divisions are re-titled in Marx's biblical parody of Stirner's work, "The Old Testament: Man," and "The New Testament: Ego." The corresponding sections of Stirner's work are also re-titled to fit the biblical theme.

When it came to dealing with Stirner, *The German Ideology* revealed both its temper and principle idea in its first introductory paragraph:

> Saint Max exploits, "employs" or "uses" the Council to deliver a long apologetic commentary on "the book," which is none other than "the book," the book as such, the book pure and simple, i.e., the perfect book, the Holy Book, the book as something holy, the book as the holy of holies, the book in heaven, viz., *Der Einzige und sein Eigenthum*. "The book," as we know, fell from the heavens towards the end of 1844 and took on the shape of a servant with O. Wigand in Leipzig.[29]

"Saint Max" (who appears more than "Stirner" in the text), is thereafter, and throughout the work caricatured in a religious parody. The final paragraph of the exhausting and vitriolic criticism follows the same thought set out in the first paragraph:

> Finally Saint Max gives us a few more examples of his faith, showing that he is so little ashamed of the Gospel that he asserts: "We really are nothing but spirit,"

and maintains that at the end of the ancient world "after long efforts" the "spirit" has really "rid itself of the world." And immediately afterwards he once more betrays the secret of his scheme, by declaring of the Christian spirit that "like a youth it entertains plans for improving or saving the world."

The apocalyptic prophet did not prophesy accurately this time. Now, at last, after Stirner has acclaimed man, one can state that he ought to have said: So he carried me into the wilderness of the spirit. And I saw a man sit upon a scarlet-coloured beast, full of blasphemy of names . . . and upon his forehead was a name written, Mystery, the unique . . . and I saw the man drunken with the blood of holy, etc. So we now enter the wilderness of the spirit.[30]

At the very outset of the *Ideology*, Marx proposes that the followers of Hegel were trying, rather desperately, to revive the "Absolute Spirit":

Certainly it is an interesting event we are dealing with: the putrescence of the absolute spirit. When the last spark of its life had failed, the various components of this caput mortuum began to decompose, entered into new combinations and formed new substances. The industrialists of philosophy, who till then had lived on the exploitation of the absolute spirit, now seized upon the new combinations.[31]

The "new combinations" are all cast in religious forms:

Gradually every dominant relationship was pronounced a religious relationship and transformed into a cult, a cult of law, a cult of the State, etc. On all sides it was only a question of dogmas and belief in dogmas. The world was sanctified to an ever-increasing extent till at last our venerable Saint Max was able to canonise it en bloc and thus dispose of it once for all.[32]

All of this rapid-fire dismissal of Hegelians, both "Old" and "Young" as being nothing more than religious idealists faced with the "putrescence of the Absolute Spirit" (a meaningless, if striking, metaphor) finds that Max Stirner is responsible for "disposing of it once for all." The polemical introduction sets the tone for the remainder of the work. Not only is Marx's scorn of the "industrialists of philosophy" taken as fully justified, but such terms as "German reality" and "material surroundings" are left undefined. Needless to say, these undefined "material surroundings" will be gathered together and later established by Marx under the label "Historical Materialism." It is a doctrine which claims to be based upon

Real premises from which abstraction can only be made in the imagination. They are the real individuals, their activity and the material conditions under which they live, both those which they find already existing and those produced by their activity. These premises can thus be verified in a purely empirical way.[33]

Hence, Historical Materialism is "realistic." It deals in "real premises" (unlike the Young Hegelians who deal in "the illusions of consciousness"). As a "realistic" doctrine, its "premises can thus be verified in a purely empirical way." It seems evident that the acceptance of these assertions, generalities without further definition is merely a matter of belief, which is exactly what Marx condemned. This literary, if not logical, introductory *tour de force* has but one intention: Marx is right, is "realistic," and everyone else is wrong.

It is certain that Marx and Engels did read Stirner's *Ego*, as almost every section of it is subjected to relentless and selective criticism. Overall, merely considering the logic of *The German Ideology*, the work is simply a running series of *ad hominum* arguments and *petitio principia* fallacies. Even Hans Mehring, the usually admiring biographer of Marx, had difficulty in finding any merit in this "super polemic." He was forced to conclude that *The German Ideology* was characterized by "hair-splitting and quibbling, some of it of a rather puerile [*knabenhaft*] character."[34] As seen, for Stirner, this "puerile" or adolescent character was characteristic of the fixed mind of the social reformer who, as Hegel had it, "fancies himself called and qualified to transform the world, or at least to put the world back on the right path from which, so it seems to him, it has strayed."

Throughout the work, Stirner is variously referred to as "Jacques le bonhomme," "our good-natured Philistine," "Sancho Panza," "our schoolmaster," "our theorizing petty bourgeois" and other labels too numerous to mention, the most common being "Saint Max"—which is used more than "Stirner." As to begging the question, Stirner is first quoted (selectively), and then, the author being suitably ridiculed, the quote is shown as failing to accord itself with "realistic" Marxian doctrine.

The second major division of the *Ideology* is entitled "The New Testament: Ego." Its third section has the title "The Revelation of John the Divine, or The Logic of the New Wisdom." It is the expected heated critique of "Saint Max" but does contain a passage of more than the usual interest, as it deals with the overall intent of the *Ideology*:

> Our whole exposition has shown that Saint Sancho criticizes all actual conditions by declaring them "the holy," and combats them by combating his holy idea of them. This simple trick of transforming everything into the holy was achieved, as we have already seen in detail above, by Jacques le bonhomme accepting in good faith the illusions of philosophy, the ideological, speculative expression of reality divorced from its empirical basis, for reality, just as he mistook the illusions of the petty [bourgeois concerning] the bourgeoisie for the

holy essence of the bourgeoisie, and could therefore imagine that he was only dealing with thoughts and ideas. With equal ease people were transformed into the "holy," for after their thoughts had been divorced from them themselves and from their empirical relations, it became possible to consider people as mere vehicles for these thoughts and thus, for example, the bourgeois was made into the holy liberal.[35]

The theme is clear: Stirner, in accepting the "illusions of philosophy" has lost contact with "reality." He deals only in "thoughts and ideas." Marx, of course, never deals in mere "thoughts and ideas" but in "reality." The terms are left undefined. The presupposition that "empirical relations" are "actual conditions" is left unquestioned throughout the whole of the *Ideology,* and how one concludes that philosophical "illusions" are divorced from their "empirical basis" is itself a philosophical assertion—if not an "illusion."

What becomes ever more evident when reading the *Ideology* is its overriding fascination with religious imagery, with Stirner's "Holy Book" being the prime critical object. However, this fascination with Stirner's "Holy Book" and all things religious, suddenly ended with the writing of the *Ideology.* Soon after it had been written, Marx became the "Father of Scientific Socialism," and in less than two years, the loving Feuerbachian "Young Marx" of the *Economic and Philosophic Manuscripts* had been transformed into the hard-fisted Marx of *The Communist Manifesto.*[36] In short, Marx had become a Marxist. Religion was reduced to a vanishing element in the "ideological superstructure" seemingly far removed from the fundamental "economic substructure." Nevertheless, the theological ghost in the scientific machine was never fully exorcised.

It also might be mentioned that there were, for Marx, certain Proletarians who did not deserve salvation, that is, the *Lumpenproletariat.* Marx first used this term in the *Ideology,* and Stirner stood at the head of the class. It would appear that Marx was compelled to modify his strict Manichean distinction between evil bourgeois and good Proletarians, by taking only the more docile Proletarians as deserving of and willing to accept Communist salvation. The term is derived from the German *Lumpenproletarier,* which means "miscreant" as well as "rag." In *The Eighteenth Brumaire of Louis Napoleon* (1852), Marx gives a full description of who comprised the class of *Lumpenproletariat:*

> Alongside decayed roués with dubious means of subsistence and of dubious origin, alongside ruined and adventurous offshoots of the bourgeoisie, were vagabonds, discharged soldiers, discharged jailbirds, escaped galley slaves, swindlers, mountebanks, lazzaroni, pickpockets, tricksters, gamblers, maquereaux [pimps], brothel keepers, porters, literati, organ grinders, ragpickers, knife grinders,

tinkers, beggars—in short, the whole indefinite, disintegrated mass, thrown hither and thither, which the French call la bohème.

Stirner refused to accept the Communist intention to treat him as a "Lump": "We want to make them all 'ragamuffins [*Lumpen*],' all of us must have nothing, that "all may have"—So say the Socialists."[37] Communism is but a

> fight which is to bring "Man" to victory and make propertylessness complete: victorious humanity is the victory of - Christianity. But the "Christianity exposed"[38] Thus is feudalism completed. the most all-embracing feudal system, that is, perfect ragamuffinism [vollkommene Lumperei].[39]

For Stirner, the ideological link between Marxian Communism and Christian belief is clear:

> The Christian age is precisely that of mercy, love, solicitude to have men receive what is due them, yes, to bring them to fulfil their human (divine) calling. Therefore the principle has been put foremost for intercourse, that this and that is man's essence and consequently his calling, to which either God has called him or (according to the concepts of today) his being man (the species) calls him. Hence the zeal for conversion. That the Communists and the humane expect from man more than the Christians do does not change the stand-point in the least. Man shall get what is human! If it was enough for the pious that what was divine became his part, the humane demand that he be not curtailed of what is human.[40]

Marx, as the heated and extensive polemics of *The German Ideology* fully revealed, was well aware of the early and fundamental threat that Stirnerian individualism posed to collectivism. Attempts to realize the unrealizable, that is, ideals such as universal property or love or freedom, will always miscarry when faced with actual self-consciousness—with the assertion of individuals.

In his lucid and incisive study of the relationship between Marx and Stirner, Nicholas Lobkowicz asks a crucial question regarding the genesis of "Historical Materialism":

> It was in the manuscript in which he criticized Stirner that Marx for the first time succeeded in outlining his mature "historical materialism." Is it conceivable, then, that it was Stirner's challenge that induced Marx to give up Feuerbach's sentimental humanism which he had embraced in The Holy Family, and to develop a quite different doctrine?[41]

Karl Löwith answers this question, and sees the effect of Stirner's critique extending even beyond the orbit of Marxism, He noted that the Hegelian historian "

> Rosenkranz appraises Die Heilige Familie of Marx and Engels as merely a "clever book," And yet it was a precursor of Deutsche Ideologie, with which not only Marx but German philosophy in general took leave of its belief in universal reason and spirit."[42]

Not unexpectedly, after encountering Stirner on the "Path of Doubt," Marx, along with others on that same path, discovered that it was a dead end—"Universal reason and spirit" were not to be found.

NOTES

1. Barnikol, *Das entdeckte Christentum im Vormärz*, 78.
2. Bertrand Russell, *History of Western Philosophy* (London: George Allen and Unwin, 1947), 383.
3. Perez Zagorin, *How the Idea of Religious Toleration Came to the West* (Princeton University Press, 2003).
4. Ego, 210.
5. MEW (Dietz Verlag), 1, 494.
6. See Frank Munk, "Communist Heresies: Hopes and Hazards," *Western Political Quarterly* 22 (1969): 921–25.
7. Hook, "Karl Marx and Moses Hess," *New International* 5 (1934): 140–44.
8. Ego, 222.
9. Ego, 263ff.
10. Letter of Engels to Marx, December 19, 1844.
11. Letter of Engels to Marx, January 20, 1845.
12. Ego, 158.
13. All citations and pagination from *The Holy Family* are based upon the *Karl Marx, Friedrich Engels Werke* (Berlin: Dietz Verlag, 1962) "*Die deutsche Ideologie*," V. 3, 13–436. English translations of these citations are taken from the "Marxist Internet Archive."
14. Engels, in "Forward," to *Ludwig Feuerbach and the outcome of German Classical Philosophy*. It was not that all "willingly abandoned" as several publishing houses were sent the manuscript to review after the publisher of *The Holy Family* had rejected the manuscript.
15. On variant critical Marxist readings of Stirner, see Laska, *Max Stirner: ein dauerhafter Dissident*.
16. Both Lukacs and Harbermas employ the term "absurd" when treating of Stirner's work. Lukacs, in his *The Destruction of Reason*, trans. Peter R. Palmer (U.K. Merlin Press, 1980) writes of the Hegelian tendency to abstraction, which "reaches

its climax which tilts over into the absurdly paradoxical with Stirner," 254–55. Habermas wrote of the "absurdity of Stirner's fury."

17. http://www.marxists.org/archive/marx/works/download/Marx_The_German_Ideology.pdf].

18. 2011 Reprint of 1939 Edition.

19. Hellman, *Berlin: The Red Room and White Beer*, x.

20. Eric Fromm, *Marx's Concept of Man* (New York: Frederick Ungar, 1961).

21. Ibid., 168.

22. Karl Marx, and Friedrich Engels, *The Holy Family* (Moscow: Foreign Languages Press, 1956), 178ff.

23. Louis Althusser, *For Marx* (New York: Random House, 1969), 33.

24. Marx, *Early Writings*, 64.

25. *Communist Manifesto*, III, c.

26. Benjamin, in 1940 essay, "Theses on the Philosophy of History."

27. Ego, 168.

28. "In Brussels Marx and myself had felt the need to set ourselves apart from the Hegelian school, we also criticized Stirner, among others—our critical book [*The German Ideology*] was as thick as the book [*The Ego and His Own*] itself." Letter of Engels to Max Hildebrandt, Oct. 22, 1889.

29. MEW, III, 101.

30. Ibid., 131.

31. Ibid., 17.

32. Ibid.,19.

33. Ibid., 20.

34. *Karl Marx* (Ann Arbor: Michigan Press, 1962), 110.

35. Ibid., 263.

36. The *Ideology* was completed in May, 1846, *The Manifesto* appeared in February, 1848.

37. Ego, 105.

38. *A reference to Bauer's Das entdeckte Christentum.* See note 58.

39. Ego, 279.

40. Ego, 256.

41. "Karl Marx and Max Stirner," in *Demythologizing Marxism* (The Hague: Martinus Nijhoff, 1969), 71.

42. Löwith, *From Hegel eto Nietzsche*, 53–54.

Chapter 9

The End of the Path

> It was Stirner who grasped what Nietzsche was to call the "turn into nihilism" in its beginning stages, presenting it as egoism.
>
> —Keiji Nishitani

As already cited, Karl Löwith understood Stirner's work as "an ultimate logical consequence of Hegel's historical system, which—allegorically displaced—it reproduces exactly."[1] The question is now, what does this "allegorisch entstellet" mean? I would propose that it is merely Löwith's way of understanding Stirner's philosophy, even if it can still be called a "philosophy" as the *Aufhebung* and completion of Hegelianism itself—the discovery of "a new world and shape of Mind [*eine neue Welt und Geistesgestalt*]."[2]

"*Absolute Wissen*," as the conclusion of Hegel's phenomenological *Bildungsroman* would not then be an "idea," but rather a state of self-consciousness resting at the term of the dialectic which had generated definitions, "fixed ideas." It was the end of the "love of wisdom" in possession of its object. In 1853, less than a decade after he had given up his critical project, Bauer noted, "The catastrophe of Metaphysics is undeniable. For the last twelve years it can be seen that philosophic writing has forever been closed and finished."[3] Bauer understood that the narrative history of consciousness had concluded, and nothing more could be said—except the endless retrospective analysis of the academic "Old Hegelians." Such exhaustive reflections upon past thought might bring to mind Foucault's *Archaeology*, a view of the issue which leads directly to Gilles Deleuze, and his understanding of Stirner's significance as "he who pushes the dialectic to its final consequences."[4] In this termination of philosophy would be found the reasons for the inability to simply "define" Stirner's philosophy. As the Protagonist of

Hegel's "voyage of discovery," he has reached the end of the "Path of Doubt" which reaches beyond atheism. He might well be the first to state what was entailed in reaching that final knowledge. Absolute Knowing, being fully independent the constraint of a defining other, beyond the last form of relating to another, would be indefinable. In Stirner's words:

> With the Unique One [Einzigen] the Kingdom of Absolute Thoughts, of thoughts which carry their own meaning, their own content, comes to an end . . . the Unique [Einzige] is the highest, the most undeniable and most revealing—phrase; it is the final capstone of our world of phrases, of this world, in which "the beginning was the Word."[5]

In the final paragraph of the *Phenomenology,* Hegel concludes his narrative in a similar manner, a conclusion in which self-conscious Spirit, as

> absorbed in itself, it is sunk into the night of its self-consciousness; but in that night its vanished outer existence is preserved, and this transformed existence— the former one, but now reborn of the Spirit's knowledge—is the new existence, a new world and a new shape of spirit.[6]

In the final paragraph of *Der Einzige*, Stirner also concludes his own Phenomenology:

> In the unique one the owner himself returns into his creative nothing, of which he is born. [Im Einzigen kehrt selbst der Eigner in seine schöpferisches Nichts, zurück, aus welchem er geboren wird.][7]

For both the long and painful story of the travails of "The Experience of Consciousness [*der Erfarung des Bewußtseins*]"[8] comes to a happy ending when consciousness recovers itself from out of its ideal worlds, from out of "*der Nacht seines Selbtsbewusstseins*" and enters into "*eine neue Welt,*" a world well beyond the dreams of the beautiful souls, and the "humane liberals." As understood by Alexandre Kojève, *Absolute Wissen* ends the history of consciousness, the ending of philosophy, and so beyond the ideals of such entities as Bauer's *Mensch*—or Nietzsche's Übermensch. It would be the time of Nietzsche's "Last Man," the Man without any ideals beyond himself—the time of a Stirner.

An answer is suggested here to the long-debated issue of Nietzsche's relationship to Stirner. Rüdiger Safranski, in his work *Nietzsche: A Philosophical Biography,*[9] takes up the issue of why Nietzsche consciously decided to act as if he knew nothing of Stirner. It would seem that Nietzsche, through his known admiration of Bruno Bauer, had indeed read Stirner, but what he discovered was an unacceptable justification of "the last man," and so the notorious Stirner was left unmentioned. This would not be the only instance wherein knowledge of Stirner was, for one reason or another, suppressed—as it was with such as Edmund Husserl, Carl Schmitt, Ernst Jünger, and others as documented in the work of Bernd Laska, *Ein dauerhafter Dissident*.[10]

But if this happy ending made the narrative of consciousness a comedy for Hegel and Stirner, it was a tragedy for Nietzsche. For him, the new world was the world of the "Last Man," and Stirner would surely qualify for that role. Stirner, being quite at home with himself, was set to enjoy himself in the here and now:

> My intercourse with the world consists in my enjoying it, and so consuming it for my self-enjoyment. Intercourse is the enjoyment of the world, and belongs to my—self-enjoyment.[11]

However, in this self-satisfaction, this stoic *Autarkie* of the free individual, Stirner's goal would accord itself with what Hegel had set forth as his own thought as to how the phenomenological "voyage of discovery" would end. It would end at that moment when

> The separation of knowing and truth, is overcome [der trennung des Wissens und der Wahrheit is überwinden]". Being is then absolutely mediated; it is a substantial content which is just as immediately the property of the 'I' [der ebenso unmittelbar Eigentum des Ichs], it is self-like or the Notion. With this the Phenomenology of the Spirit is concluded.[12]

Hegel's "*Eigentum des Ichs*" anticipates Stirner's "*Einzige und sein Eigentum.*"

The Political Scientist, Saul Newman has recently affixed a label upon Stirner—he is a "proto-poststructuralist" and so taken as the political ancestor of such post-modernists as Foucault, Lacan, Deleuze, or Derrida. This is fine as far as it goes, but among them Hegel is barely recognizable in the thickets of Marxian political theology. It can be held that Stirner is more than merely an ancestor of the latest political fashion, for he has concluded Hegelianism itself—not that of Marx nor Feuerbach nor any of the other Hegelians, Young or Old.

Jean Hyppolite, in his study of the *Phänomenologie*, understood that for Hegel, "The history of the world is finished; all that is needed is for the specific individual to rediscover it in himself."[13]

Stirner rediscovered *himself* as that "specific individual"—*Der Einziger*.

NOTES

1. Löwith, *Von Hegel zu Nietzsche*, 18.
2. *Phänomenologie*, 564.
3. *Russland und das Germanthum* (1853); Cf. Löwith, *Die Hegelsche Linke*, 100.
4. Deleuze, *Nietzsche et la philosophie*, 184.
5. Kleiner Chriften, *Max Stirner: Stirner's Critics*, trans. Wolfie Landstreicher (Berkeley, CA, LBC Books, 2012), 57.
6. *Phenomenology*, 492; *Phänomenologie*, 564. *In seinem Insichgehen ist er in der Nacht seines Selbtsbewußtseins versunken, sein verschwundnes Dasein aber is in ihr aufbewahrt; und dies aufgehobene Dasein,—das vorige, aber aus dem Wissen neugeborne,—is das neue Dasein, eine neue Welt und Geistesgestalt].*
7. Ego, 324; *Der Einzige und Sein Eigentum.* 412.
8. Original subtitle to the *Phänomenologie*. See John Stewart "Zur Feststellung des Textes," in *Philosophy and Phenomenological Research*, Vol. 55, No. 4 (Dec., 1995), pp. 747–776.
9. Trans. Shelly Frisch (New York: W.W. Norton, 2002).
10. Nurnberg, LSR—Verlag, 1996.
11. Ego, 282; Der Einzige, 358 *[Mein Verkehr mit der Welt besteht darin, daß Ich sie genieße und so sie zu meinem Selbstgenuß verbrauche. Der Verkehr ist Weltgenuß und gehört zu meinem—Selbstgenuß].*
12. *Phenomenology*, 21; *Phänomenologie*, 32–33. "*der trenning des Wissens und der Wahrheit is überwinden. Das Sein ist absolut vermittelt:—es ist substantieller Inhalt, der ebenso unmittelbar Eigentum des Ichs, selbstisch oder der Begriff is. Hiermit beschließt sich die Phänomenologie des Geistes.*"
13. *Genesis and Structure of Hegel's Phenomenology of Spirit*, trans. S. Cherniak and J. Heckman (Evanston: Northwestern University Press, 1974), 40.

Addenda

All translations contained in this Appendix are those of the author. These three translations are relevant to the present study. Other translations by the author less relevant to the present study, although dealing with Young Hegelians are found in *Young Hegelianism, an Anthology* (Cambridge University Press) Bruno Bauer's 1843 book, *The Trumpet of the Last Judgment: Against Hegel, Atheist and Antichrist* (. . .)

I

A Review of Stirner's final work: DIE GESCHICHTE DER REACTION

The *History of Reaction* [*Die Geschichte der Reaction*][1] appeared in January or February of 1852. The work, with some notable exceptions, has hardly been noticed

Expectedly, among the first to take note of the work were Marx and Engels. In a letter to Marx, which he wrote even before he had read Stirner's work (if he ever did), Engels summed it up in the usual sarcastic tones expected whenever he dealt with anyone who disagreed with Marx:

> Stirner's *History of Reaction* is, according to the *Augsburger Allgemeinen Zeitung* a miserable compilation, or better yet, Stirner's gleaning from his printed and unprinted newspaper articles—these "rejected leaves and flowers" dealing with everything in the world and then some. The second volume closes with the threat that the third will contain "the foundation and system." His own commentary, by which he would ascend to holiness, are far more suited for a elegant girl's school [*höhere Töcherschulen*][2]

Figure A.1 Stirner among the "Frein" during a contentious visit in 1842 by the poet Ludwig Buel. Sketched by Frederich Engels. Stirner is seen here as leaning on table, smoking a cigarette, Bruno Bauer is sitting at the table. This is one of the two images we have of Stirner.

It might here be noted that Stirner made no such "threat" at the end of his work—but Engels relied entirely upon a newspaper item. Hans C. Helms, a latter-day Marxist, is equally unhappy with Stirner's work, but might have at least read it in part and was less inclined to falsify it. Here is Helm's remark: "Overall, it is, frankly speaking, a compilation of the contemporary writings of others. The curt connecting comments, transitions and annotations allow no insight into Stirner's thoughts."[3]

A more favorable view of Stirner is held by Roberto Colassa, who, in his recent work, *The Forty-Nine Steps*,[4] devoted a full chapter, "Accompaniment to the Reading of Stirner," toward setting Stirner within a complete cultural context. For Colassa, Helms, "being "propelled by hatred," willfully distorted Stirner's thought. As to *The History of Reaction*, Colassa's brief remarks are in accord with the general consensus:

> The two volumes of the *Die Geschichte der Reaction* conceal behind the inviting title a work of compilation, an anthology with a vague outline, in which

Stirner appears mockingly in a few hidden lines. One can say that after *Der Einzige* and the two replies to his first critics, Stirner declared Silence and, moreover, maintained it. And meanwhile the world declared it on him.[5]

The *Stanford Encyclopedia of Philosophy* presents a brief but quite typical summation of the work: "In 1852, he [Stirner] published part of a *History of Reaction*, mainly consisting of excerpts from other authors, including Edmund Burke (1729–1797)." A similar reading is found in the *Routledge Encyclopedia of Philosophy*: "An incomplete work largely compiled from the writings of others, including Burke, Compte, Hengestenberg and Florencourt." These entries are perhaps all that most readers, including even those who have read *Der Einzige*, know of the *History*—and perhaps they are enough.

It would be difficult for anyone, no matter how highly they might estimate Stirner, to hold that his *History* is a work that in any way can compare to *Der Einzige*. Even John Henry Mackay, whose biography of Stirner approaches a hagiography, was constrained to admit that the *History* which was published was essentially "unfinished," and was not what had been originally planned.[6]

As its introduction indicated, the *Geschichte der Reaction* was intended to bear the title "*Reactions-Bibliothek*," with each of its two parts, or volumes, being divided into two sections, the first part being "*Die Vorläufer der Reaction [Precoursers of the Reaction]*," the second being "*Die moderne Reaction*." It turned out otherwise—only the first sections were printed. It is not clear as to why the second sections of each part were not included. But in any case, the final "finished" version of the "*Geschichte der Reaction*" comprised two volumes, the first running to 315 pages, and the second to 348.

With this work, there is a persistent problem for any reader not only to determine just where Stirner's commentary (usually too brief) begins or ends, and where the cited texts (usually too lengthy) begin and end. There are no reliable typographical aids here, such as paragraph indentations, type styles, symbols, or spacing. There are a number of dashed lines of various length that often will separate Stirner's writing from that of the others, but this is not always the case and quotation marks are employed, but Stirner seldom indicates who is the author of the text quoted. Unless one reads with great care, a question is always present: is this Stirner or Burke, or Compte, or someone else who is writing the text? The work does not lend itself to random reading. Much of this confusion could have been eliminated had the extensive material drawn from other writers been formally referenced to its original published source.

The *History* was written just a few years before Stirner's death, at a time when he lived in poverty and, as one might suspect, depression. Marx later told Engels that Stirner had "literally starved."[7] In 1853, Stirner, moving restlessly from place to place to avoid his creditors, was twice imprisoned for debt. After a brief period of notice, his major work, *Der Einzige*, was ignored, and then forgotten. Given the circumstances, it might be wondered how he could even have written the *History*—let alone "well."

At this point it might seem reasonable to immediately cast Stirner's work aside as perfectly useless—which was just what a German doctoral student in Political Science did.[8] Still, as Roberto Colassa observed, in that Stirner "appears mockingly in a few hidden lines" the text might be worth at least a reading—if only with the hope of seeing just what Stirner might have had in mind.

There has been, at least to this author's knowledge, only one favorable review of the *History*, that of Bernd Kast found in his excellent work, *Die Thematik des "Eigners" in der Philosophie Max Stirners*.[9] Considering the short shrift given to work by the few others who noticed it, Kast's review is not only well-researched but relatively extensive.

As the title of his work indicates, Bernd Kast is principally interested in the meaning and development of the term *"Eigners"* as it occurs in the writings of Stirner. After his short review of the *History*, Kast concluded that "For our purposes and the *Eigner* theme, the "*History of Reaction*" provides no new insights." However, although of little meaning for Kast's project, the *History* might well provide an insight toward concluding that Hegel was indeed Stirner's mentor. In the *Preface* to his work, Kast observes that "Stirner's philosophy is, in a wide measure, an oppositional Philosophy, Philosophy in opposition to Hegel and to the Hegel school"[10] However, to be in opposition to the Hegel school might be just that—an opposition to the way in which that school understood Hegel. It does not follow that if a reading of Hegel opposed, then Hegel must be opposed. In the *History* there is little doubt but that Stirner was guided by what he understood to be the "correct" reading of Hegel, and did not set out any radical revision of Hegel. This sort of thing is found in his earliest disciples, such as Marx [who "stood Hegel on his feet"], or Feuerbach or Bauer, who reduced Hegel's "God" to "Man." August von Cieszkowski even had the intention of correcting Hegel, of making him, as it were, into "A better Hegelian." In his opposition to the Hegel school, Stirner had no such intentions to "revise" or "correct" Hegel, and there is Hegel in the *History*.

One of the reasons that might have been a *prima face* dismissal and definition of Stirner's *History* as a work "mainly consisting of excerpts from other authors" is that the first volume is indeed just that—"an anthology with a vague outline." It is only the second volume, in the *Forward*[11] that Stirner, somewhat apologetically, is aware that the first volume, since it was "limited [*beschranken*]," "appears to be a mere collection, a string of reactionary literature." This is immediately followed by a question which addresses the overall purpose of his work: "How would that be possible, if there would be no basis [*Grunde*] to determine just what is reactionary and what is not?" In brief, Stirner seems to mean that the "mere collection" of the first volume would have no meaning without understanding just what is "reactionary and what is not."

Historically, the "reaction" to which Stirner is referring began with the 1815 Treaty of Vienna, when the European powers which had defeated Napoleon embarked upon the restoration of the "Old Order" which had been seriously threatened by the promulgation, in the form of the "Napoleonic Code" the revolutionary doctrines contained in the 1789 *"Declaration of the Rights of Man."* As the victory over Napoleon was supported by the many young Germans who had fought against the French, King Frederick Wilhelm III had promised them a national constitution.[12] The promise was not fulfilled. In 1830, another French revolution finally wiped away the last bits of aristocratic power, and the French example encouraged the German liberals to renew their efforts to establish a constitutional government. A Parliament (the "Vorparlament") was set up in Frankfurt, but their liberal proposals were soon rejected by Frederick Wilhelm IV, the King of Prussia. The reaction, the counter-revolution was victorious. The age of Bismarck was on the horizon. Needless to say, German liberals were enraged—but impotent.

In his introduction to a set of historical documents compiled under the title *Revolution and Reaction: 1848–1852*.[13] The editor noted that "As swiftly as it had risen, the tide of revolution began to ebb . . . in studying the revolutionary movement of 1848 it will be interesting to ponder whether it failed because it came before its time or because it came after its time." But for Stirner it was not merely a matter of chance and circumstance, but rather the necessitated dialectical articulation of political history, the self-alienation of the political consciousness into polar opposition.

Stirner's *History*, "in opposition to the Revolutionary Tribunal,"[14] was to be a "Reactionary Tribunal." The purpose of this would be to bring the reactionary mind into self-consciousness, into an awareness of what it its intentions would ultimately obtain:

"Reaction, before it reaches the last judgment, has still one more judgment to undergo, which is, namely, to judge itself. As a Spirit [Geist], which will seek to develop itself in the course of history, it finds itself necessarily caught up in a process of cleaning and separating itself from everything that is not reactionary. This it must and will continue to do if not under the pressure of external restrictions [*der Last von Fremden*]. *"Pure Reaction"* is the goal of their strivings, to which reactionary spirits are more or less consciously driven; this "pure Reaction" is the singular tribunal of reaction, it is, in opposition to the Revolutionary Tribunal, the—*Reaction Tribunal*."

Stirner's intention (but only partially realized because of the incomplete text), was "To set the Reaction itself before the Reaction Tribunal and to see if it can justify itself, and if it can hold itself as valid [*und ob sie in sich selber Stich hält*]." By considering a series of various reactionary and revolutionary texts, most dealing with the German reaction to the German Revolution of 1848, Stirner concluded that both parties in the dispute tended to their own self-destruction, as the total victory of one would put an end to the common ground of each—their political life. Unhappily, Stirner often did not make either his intention clear or his historical documentation as supportive of his thesis as might have been. But the *History* has the merit of being written after 1848 and, if only for that reason, support the contention of the *Ego* that the revolution would be transformed into a reaction.

It was not sophistry which lead Stirner to question the accepted and common understanding that "Reaction is the opposite of Revolution."[15]—and its converse, "Revolution is the opposite of Reaction" For Stirner, this common understanding did not perceive that these apparent opposites both emerged from the same ground:

> Reaction steps into the world at the same time in which Revolution comes into the world: both are born in the same instant [Die Reaction tritt in dem Moment ins Leben, in welchem die Revolution zur Welt commt: beide werden im selben Augenblick geboren].[16]

In short, the opposition of these two political attitudes is not absolute nor is either one capable of being "in itself" without the other, a matter of "co-existence." As in the case of an the opposition between Catholic and Protestant, in which both share an identical religious consciousness, the alternatives of "Conservative" and "Liberal," rest within the common realm of politics—and both are defined by and created by their opposition. This is a purely Hegelian viewpoint.

The major theme (or "vague outline") of the *History*, is the echo of what was stated in *Der Einzige und sein Eigentum*:

> If the Revolution ended in a reaction, this only showed what the Revolution really was. For every effort arrives at reaction when it comes to discreet reflection, and storms forward in the original action only so long as it is an intoxication, an "indiscretion." "Discretion" will always be the cue of the reaction, because discretion sets limits, and liberates what was really wanted, i. e., the principle, from the initial "unbridledness" and "unrestrainedness." Wild young fellows, bumptious students, who set aside all considerations, are really Philistines, since with them, as with the latter, considerations form the substance of their conduct; only that as swaggerers they are mutinous against considerations and in negative relations to them, but as Philistines, later, they give themselves up to considerations and have positive relations to them. In

both cases all their doing and thinking turns upon "considerations," but the Philistine is reactionary in relation to the student; he is the wild fellow come to discreet reflection, as the latter is the unreflecting Philistine. Daily experience confirms the truth of this transformation, and shows how the swaggerers turn to Philistines in turning gray." So, too, the so-called reaction in Germany gives proof that it was only the discreet continuation of the warlike jubilation of liberty.[17]

This sentiment regarding revolutionary enthusiasm also finds place in the *History*:

The Kingdom of Truth had come, the Spirit dominated. . . . Philosophy was given its rightful place, and had in its hands the power to rule a great Kingdom.[18]

One is reminded of Hegel's description of the revolutionary gathering of German students in 1818 at the "notorious" Wartburg Festival. He condemned Professor J. M. Fries as the "Ringleader of these hosts of superficiality."[19] Although Hegel's criticism of the event improved his image in eyes of those in Berlin who were considering his appointment to the University, he nevertheless, "had as little sympathy with Romantic [i.e., liberal revolutionaries of the time] as he had with Reactionaries."[20] Both Stirner and Hegel shared the same attitude when it came to extremes.

The curbing of revolutionary "indiscretion" which began shortly after the Wartburg Festival, was an early sign that the reaction was taking hold. For Stirner, this curbing and restraint is fundamentally based upon religious belief, in this case, Christianity. "The Reaction is only the reaction [reagirende] of the Christian man; what is not Christian is,—openly or hidden—revolutionary."[21] Among the Christian leadership, such as Ernst Wilhelm Hengestenberg, the coming of revolution was the coming of atheistic anarchy. His public popularity insured that his fears were taken up by the Aristocracy as well as the people. The patriots and those who set order above any "new found" freedom were soon turned from being conservatives to being reactionaries. Stirner, with humorous irony, presents a series of anxious questions which would have been heard among the fearful order-loving people and their traditional leaders in the nervous days before the 1848 revolution (and, with modifications, before every revolution). Here is but a small part of the exhortations:

Should not the Christian World of the German Nation react to the fact that her thankless son, the State, his Mother, the Church (since Germany as a Kingdom, as a Nation, has its proper Mother in the Christian Church) that this same State drives this honorable Mother out of her house and then surrenders the house to street mobs and thieves? Should it not react against the domination of the Jews, of German Catholics, of pantheists and atheists? Should our Christendom, should German Law, should German Freedom not react against the tyranny, which already dominates and expresses itself in the self-appointed Parliament and the fifty clubs of Frankfurt?[22]

It is not long before the reaction emerges, first draped in the concern of the religious for its "sinful" character, and then:

> Finally there falls upon the revolution a proper and concluding sentence of damnation, the judgment: It is a sin! Thereafter the full break with the revolution is confirmed, and every concession will vanish and be set aside, even the thought out of this sin perhaps some good can emerge.[23]

The eventual reduction of the revolutionary movement into that of a negligible "obedient opposition [*gesinnungstüchtigen Opposition*]"[24] which collapses into the power of reaction, was, for Stirner, was to be expected:

> the concept: "Reaction" . . . exists in every Organism in which something strange is acting in it, and which it cannot immediately assimilate. An organism, even the highest organism, the personal spirit, will strive for unity in its diversity [nach Einheit in der Manngfaltigkeit] and so whatever enters into it must be taken into its unity and be assimilated and transformed or, if it persists in its otherness [oder wenn es in seiner Fremdigartiges beharret, aus gestostossen warden], then it must be cast out."[25]

Stirner was neither a "revolutionary" nor a "reactionary" but understood that both reflected the same oppressive wish to dominate, if not eliminate, individual freedom. Unlike either Bauer or Feuerbach, who had taken part in the revolution of 1848 (Feuerbach being one of the delegates to the Frankfurt Parliament), Stirner sat back—a pose redolent of Engel's sketch of him during an uproar in the pre-revolutionary club known as the *Freien*.

There can be little doubt that Stirner favored the revolutionary mind, as his major work can hardly be characterized as "conservative," but he well knew that the revolutionary mind reflected, and was reflected in, the mind of the reactionary. His political views regarding the party system of conservative vs. liberal might be simply summarized as "a pox on both your houses." In this dim view, he stood against all of his own Young Hegelian contemporaries, particularly such as Arnold Ruge or Karl Marx. He held to "an oppositional Philosophy" which would restrain ideas from being held as "absolute"— either conservative or liberal ideas.

Is the *History* worth reading? Yes, but it is not an "easy read." Much of what he had to say about Reaction and Revolution can be found, more easily and more lucidly, in *Der Einzige*.

II

Author's Introductions and first translations to three of Stirner's articles

II A

THE FREE ONES

Stirner's article *"Die Freien"* first appeared in the *Leipziger Allgemeine Zeitung*, No. 195, July 14, 1842. Republished in Stirner's *Kleinere Schriften* hrs. John Henry Mackay (Berlin: Bernhard Zack, 1914); republished (Stuttgart-Bad Cannstatt: Friedrich Frommann Verlag, 1976). pp. 132–141.

TRANSLATION

The *Königsberger Zeitung* was first to report the existence of the club "Free Ones," and their report was soon followed by a series of others directed to this same topic by almost every other newspaper. The club has had to suffer such vehement and fanatical attack that even any opponent of the group, if he did not consider violence a virtue, must ask, that given such enemies, if this club really has no rights whatsoever. Certainly, this club might be considered worthy of attention by anyone who understands the importance of intellectual trends; but in any case, it must be quietly considered, and one must presuppose the best, as it is with this presupposition that one must begin in every court proceeding and with every criticism. Most newspapers broke out in a furious storm against the "Free Ones," with the lead being taken by the Spenes'sche[26] with its frightening call that "The Autonomy of the Spirit[27] is the fruit of a childish conceit and a sinful misjudgment of the limits of human understanding, and in that Christian community, wherein whose womb such a propaganda of disbelief would have nourished itself, a judgment of a deeper degeneracy can be pronounced." They ring out storm bells against the heretics and clearly enough point out the club [Knüttel][28] to the people of Berlin by which they can also re-enact in our own Market that lovely mob-scene held against Strauss in Zurich.[29]

> Certainly, in our city, the deepest contempt of its fellow citizens would greet those who would openly teach the adoration of the human spirit rather than

devotion to the church! They would not tolerate the tendency of a group, whose opinions are only employed in order to undermine the moral grounds of civil society, nor allow its gates and doors to be open to the entrance of this most capricious and be opened for principles whose practical consequences would require bullet-proof vests under coats and to completely lock up both home and family for their protection.

The "Kolnische"[30] dressed up these few crude words and paraphrased them into three large columns. However in so honoring its sister, it lowered not only its own honor but those it represented as well—the educated and Christian world. No, those who consider themselves to be permitted to make a public statement over the merits of the intellectual currents of their time, should at least have a measure of culture, and in their exposition betray at least some attempt to penetrate into the subject matter.

Indeed, the public does not read newspapers in order to commiserate with some shaking statements of cowardly fears, but to read important and well-written reports. How much more worthily has the *Aachener Zeitung* conducted itself, for although it is otherwise opposed to the *Freien*, it nevertheless has stood up with faultless candor and has declared itself against all intervention by "governmental actions." But your newspaper has already taken up this matter in a series of leading articles which on every occasion display prejudice. For us, who draw upon all forms of liberalism, forms so heavy and meaningful in our changing times, and who would seek to overhear the fundamental issues and to secure our relative right against obstinate fault, there is no sound so fitting than that of the quiet and more fearless reflection that you have loudly criticized. Whoever looks danger in the eye, overcomes it, or at least it frightens them no more.[31] You have already reported that a club, the "Free Ones" exists, and in the manner it does exist. I'll pass these reports along as they come in, but at the moment I will only state that the majority, as well as the leading voices of the group, fear that the absurd ideas of the club being developed will rob them of something they hold very dear. Certainly, the *Königsberger Zeitung* bears some blame for its fragmentary and hurried representations of the intentions of this group.

Now, let us see what the "Free Ones" really want—what "they openly present as a valid principle." First off, in what does this principle consist? In this: "To raise the banner of the 'Autonomy of the Spirit' and to be fundamentally committed to leading modern philosophy from out of its restricted sphere as a science into the wider circle of modern life." This is certainly not the place to simply state this fundamental commitment, and then to merely recognize it or cast it aside. The principle is actually found within the scientific work of modern philosophy itself and will find its enemies in this field and can only then either claim victory or be defeated. No one can deny that, first and foremost, it is a "commitment," and if the "Free Ones" would claim to represent this, then no one can either rebuke or damn them except with the weapon of commitment itself. Only the "Free Ones" wish this principle "introduced in the wider circle of life," and this appears to be the immediate meaning of "making it valid in the world." On the other hand, one cannot understand what could be the object of those who hold a certain conviction, one that would lack the strength to be maintained, could gain by confronting others who hold opposing viewpoints.

The mutual exchange of viewpoints and convictions must be free. If, for the moment, the pressure of the press hampers this exchange rather than permitting it to happen, there still remains the trade route of vocal traffic, an open and direct route all the more eagerly taken when the roads of literature are guarded against smuggled goods.[32]

What is told into the ear of another penetrates more deeply into the heart than the roaring tangle of a thousand passing voices. One can hardly think of a more favorable condition to really excite and inform people with this or than forbidden viewpoint than that given by present press restrictions—it only requires the privileged party to talk, that party will soon lose all credibility, and what it defends and praises will gradually be rejected and distained by its readership. Indeed, each ounce of freedom that is taken from anyone who wants to present their conviction will add, in the scale of public opinion, a pound of trust in that very conviction and would expectedly add a hundred pounds of distrust against those who erect barriers against free expression. So then, if the "Free Ones" were to be allowed to spread their convictions, who could hinder them? Anyone attempting it would simply help spread this viewpoint even further, and excite even more hunger for it: Forbidden fruit is the sweetest.

If the "Free Ones" were to establish a "Union" toward this end, or even if one is needed, is another question. They at least know that for the moment by taking up this name a spiritual fear has been raised which has closed any attempt to open a discussion. In this respect, how should this Union be considered? It would not be illegal, but rather unwise. There also seems a second reason which would move these "Free Ones" to form a Union: "The group intends to publicly exit the Church and to affix the signatures of every member upon their statement." This is a total misunderstanding. The Church, at least our Protestant Church, has no power to put any pressure upon any individual: the church can neither force a baptism, a confirmation, a wedding, and so on. If it were to employ force, then clerical force would have to be recognized. But as it stands, for example, one who did not seek confirmation, can only expect a civil penalty that would follow from some damage to a civil law. But if the state, through its police power, does not hold a person to be legally bound to the requirements of the church, then the Church cannot punish anyone even if, after being baptized and confirmed, that person never again enters a Church. Indeed, what is even more, people who live in such an unchurchly manner are not a hair less respected for that. Among others, this was seen to be the case with Jean Paul,[33] who didn't care in the least about the approval of his fellow citizens of Bayreuth when it came to attending church or taking communion.

The Protestant Church has lost that power which, at the time of its full bloom and energy, it had once exercised over people, and has now become invisibly and inwardly transformed. What might it now mean if this invisible and inward church would express itself openly? The Church has no power over those who do not wish to hear a sermon, or take communion, or indeed to leave the church. Thousands do this throughout their lives and no one questions it, and otherwise, if they are respected, such as Jean Paul, they are honored by their fellow citizens and are set among the immortal geniuses of the human race. One feels that going to Church is a personal affair, and that each one must deal with it as they will, and be responsible to no other. To attempt to restrain such a harmless and voluntary matter as this, as the Church would attempt, is both pointless and quite contemptible. Since I have thought about setting out the truth regarding "The Free Ones," I know it is not what their scornful enemies, in a poorly chosen expression would presuppose it to be—as merely a "childish pride" with the basic intention to "exit from the Church." This viewpoint is not contradicted in the *Königsberger* article. But just this sort of miserable language has generated a great deal of hate and enmity for them. One would think that with their exit they wish to make enemies of all those who would protect and keep from change their understanding of Christian belief; one would think that they wish to destroy the Church that every Christian needs, to take away that which is indispensable. This wish does not in the least find any place in their words, and it seems to me that that one must have a very fearful and despondent heart if this is seen as underlying them.[34]

The "Free Ones" also promulgate the view that the "basic conviction of modern philosophy is the Autonomy of the Spirit." Indeed, it might well be the result, for anyone recognizing the Autonomy of the Sprit, that they would no longer have need of the Christian Church. Whoever is won over to this conviction will do what many have done and still do all the time: the Church will be left out of their needs. What will follow for those who remain undisturbed in their fundamental convictions? For those who continue to live with this conviction, although the Church be shattered, will Christianity be taken from them?

Where is it stated that "The Free Ones" would destroy culture, and who has the right to that barbaric reproach? They only wish to introduce their "conviction" into life, and believe that by their exit from the Church they have already presented part of the proof that the Church is not absolutely necessary. Does this mean that they intend to empower those who are convinced just as they are that they should destroy Christendom for all of those who still depend upon it? Not at all. It means nothing other but that they express, in a direct and honest manner, their convictions. In a word, it means, they follow upon the way of their convictions, and not upon the way of storms and revolutions.

It might do well to consider that those opposed to the "Free Ones," those who need force and prohibitions, might well be even more dangerous and worse revolutionaries. Be that as it may, this "exit from the Church" is meaningless, and the anger directed against it should be completely ignored. The exit is inward, not outward. If we look more carefully at this, it was also the case that the *Aufklarung* was not directed against the Church but against the State, not against the impotency of the Church, but against the power of the State. Indeed, the "Free Ones" have been credited with accepting the statement of the Philalethen[35] that they also "have cast aside as unnecessary such clerical requirements as Marriage and Baptism whose enforcement rests upon the State." These "requirements" would be necessary if any group needed correction.

In all this we see evidence of the weak against the strong, of a small minority setting out against a huge majority. Who runs the greater risk and danger? Not those who, without material power, would try to set up an opposition, but rather the majority, who must stand with the Devil and so validate his evil principle "Might makes Right." I have heard some say that it is not good that the State should alter a law or an organization because some minority wants it changed. Quite to the contrary, even the will of one man might overturn a law of a thousand years if that law be wrong and unjust. For a long time, among the English, many old laws, whose application would be an injustice, have been either adjusted, or better, simply cast aside. Indeed, what the "Free Ones" seek, which is simply that the State should no longer tie its citizens to one religious confession, is no longer merely the wish of a few. The Jews well know, if they trace their wish for Emancipation back to its ultimate ground, leads to nothing less than to the separation of Religious confession from citizenship.[36]

One of the most important matters of contemporary political life is drawn from the unconcealed and open assertions of the "Free Ones." In the last analysis they revolve about the issue of whether or not the modern European State is to be either "Christian" or "Human." It is said that "All of our European States have a Christian foundation." Proof? "It does not require one, it is an indisputable axiom!" A beautiful thought, but although a mathematical axiom requires no proof, a worm-eaten conceit cannot pretend to be an axiom. To claim that Christianity is the foundation of our states is not only a sign of historical ignorance, but an even greater sign of incompetent thinking. To demonstrate that our states are not Christian, although an extensive task, is not all that difficult, but it does require that the prejudices of a Balde[37] be swept away. That our states cannot be Christian will be soon be seen. Here, the limits of space only permit a few short remarks.

It appears to be quite clear, that insofar as we are Christians, our state would also be the product of Christianity, and yet this is little a fact as a Christian development of physical science or as fully developed German Philosophy is a Christian Philosophy. It is rather the case that the State rests upon the principle of "Culture, of Civilization." The State is based upon a "Secular" principle, Christianity upon the "Kingdom of Heaven" ("My Kingdom is not of this world"). Christianity is completely indifferent to what the State holds of the greatest meaning; everything appears indifferent to it, even Freedom. With compassion, the "Children of God" look down from their height upon all other freedom as something "other." It does not disturb the Christian if one be noble or a beggar, master or servant, free or slave, poor or rich, crude or refined, and so on. A slap in the face, given to either the Count or the beggar, is not punished in different ways: the Count just as the beggar must turn the other cheek. The secular should not cause the Christian any concern, for they should only recognize it in that they are driven to do so by inexorable need.

Regarding our culture, all of our present relationships, all of our common civic life, must now be taught that the false axiom ["All of our European States have a Christian foundation"] be transformed into this: "All of our European States have cultivated reason [*Bildung*] as their basis." It must be admitted, although this is not the place for any further explanation, that "developing culture" will indeed support the faith—even though this idea might not be understood here.

Believers will always have something to believe in if only it can be believed. On the other hand the truly educated person is a free spirit, a free spirit in the purest meaning of the term. The solid and full development of rational culture can only be grounded in free knowledge and free will

What the "Others" [the "Free Ones"] are really opposed to is not the Church, but the State, and this opposition to one of the institutions of the State is a loyal opposition. They are as loyal, for example, as those who speak against the censor, and so would make their convictions valid: it is a "legal opposition."

II B

"DIE MYSTERIEN VON PARIS VON EUGENE SUE"
Berliner Monatsschrift Erstes and einziges Heft, Juli 1843. Mannheim 1844. pp. 302–332; *Kleinere Schriften* pp. 278–295.

TRANSLATOR'S INTRODUCTION

Now seldom read, Eugène Sue (1804–1859) was the leading French popular novelist of the 1840s. Born of a wealthy upper middle-class family and inheriting his father's wealth in 1830, Sue developed as a popular writer of roman-feuilletons—serial stories appearing as installments in newspapers.

Sue's early works were principally given over to adventure stories, or to picturing, as with his 1837 work, *Lautréaumont* the complex and tedious social interplay of characters residing in the decaying world of French aristocracy. But in the early 1840s, upon reading Fourier and Proudhon, Sue converted to socialism. It proved to be a lucrative conversion, as once he became aware of the miseries of the urban poor, which he as all socialists, took as the necessary by-product of the "cruelties of capitalism," he had found a popular subject fitted for his particular style. In a short time his melodramatic novels earned Sue a great amount of money, considerably more than his contemporary Dumas. Needless to say, his money came from a newly created class, those able to read, the capitalistic bourgeois.

After he had found his subject in the urban poor, his first major novel was the lengthy *Les Mysteres de Paris*. It ran to over 1,300 words, and was published as a serial in the *Journal des débats* from June 19, 1842 until October 15, 1843. With this work he said the right things in the right way to the right people, and it insured him both continued wealth and reputation. Fortunately for him, the French Industrial Revolution had provided what his high romanticism most needed: the inherent drama found in the confrontation of two new classes, the satisfied urban capitalists and the unhappy working masses. From the point of view of liberals, such as Sue, the guilt naturally fell upon those who had wealth against those who did not. Similarities, both in style and sympathy for the poor, are shared by both Sue and Dickens, and Sue has even been referred to as "The Dickens of Paris." However, Dickens had actually shared in the trials of the poor but Sue had not, and this might be the reason that Dickens is still read, and Sue is not. No amount of lurid and exaggerated bathos, high sentiments and piteous expressions can substitute for the understanding gained from suffered. Nevertheless, Sue did know how to write a dramatic work, had an eye for detail, and plotted his work in a manner that held the reader's interest from one episode to the next. And so, even if the *Mysteries* might be said to have a false ring, the work was happily welcomed by Sue's bourgeois readership, for which he revealed the mysteries and sufferings of a class which they otherwise would ignore. With Sue as their moral guide they could look down with pity mixed with moral satisfaction upon the miserable underlings who lived in the slums of Paris, in their fallen and impoverished world, and yet have the satisfaction of being told that their fall was more the result of the devil than of economic forces—or their own avarice. That his work would have the requisite happy ending, at least for the virtuous, Sue provided a *deus ex machina* which insured the final triumph of good over evil: he simply provided a rich and powerful Savior. In the last analysis, as Stirner well knew, Sue had written a morality play. Presented in the luridly romantic tones thought appropriate at the time, and reflecting Sue's own sense of moral righteousness, the novel proved to be an irresistible bait for myriads of readers—particularly the *Nouveau riche*. After all, was it not just this morality play that the bourgeois would want to read? For whom among that readership could imagine that they would not, were they able, go forth and help the save the deserving poor from evil, and who would not think that they themselves, were they able, would be as just and powerful as the mysterious benefactor created by Sue? In this regard, the novel can be looked upon as the prototype of today's fantasy "savior" stories, featuring the cryptic but powerful hero who comes upon a scene of injustice and immediately sets about righting matters. One thinks here of fictional heroes from Batman to Zorro, but in Sue's novel he appears as the mysterious Prince Rudolphe of Gerolstein—and he also wears a black cloak!

Stirner's reading of Sue's *Mysteries of Paris* is clearly based upon Hegel's *Phenomenology of Mind*, in the short section entitled "Virtue and the Course of the World." Here, the conflict between Virtue and Vice ("the way of the world") is comprehended as a dialectical engagement in which the seeming antithetical character of both is revealed as essentially the same. As the conflict is initiated, the discipline of abstract law (virtue) is set against individual reality found in "the way of the world." As Hegel puts it, in this opposition, the "true discipline of law requires nothing less than the sacrifice of the entire personality as proof that individual peculiarities are in fact no longer insisted upon. Stirner well understood the one-sided morality of Sue's novel in which abstract generalities (such as the "good" or "virtue") were to overcome the particular desires of specific individuals. Sue's Prince Rudolphe must have seemed, to Stirner, as but a fictional recasting of Hegel's "Knight of Virtue" ["*Ritter der Tugend*"]. Rudolphe, as that "Knight of Virtue" was expected to be admired for setting out upon a crusade to conquer vice—"the way of the world" in Sue's Paris. But Rudolphe was, just as Hegel's "Knight of Virtue," blind to the reality that in this battle he was ultimately engaged in a struggle against his own individuality. He was, just as Hegel's "Knight of Virtue," engaged in a "sham battle" [*Spiegelfechterei*] which could only conclude with the self-inflicted defeat of virtue itself. Sue himself, as Stirner indicates in his critique, was unable to follow through to the final paradoxical consequence of his own fictional vision of the triumph of virtue over vice. Virtue would end in vice. However, the self-righteous optimism of Sue's readership, who had a high regard for their own virtues, precluded any defeat of Rudolphe's crusade. This was to be expected, and, as Stirner had it, "It is no miracle that the mysteries have received so much approval. Indeed the moral world has seized upon this winning production of Philistinism as the true image of its own humanitarianism."

The story begins when Prince Rudolphe, in seeking to do penance for a sin against his Father, arrives (in disguise) in Paris to "work for the Good." He immediately sets about his moral crusade among the inhabitants of the dark slums near Notre Dame Cathedral. It is here that Rudolphe finds himself confronted with a myriad of striking and exaggerated characters—either angelically good, as the worker Morel, or diabolically evil, as the old woman, *La Chouette* (the Owl) or Ferrand, the notary, whose greed drives families into poverty. In his crusade, Rudolphe encounters a beautiful young prostitute, Fleur de Marie. Both are unaware that she is his daughter, the child of his first love. Miraculously, Marie has somehow remained innocent and free from the stains of the pervasive immorality surrounding her. For Rudolphe, she is in need of salvation. This is the point from which Stirner takes up to illustrate how "the interplay between virtue and vice drives this novel." The play continues on to the end of the lengthy novel. Finally, Maria is recognized as his daughter by Prince Rudolphe, and becomes the Princess of Gerolstein. However her natural happiness has been eroded by a bad conscience, and she gradually falls under the baleful piety of a certain clever Madame George and a sinister Priest, Laporte. More and more, Marie becomes convinced that her past sins are unforgivable. In her words:

> When Rudolphe took me away from the Cité, I already had a vague consciousness of my degradation. But the education, the advice and examples I got from you [Laporte] and Madame George made me understand . . . that I had been more guilty than unfortunate. . . . You and Madame George made me realize the infinite depth of my damnation.

Marie then withdraws from the world by entering into a convent and it is not long before she dies. Over Marie's grave a final pious statement is intoned by a Priest: "Inwardly pure as human beings seldom are, she has closed her eyes to this world."

Stirner was the first among the "Young Hegelians" to write a review of *Mysteries of Paris*. Under the name of "Max Schmidt" his review was published in the *Berliner Monatsschrift* of July, 1843. Almost a year later, in June, 1844, another review appeared in Bruno Bauer's *Allegmeine Literatur-Zeitung*. It was written by Bauer's follower, Franz Zychlin von Zychlinski—known as "Szeliga." One year later, in early 1845, Marx, joined by his new friend Engels, wrote *The Holy Family: or Critique of Critical Criticism. Against Bruno Bauer and Company*. In it, and at some length, Marx discussed Szeliga's review. This was Marx's first and only study of a literary work, and

Stirner was left unmentioned. For Marx, the redemption of Marie lies not in responding to Rudolphe's "itching to moralize" but simply was another consequence of class oppression:

In natural surroundings, where the chains of bourgeois life fall away and she can freely manifest her own nature, Fleur de Marie bubbles over with love of life, with a wealth of feeling, with human joy at the beauty of nature; these show that her social position has only grazed the surface of her and is a mere misfortune, that she herself is neither good nor bad, but human.

Stirner' remark, in his review, that "one is not freed from an illusion until one overcomes it in theory" sets him in direct contrast to Marx's focus upon theory as being determined by practice, of ideology being determined by productive forces. For Stirner "interpretation" is all, and the external struggles of social classes merely reflects the internal struggle of the human mind between received ideas from the "other" and reflected ideas of our "own." Stirner stands on a more philosophic plane than Marx, and takes Sue's work as illustrating the deadly effect of all "fixed ideas"—even "good ones":

Is it perchance only people possessed by the devil that meet us, or do we as often come upon people possessed in the contrary way—possessed by "the good," by virtue, morality, the law, or some "principle" or other? Possessions of the devil are not the only ones. God works on us, and the devil does; the former "workings of grace," the latter "workings of the devil." Possessed [bessessene] people are set [versessen] in their opinions.

For Stirner, the sad fate of Maria, who was caught up and crushed between the fixed ideas of virtue and vice, would be a clear justification for Hegel's contention "that the present task consists in freeing determinate thoughts from their fixity."

A final note: the novel ends with Prince Rudolphe returning to Gerolstein. This caused Dumas to doubt the whole moral stance of the novel, insofar as Rudolphe gives up his role as defender of the lower class to claim his hereditary place as ruler of Gerolstein—a case of self-interest overcoming idealism.

TRANSLATION

The "mysteries" have created a great sensation in the world, and a crowd of imitations have already appeared. Everyone wants to know about the hidden "lowest level" of society, and all look about, with curiosity, into its darkest and most dreadful corners. But with what eyes does one look into this?— With the eye of secure modesty, and with a virtuous shiver. "What an abyss of corruption, what horror, what a pit of depravity! Lord God, how can things so wicked be allowed in your world!" But soon Christian love is awakened, and it arms itself for helpful and pious action. "There must here be a salvation, and here action must be taken against the cunning of Satan! Oh, yes, there are many to save and many souls to win for the Kingdom of the Good [*dem Reiche des Guten*]."

Now thoughts are busy, and a thousand ways and means are planned to cast out the evil, and to put an end to the boundless depravity. Isolated prison cells, public housing for unemployed workers, education for fallen and penitent girls and countless other remedies are now not only proposed but actually undertaken. Charitable organizations will be gathered together and expanded in scope as never before, and there will be no lack of sacrifice and charity. Eugene Sue presents Rudolphe, the Grand Duke of Gerolstein, as the shining image of this impressive display of neighborly love.

What evil then would be cast away?—Immorality, sinful lust! The wells of evil should be dried up by needed reforms, and misled souls taken away from them and persuaded to seek a moral life. But who would want to take up this great work, and rob sin of its victims and servants? Who, if not those who love virtue and who understand that the true calling of man, are to follow the true moral way of life?

And so it is that virtuous people are to direct the immoral onto the right path, and the servants of the Kingdom of the Good are to seek the destruction of the Kingdom of Evil.

Are we not all of the understanding that there is nothing greater and more noble than to honor the Good? But yet, do not all of you have a fault, something that is disturbing and regretful, and which all-too-often turns you from the path of goodness and is "sinful"? Has the question ever occurred to you to ask if the Good might indeed be worth the cost, that to be on the path of goodness is the only thing for which a human being must do throughout their whole life? Do you just as little ask this question of yourselves than those who have fallen and have forgotten God question their own knowledge? (even if, on the other hand, they are—"sinners").

But you, who would save and convert sinners perhaps might be just as incorrigible and unredeemable as they are. Have you never doubted as to whether or not the Good might be—a mere fantasy? What if you were to admit that? Just as the Philosophers who love Wisdom, but never obtain it, would you also still believe that sinners can be made good and able "to do good"? Could you turn sinners away from desiring Evil? Might it then be possible even for you to turn from away desiring the Good? Do not ask yourselves what the Good is, but rather IF it is. If you really think it is, then ask yourselves first of all if it might be only be your—imagination.

Perhaps your proofs of the Good might be more convincing if you would use some examples, such as: "Lying is bad, but honesty is good, impenitence is evil, but contrition and remorse are good, not being chaste is a sin, but chastity is a virtue, etc." On this, let us look into the "mysteries" and observe how the interplay between virtue and vice motivates this novel.

Now, I won't say anything about the details and the development of this novel, as I can suppose that you have read it. And even less will I speak of the so-called aesthetic value of this book. For if a Juggler were to perform some very difficult act, or a Magician would achieve the most astonishing of effects, even if be said that such effects were an excellent display of the arts of the Juggler or Magician, yet no one would hold their arts in particular respect. So I also find no need to deal too closely with our author's skill in portraying social contrasts and characters—although his skill has hardly satisfied all connoisseurs of the fine arts. I do not think so highly of the talent displayed in this work that it would blind me to its total lack of any profound and compelling insights into the nature of society. Görres had also a beautiful talent, and died, as so many others, in a childish tottering about in the fixity of stupid thoughts.[38]

Now, although the Grand Duke of Gerolstein cannot be regarded as the hero of the novel, as the whole mechanism of the novel is not set in motion by him alone, he nevertheless does represent the elevated views and thoughts to which Sue himself aspires. The high ideal of morality is the viewpoint from which every thought and deed is measured. It is a literary work of fiction which is totally worked out from the standpoint of morality, and it presents the sort of men that would be created in the light of this viewpoint, and what would transpire under its dominion.

Prince Rudolpfe, in a momentary fit of fury, drew his sword against the sacred body of his Father. This he considered a sin, and because of it he felt compelled to choose a very heavy penitential duty. He decided that this duty should be "working for the power of Good." In time, following upon this, he was led to Paris where he visited the dark slums of poverty and criminality. There he would do whatever he could to help to relieve suffering, to soften hard hearts, and to bring fearful and just punishment upon criminals. With his princely means, he easily succeeded in alleviating some physical suffering, such as that endured by the impoverished Morel family. For this, they were indebted to him for their future happiness. But even more than his desire to eliminate physical dangers, and closer to his heart, was his desire to eliminate moral dangers. And it is this desire which brings him into contact with the heroine of the novel.

Fleur de Marie (*Marien-Blume*), or as we can simply call her, Marie, is in prison. Rudolph has no idea that she is the child of his first love. She is a lovely girl, who grew up in the custody and in the frightful hands of "*la Chouette*" [The Owl]—an evil woman. Pressured by poverty, pimps [*Kupplerinnen*], and other miserable circumstances, the growing girl finally decides upon the trade of a prostitute. But nevertheless, she remained untouched by the lustful pleasures of this way of life, she is stained without being stained. From the beginning, she was detached from either the desire for the trade of prostitution, or the fear of enslavement to it, and she would have had the strength to resist it. But then she encounters Rudolphe, and with him, the very thing that vice cannot resist—the temptation to be virtuous. The poor child is tempted by virtue, which, if it would overcome her, will replace her vice. And so it is, that in the hope that he can bribe her, Rudolphe presses every promise and reward of virtue upon her easily excited imagination. However, although she has not completely "fallen" into the center of an intoxicating life of vice, she is still able to resist the sweet solicitations of the promoter of virtue, and so "falls." Yet there remains the temptation not to fall, to be virtuous. So, how then can Sue, the novelist of a liberal and virtuous civil society, find even more temptations to make her virtuous? Can she ever be raised up from being fallen if she refuses to take refuge in the comforting lap of the only morality able to make her divinely happy? And if one thinks that she should be delivered over into blessedness, then it must be delivered in full measure. It can only be that sort of morality leading to a blessedness in which both true piety and true virtue are inseparably linked. This is the case even among those Moralists who deny a personal God, for they still hold to the Good, the True, and the Virtuous—to their God and their Goddess.[39]

Still, I am not the opinion that Marie, even after her fall into virtue, would ever ascend into blessedness. As our novelist knows of nothing higher than this sort of blessedness, and insofar as anything higher is well beyond the limits of his thought, his creations could never ascend beyond his level—as even the best among them would simply be unable to rise higher *than* their creator. Marie, who was recruited by Rudolphe to serve the cause of morality, would thereafter, as the devoted and obedient servant of her author, only be committed to cause of morality. And so, whatever might be revealed in the later history of Maria, it could only happen to her in that she was the true servant of her creator, and as such would hold to the fate which her Divinity had imposed upon her.

In escaping the "claws of the owl," who was only able to despoil her body, Maria then fell under the power of a Priest, who despoiled her tender soul with the pious teaching that her life must now be that of a penitent—if future forgiveness was to be gained. This teaching determined her future. This worm of thought, placed in her heart by the Priest, gnawed steadily away, and finally corroded and destroying her God-given heart [*das gottergebene Herz*]. This inner corrosion ultimately forced her to totally renounce and withdraw from the world. The actual doctrines of morality are found in the pious teachings of this Priest and they finally silenced even Rudolphe's "sensible" objections.

Every day, Rudolph gave himself over to the sweet hope and longing for an intimate family life in the Court of Gerolstein, and to have the joy of a Father sharing the bliss of a life with Maria, his delightful young daughter.

He, as only a princely Father could, would compensate the well-behaved and virtue-rich princess with new offerings of love to replace the early miseries she had endured. All the pleasures of a world that a great ducal court could offer her should now stand open to her.

But what would be Maria's cost for the purchase these worldly pleasures? It could only be that no one should ever discover her former life, and henceforth, everyone must only recognize the goodness of her present life. If her former life were ever revealed, then no brilliance from the ducal crown would be able to protect the poor Princess from the poisonous looks and disdainful shrugs of the relentless admirers of moral purity. Rudolphe knows this quite well, and so he quietly keeps his own misgivings over Maria's earlier days to himself. What sensible human being would deal with this any other way? Everyone would—except an Ultra,[40] as it would not be moral!—just as a moralizing liberal would also say.

But how can Marie, the pure priestess of moral principle, now having entered into the moral world despite her misdeeds, still prove her salvation through a lie? Can she, through a deception, pretend to be purer than she really is? "Deception, always deception," she calls out in despair, "always fear and lies, always shaking before the gaze of him whom one loves and respects, as a criminal trembles before the relentless eyes of a Judge!" So, can it be accepted that Maria, a servant at the altar of morality, be permitted to lie?

Lying is a sin that no moral human can forgive. As much as he will, a person might ask forgiveness because his lie was necessary, but a necessary lie still remains a lie. But how can the truth serve, if even under temptation, it still leads to falsity? No morality can ever teach the justification of a lie, yet so many moral people actually do lie, that this surely proves that neither ethical principles nor the good itself is strong enough to direct actual life. This is the reason why humans are unconsciously led into actions which scorn these petty moral principles, into actions which might even encourage them to break away from the compulsion of these very principles themselves. But yet, one is not freed from an illusion until one overcomes it in theory.

Once won over to the cult of the good, Maria is too modest to argue any exception to its rules. So, she cannot lie. But how can she confess to this "relentless judge"? If the moral world does not know what she has done, then how could she be judged? The world of the "good" could not exist without having "goods," and among good things is Chastity, whose loss they can never forgive—in a woman. Yes, an enduring humility will allow for the healing of the painful wound, but time alone cannot wash off the mark of its scar. But that world, that world which believes in morality and its goods, can never forget the loss. Its goodness is valuable to it, and for those who lose even one good, even among those who would yet hang onto the illusions of this morality, however they might twist and turn, their sense of loss and criminality can never be fully forgotten. A woman who has given up her chastity, who has lived among the "castoffs of society," who has been "demeaned" will forever be looked upon with disdain. She is "stained," "fallen," "shameless"—she is "dishonored." The moral world will demand permanent shame as her punishment, a shame that they will awaken within the penitent woman.

Perhaps one might think that this is but an exaggerated and false shame and that if one were not overly-sensitive, it might, by a mature person, be easily cast aside. But then we must ask as to what this world, in its actual moral judgments, holds of higher worth—whether the human person—or his goodness. There is a profound connection between the rising concern with ethical behavior and the rise of the bourgeoisie: the Banker and the moralist judge a man from precisely the same viewpoint—not what he is in himself, but rather what he possesses. "Has he money?" And along with this question runs a parallel question: "Has he virtue?" Who possesses no money can have no connection to the Banker, it "makes him disgraceful," who does not "posses" the virtues of the honorable citizen must not approach that citizen. Both measure according to possessions, and the lack of property is, and will remain, a lack. Just as a horse, who might possess all of the virtues of the best horse, but possesses the blemish of a bad color, so also with a woman, who although otherwise pure has yet been once impure, and so will be forever condemned for that. Rightly so, as she does not possess one of the major goods which makes for the honor of a moral woman. If Marie is now chaste, this has not always been the case, and if she is now innocent, she was not previously so. Innocence is so tender a nature that it should never be allowed to be touched; once touched will forever vanish [*Die Unschuld ist so zarten Wesens dass sie niemals berührt worden sein darf; einmal verletzt ist sie immer verschwunden*][41] Innocence is one of those fixed ideas which turned Moral[42] into a lunatic, and Maria into a sick woman [*Betschwester*]. But so it must be. The fixed distance between the impure and the pure, the immoral and the moral, is simply expressed in the inward and hidden feeling in Maria. She is—"desecrated."

Might there be an objection intended to show that one is not guilty of what was done long ago, and so deserves greater leniency? First of all, although this objection might be generally disputed, still no one today is punished by the Church, certainly less so than during the lax morality of the *ancient regime*. Then, when the great mass of people had thick skins, there seemed little concern regarding the hard consequences following upon their religious doctrines [*Glaubensartikel*]. So then, must a serious thinking person with the fine sensitivity of Maria be ruined by the mundane views of the common man?

However, we must recognize, that she would, feeling the inner pressure of moral directives, do all that she could do, and so her withdrawal from the world was inevitable. She could not, without acting immorally, be allowed to deceive the world. It could not be allowed that she could ever admit of this deception, for if she did, rather than joy, she would only reap the scorn and ridicule of the world. Every joy, which the future might have offered her would have immediately been poisoned by the thorn of shame. Feeling this, she then remembered what he, whom she loved, had said of his Father, Prince Heinrich, "They wish me to die, to see me debased in his eyes!" She thought she must either hold something back from the world, or hold it in her own conscience, she could hope for nothing more—they had ruined her.

But why does she take refuge in God? Because neither the world nor she herself could remove her sins. Only God can forgive her. Men must act according to the Rules of the Good Book [*Gesetzbuch des Guten*] and so are but servants in the Kingdom of the Good. Here God alone is the absolute King, under whom the Good is subordinated, and when he wishes to pardon, it is not the Good which is addressed, but only his unlimited will. What is in this turn of Maria to the Lord? Nothing more than but she feels, as no justice can be found in the rule of morality, that she must have another rule and another judgment. She seeks absolution from God at the cost of a life of remorse. This remorse will be the work of the devout Priest, who is, of course, not allowed to tell her that "Who enslave themselves are slaves, and who release themselves are free." So, what she was able to do for herself, she seeks outside of herself; however, she would be neither moral nor pious were she to seek it elsewhere.

But how could this good maiden ever forgive herself for her unchastity and lies? If she did, then her forgiveness would go beyond morality, and all of the charming construction of E. Sue would collapse into a ridiculous nothingness—if the Good were no longer be taken to be the Highest. If this could be, then the human being would rise beyond virtue and vice, beyond morality and sin.

This whole struggle is based upon how a few bigoted people have a manic fixation upon the illusion of Good and Evil. As the world judges, we are allowed to do this and that, because it is good; but other things, such as lying, we are not permitted, because it is bad—and so thinks Rudolph, who intends to lead Marie to virtue.

The poet didn't impose his own virtues and morals upon Marie, but she imposed them upon herself, she became her own measure of virtue. It is as if one would measure a Lion not according to human properties, such as being magnanimous, but rather to take it according to its own animal nature; perhaps the dishonorable transformation of Maria from being a free and hopeful person into a miserable and lost child was but the startling result of her coming to know and to devote herself to virtue in the time that she was yet a free and hopeful person. Her dedication was more than superficial, as the poor girl not only accepted and joyfully agreed to the unhappy link between virtue and remorse, but that she immediately become an oppressed slave in that moral world and submitted herself to its requirements. As she had been cast under the fated pressure of circumstance, the evil angel of conversion had seized upon this tender child. If she had but had the lucid and sensuous spirit of a Bajadere,[43] she would have been able to gather up her scornful passion and would have cast off the weight of a solidified world, and, rising up from her humiliating status—and rebel. But who has the courage and the spirit to avenge this loss of a girl's chastity [*Keuschheit*], to avenge this and every other loss in this whole guilty world?

But such as Sue know of no other happiness than that of honorable people, no other greatness than that of morality, and no other worth for man than being virtuous and devoted to God. And so, a human child, from whom might emerge a free human being, must be first enrolled in the service of virtue— and a yet unspoiled nature must be poisoned and spoiled with the hallucinations of "good people."

If a novelist can present his heroine as one who can lead her life in the center of a confused mass of the dirtiest vices, paying for it with the bloom of her body, but not as *Chouette* or the Schoolmaster,[44] who would convert her young friends into the servants of vice, then why cannot an Atheist, who, although pressured by religion remains perfectly free, be thought of as one who might lift her above the influence of virtue? But no, the maudlin writer, dreaming of a "true and proper bourgeoisie society," rather than having this girl assertive in the face of vice, renders her into a weak and sentimental creature whose feeble resistance against a craving for the "Good" will welcome, both in body and soul, the slavery of virtue.

There is no one to be found in this whole novel who could be termed "self-creative." There is none, who, by his own omnipotent and creative power, creates himself. There is no one who can act without restraint against their own instincts, nor against the pressure of beliefs (belief in virtue, morality, and so on—as well as vice).

The first type of Sue's characters are those who blindly follow the direction of their heart, their disposition, and their natural inclination such as Rigolette.[45] She is as she is—a contented nature, a happy mediocrity, and she will always remain so. Her nature is undeveloped, just as her canaries. They also can experience their fate, and suffer, but they can never become anything other than what they are. The other side of Rigolette is the child, Lahme.[46] He is a malicious child who now enjoys seeing misery, and who will, as he ages, only get worse—until his life ends on the scaffold. He will find an unknown grave, just as Rigolette, who will find a respectable grave. It makes no essential difference what sort of a life style dominates the individual, with Ferrand,[47] it is greed, with the prisoner German,[48] an impotent gabbling, and so on.

The second type of undeveloped and servile humans, are those who are not so much governed by their natural instinct, than from a belief, a fixed idea. Eugene Sue, himself a servant among servants, knows nothing better than how to apply pathological exactitude upon those driven by virtue. Above them, the faithful believer in virtue, stands the Duke, who belongs to the "Order of the Benefactors of Suffering Mankind," a decoration not on, but in, his breast. Rudolphe, this "Brother of Mercy," is committed, with mildness and strength, to the improvement of mankind, to give himself over to the "betterment," both physically and morally, of those who suffer in a cesspool of sin, and to reward those who are stained and hopeless, and, by a careful search to find those who corrupt souls and—punish them. He then moves to Paris, and sick from his lunacy, leaves it after he has led his daughter into the divine house of virtue [*das Gotteshaus der Tugend*] and has robbed her of the last possibility to become an individual human being.

As virtue finally robs this child of both understanding and life, the Brother of Mercy, finally sees that he has, in his priestly duty, not sacrificed his unhappy daughter to moral idols, but rather for the "Justice of the inscrutable God." His attack upon his father has been avenged by the loss of his daughter. This fighter for virtue and religion is so insanely driven to apply his own principles that he cannot recognize the consequences of this treatment upon his daughter, and so can only admire the "stern judgment of God." Marie is a complete and perfect challenge to morality and religion. Her father must confess that "his unhappy child resists, with such relentless logic, all that is required for a tender heart and honor, that she cannot be converted" - - and he "gives up lecturing her, as all reason is impotent against her unconquerable conviction, which comes from a dignified and elevated feeling." Yes, he also understands, that he, in Marie's name, would also treat the matter with "courage and decorum"—so now then, what does he see in this uncompromised and completed morality of his daughter? Nothing but a "chastisement" of God, who gives him the goodness of his child as a "a punishment"! Truly, the cowardice of our liberal age, the "*juste-millieu*," could have been presented no more hideously nor more scornfully than what, instinctively, this spineless member of the age does here. The good Prince, after his penitential experience, had "learned nothing and forgot nothing."[49] As a man without development or self-creativity, he merely experiences hard destiny, for which the service of virtue prepares its disciples: he had only theological experiences, not human. Does it ever happen that he would seek to question the Lord, which he serves? Does it ever occur to him to seek out the kernel within the ideas he labors for—of "morality," "religiosity," "righteousness," and so on? He places himself within rigid limits, his understanding fixed in place, and from this place any further movement, any release from his Lord is, for this judgmental Duke, impossible. So intent upon proving himself to be a moral man, and yet so completely incompetent in judging men, he is a faithful image of his own creator—a miserable priest of virtue.

The opposite belief was fanatically held and incarnate in Mother Martial. Criminals have, and must also have, their fanatics, who believe in crime, and would bring it honor. Mother Martial is one of these—a Heroine of Vice. She lives and dies for crime, her ideal. But just as the believers in virtue, so also the believers in vice, who, in being possessed by a fixed idea, are also deprived of their own development and self-creation. As miserable as she is under the idea of vice, she yet cannot rise above it. And so, for her it is also the case: "Here I stand, I can do no other."[50] Ossified and gray in her belief, she is the Critic,[51] offering a singular salvation for those who suffer under the illusion that they can yet reach unreachable holiness, she yet is impotent, just as any other believer. Indeed, as is the case with lunatics, every reason she gives to free them from their lunacy serves only to strengthen it. There is no other experience for her except that fated for her. Her madness, winding about her, fully possesses her, and she can have only immoral and unholy experiences—just as her counterpart can only have moral and holy experiences.

Rudolphe's spirit has become a fixed attitude of belief in virtue. Vice is represented in the fixed attitude of Mother Martial. She levels a fearfully harsh judgment against her "misguided" son who wants to know nothing of crime. As a woman of principle, she fully impregnates the household with criminal standards, just as other family leaders fill their own homes with standards of goodness; she exercises demanding rules which have stifled the fatherly feeling of her son Brutus. And so, are the commands of virtue essentially other than the commands of vice, are the fixed principles of one more bearable than the other? In his earlier novel, *Atar Gull*,[52] Eugene Sue might well have learned something: that the feeling of revenge and the feeling of rectitude are one and the same, for good and evil collapse into a unity.[53] But for Sue, the black Moor is the Devil simply because he is black, and the white Parisian, as pure white, is virtuous only at the cost of accepting God. However, the good author can be so little improved upon as his fictional characters, for if they do convert, they become even more pitiable and slavish than they were.

As we can see, the central figures and some of the others are but repressed and slavish characters, so dominated by their own beliefs and habits that they are robbed of their self-creativity and self-reliance. This being the case, there is really no need to deal with the other slaves.

It is clear that the author employed only biased characters, those whose fate was prepared for them by their wishes or doctrines, by their uncultured nature, or their unnatural culture. Such is his world, but Sue has only proven that he can fashion complacent people within his world, but not that he is able to lift them out of its restraints—and so free them.

It is no miracle that the mysteries have received so much approval. Indeed the moral world has seized upon this winning production of Philistinism as the true image of its own humanitarianism. It echoes fully the same lust to reform, as well as the same complaint that has broken out among the Turks—that there is hardly more left to reform. The good will of a Mahmud II.[54] is not needed for our age, for our present day liberals now honor and hold the greatest expectations for today's Turkish liberalism[55]—and who, be they high or low, would not be a liberal! "Our time is sick!" one friend, with sad eyes, will speak to another, and then both immediately embark upon n botanical expedition seeking out the sweet herbs which alone can cure the sickness of the age.

Friend, your time is not sick, it is over. So, don't bother to look about for a cure, but rather ease your few final hours by allowing them to hurry by, and then—as the time can never be recovered—allow your age to die.

"Everywhere there are needs and sufferings!" This thought encourages anyone, even those in doubt, to open up the *Mysteries* and so observe the full wretchedness of suffering. But just try, just once, to "reform" Turkey. You hope to reform it, and it will become yours—to tear apart. Turkey, just as an old man, lacks nothing. Of course, an old man lacks the strength of a youth, but if he did not, then he would not be an old man. The good will of such as Mahmud II and our Liberals would attempt to cure this "lack" in the old man, and so rejuvenate him, to make his tottering body once again strong and straight. But our time is neither sick nor able to be cured, but rather it is old, and its final hours have already sounded. But despite this, a thousand Sues spring up to offer their charlatan cures.

Now, should we not conclude with a word of praise for the splendid gifts of aristocratic benefactors, and the philanthropic suggestions of the novelist? Indeed they do rush about, and, by taking as long as it takes, and by offering rewards and punishments, "guide" the people into making Virtue their Master! Countless proposals for the improvement of the Church were made before the Reformation, and are now made for the improvement of the State: improvements, where there is nothing more to be improved—

II C

Stirner's review of Bauer's "Trumpet of the Last Judgment"[56]

TRANSLATOR'S INTRODUCTION

One of the earliest responses to Bruno Bauer's *Trumpet* [*Posaune des Jüngsten Gerichts*] was a review written shortly after its publication in

November of 1841, shortly before Stirner met Bauer. The forced attempt to mimic Bauer's ironic tone of Christian shock and concern, with all of its heavy-handed ironies and ambiguities have made its translation difficult. In a few instances, faced with an intractable and convoluted passage, the translator felt justified in recasting it in the form of a more lucid and less complex statement—but in no instance was Stirner's meaning distorted or lost.

Stirner's review first appeared in the *Telegraph für Deutschland*, January, 1842. Republished in Stirner's *Kleinere Schriften* hrs. John Henry Mackay (Berlin: Bernhard Zack, 1914); republished (Stuttgart-Bad Cannstatt: Friedrich Frommann Verlag, 1976). pp. 11–25.

Über B. Bauers "Posaune des Jüngsten Gerichts

What should not be tolerated, equalized, and reconciled with everything else? We have endured this accommodation, this easy acceptance which, as it can be imagined, has brought us to a state of exhaustion, which has divided our inner hearts, and which only needed intelligence to let us know that we have spent our honorable time in useless attempts to bring about concord and unity. The accusers are right: "How can one reconcile Belial with Christ?" The devoted Zealot has never known any other goal than exterminating the spirit of the new age which is pregnant with threatening storms. He is just as the Emperor of the heavenly empire who thinks only of the "extermination" of his enemies, and as an Englishman he only wants to have no fight except the crucial one of a fight unto death. We allowed the Zealot to rant and to rave, and saw nothing in him but—a humorous fanatic. Did we do right with this? Insofar as the Zealot in the face of common sense always lost his case, and even if reasonable folk do not particularly rebuke him, we could then, in confidence, leave the affair to the sense of those who lay down the rules, and so be confident in following this sense. But this toleration has rocked us into a dangerous slumber. Admittedly, the complaining Zealot didn't do us any harm; but still, the believer and the whole flock of the religious were behind the complainer, and—what is the worse and the oddest—we ourselves were also set behind him. Indeed, we were liberal philosophers and didn't let anything impose upon thinking: thinking was the all in all. However, how stands it with belief? Should it somehow give way to thinking? Heaven forefend! There can be no enmity assumed between the freedom of thinking and belief! The content of belief and that of knowledge is one and the same content, and whoever would injure belief would not understand himself and would be no philosopher! Didn't Hegel himself take the purpose of his lectures on the philosophy of religion to be the reconciliation of reason with religion? And would we, his disciples [seine Jünger] want to subtract anything from his belief? That would be far from us! Know, ye faithful hearts, that we are fully at one with you regarding the content of belief, and that we have only set ourselves upon the beautiful task, of which you have so misjudged us, of defending disputed beliefs. Or do you still more or less doubt this? Observe how we justify ourselves to you, and so read our conciliatory writings on "Belief and Knowledge," and on the "Piety of Philosophy against Christian Religion," and dozens of similar writings, and you won't have any further malice against your best friends!—

So then, the good-hearted, peaceful philosopher fell into the arms of belief. Now, who is so pure from this sin of belief that he would cast the first stone against the poor philosophical sinner? The period of sleep-walking was so universal, so full of self-deception and illusions, the press and urge after reconciliation so general, that only a few held themselves free of it, and these few perhaps without any support. It was the time of peaceful diplomacy. Just as the diplomacy of this time it was understood that there was nowhere any real enmity, but everywhere irritation and a seeking of advantage, a purposive incitation, with persuasion balanced by a sugary peacefulness and a friendly mistrust, an artificial sensibility, a serious and willful earnestness by means of superficial balancing and juggling acts, a thousand fold phenomena of driving self-deception and illusion in every area. "Peace at all costs" or better "agreement and accommodation at all costs," that was the paltry heartfelt need of these diplomats. It might here be the place to sing a little song, if this would not be forbidden, of this diplomacy which has made our whole life so feeble, and which has by its skillful hypnosis lulled our reason to sleep in a drowsy trustfulness, and has left us staggering about—

But beyond this, we are now prepared to announce a book, a book which has been anticipated by our previous remarks, and which is the final and definitive overthrow of the diplomacy here discussed:

The Trumpet of the Last Judgment against Hegel the Atheist and Antichrist. An Ultimatum.—Under this title appears an small work of eleven Bogen, published by Wigand, whose author is not difficult to discover by anyone who knows his literary work and from it his scientific point of view—that which motivated him to address "His Brothers in Christ" and to say that "We would remain still concealed, so that it would not appear as if we sought any other honor than a Heavenly Crown. When the struggle, which we soon hope to see end, when the lies receive their punishment, then we will personally encounter him and warmly embrace his decision. This book is an excellent mystery! A man of the most devout fear of God, whose heart is filled with anger against the despicable pack of young Hegelians, turns back to their teacher, their origin, Hegel himself and finds—horrors! That the whole revolutionary wickedness, that is now bubbling forth from his depraved students had already been in this morose and hypocritical sinner, who had been long taken as a keeper and a protector of the Faith. The author, with righteous scorn, just the Clergy from Constance dealt with Huss, tears the priestly garments from him, and, painting him in flames as the devil, sets a paper hat upon his shaved head, and hounds this greatest of heretics through the streets of an astonished world. Such a confidant and versatile philosophical Jacobean has never been hunted down. It was the undeniably excellent and radical attack by this determined Servant of God that he has seized upon and bitten Hegel. This servant has served well, and out of the right instinct, has never lost sight of and never lost the smell of this Arch-Heretic, and the Anti-Christ of their Christ. Unlike those of "good intention" who hold a lightly-held belief, and neither with faith nor with knowledge would wish anyone harm, he, on the contrary, holds, with inquisitorial severity, the heretic in sight until he is caught. He does not allow himself to be deceived and duped—as dummies so often are—and can rightly claim that he be considered the best expert regarding the dangerous aspects of the Hegelian system. "You know what protective steps must be taken, don't look for any other!" The wild beast knows quite well that he has most to fear from Man.

Hegel, who would and has elevated the human spirit into the all-powerful Spirit, and has impressed this teaching upon his students that no one has to seek salvation outside of or beyond themselves, but rather are each their own Savior and Deliverer, has never made it his particular interest to lead a so-called "small war [kleinen Krieg]" and to hack out of its fortress the egoism which in a thousand fold forms liberates individuals. One can reproach him for this disregard, and charge him that his system lacks all morality, and it could really be said that he lacks any charitable sense of advice [*Paränese*] or pedagogical paternity—which could cultivate pure heroes of virtue. This man, whose task has been to overthrow the whole world by constructing a new world, a world for which the old had no space, has, as a school master, aroused the base ways of the young, and the course of malice and anger at moral teaching and the rotting huts and palaces—all of which, nevertheless, must collapse as soon as Heaven gathers up its comfortable [*wohlgenährten*] Olympians and casts them out. But that is of little concern for the one who can only feel exhaustion from wishing to have the emptiness of a life outside of himself. But this is not so with the brave person, who only requires one word—the Logos, for in it he has all and can create all out of it. But because this Master, this powerful creator of the word, on occasion falls into a rage over this or that minor restriction and the loss of this or that reward, he loses his control, and then, unrestrained, he destroys the nature of the whole world, and separates God from his Throne, and scatters the whole host of angels into nothingness, those who do not know that they have been overthrown by "The Trumpet of the Last Judgment." So now, after the death of the "King" a busy activity develops among the "garbage collectors [*Kärrnern*]." But did not a few dear little angels survive? "I could just eat them up, the lot of them."

To find any comparison to them would be indeed quite grand! But if only to make it more down to earth, something more appropriate might be fitting!

"You waver to and fro, please try descending,
A bit more worldly-like your sweet limbs bending;
Though gravity, I grant, sits well on you,
I'd like, just once, to catch you smiling, too;
I'd cherish the delight of it always;
I have in mind the way that lovers gaze,
A dimpling near the lips, and it is done.
You, lad I like the best, so lean and tall,
That curate's mien becomes you not at all,
Give me a little wanton wink, come on!
You need a decent naked fashion, too,
That long enfolding robe is over-prim –
They turn around—now for a backward view!
I could just eat them up, the lot of them.[57]

The lust for affirmation has increased, and individuals, by order of the World Spirit [*Weltgeist*], have been admonished to go forth and continue the work of Hegel, an order which occurs and is exemplified in the conclusion of his *Lectures on the History of Philosophy*:

> It is my desire that this history of Philosophy should contain for you a summons to grasp the spirit of the time, which is present in us by nature, and—each in his own place—consciously to bring it from its natural condition, that is, from its lifeless seclusion, into the light of day.

However, the Philosopher himself does not help the present world to solve its problems: "How the empirical present day is to find its way out of its discord, and how things are to turn out for it, are questions that must be left up to it and are not the immediate practical business and affair of philosophy." He merely extends the heaven of freedom over the world, and now "leaves" it to others as to whether or not they would wish to cast an idle glance heavenward. The matter is, however, quite otherwise with his followers. Since this "empirical present day is to find its way out of its discord," and in that they belong to this empirical present day, then they must, as the first of the enlightened, enlighten others. But at first they cringed and turned from this task, and became diplomats and peaceful mediators. What Hegel had completely and wholly torn apart, they thought to rebuild again in its particulars. He had not been particularly clear as to his rejection and destruction of each and every particular. He was often as dark as Christ himself when it came to details, and, as it is said, in the darkness there are whisperings, and in it much allows itself to be interpreted and re-interpreted.

It is likely that the dark decade of diplomatic barbarity is over. It had its good aspect and had to happen. We first had to absorb all of the old and sick things and then expel them so as to despise them, and so learn of our ownership and ourselves. But now, as we climb strengthened and revitalized from the humiliating mud bath which has soiled us with all sorts of prudential impurities, we cry out "Let the barrier between us be torn down! Let there be war to the death!"

Anyone who now would be diplomatic and would seek "peace at all costs" should take care that he doesn't fall between the swords of combatants and becomes a bloody victim of his own "well-meaning" half-measures. For us, the time for reconciliation and sophistry is past. The "Trumpet" has sounded the full battle cry of the last judgment. It will sound in some drowsy ears, but some will not awaken, and some will still imagine that they can remain behind the battle lines, and some will think it only a meaningless noise which is but wasted on war and not spent upon peaceful words—but there is no longer any hope for them. If the world stand armed against God, and the noisy thunder of battle breaks out against the Olympian himself and his army of sheep, then only the dead will be able to sleep, for the living will not surrender their position. We wish no more diplomatic "reconciliations," no mediators, no settlements, but only that each hostile camp should stand over and against each other, and that the godless will stand face to face against those who are God-fearing, and they will know that they are opposed to one another. And here, I repeat, in the sharpness of this enmity, the religious zealots will have the advantage; for they never have had any instinct for friendship. There could be no more skillful and at the same time a more righteous way of unveiling Hegel's great heresy, than that of this author, who, with faithful zeal, has sounded the doomsday trumpet of the last judgment. They wish no "reasonable resolutions" but a war of annihilation [*Vernichtungskrieg*]." They have a right to this.

But what can the God-fearing Hegel find vexing? With this question we will come to the book itself. God-fearing? Who threatens them more with destruction than he who annihilates fear? Yes, Hegel is the real advocate and creator of that bravery before which cowardly hearts have trembled. "*Securi adversus homines, secure adversus Deos* [Confidant adversaries of men and gods]," so Tacitus described the ancient Germans. But their confidence, as the God's adversaries, went astray and was lost, and the "Fear" of God then nested itself in their broken natures. But finally, because they have found the word, they have re-discovered themselves, and now have mastered their chilling fears. Henceforth, they will no longer divide the eternal word, and will struggle and fight so that it will become one again and immanent in all.

They have found the eternal word and it cannot be destroyed. An authentic German, *securus adversus Deum*, has spoken it, the liberating word: Self-satisfaction [*Selbstgenügen*], the Absolute Sovereignty [Autarkie] of free men. The French were the first to emphatically declare the world historical idea of Freedom, and we have now been freed by the French from all sorts of ideas about fear and respect for authority, and have seen these ideas fall into nothingness, into absurdity. But once again, these ugly hundred-headed Hydra ideas have re-appeared—and, once again, has not brave self-confidence shriveled up in the face of countless fears? The French have brought us a salvation which is as little complete and stable as that which the fiery signs of the Hussite Bohemian storm once gave to the German Reformation. The German alone is the first to proclaim the historic task of Radicalism, for only he alone is radical, and he is alone is—without injustice. None are as determined and as ruthless as he is, for he does not simply overthrow the existing world, he overthrows—himself. Wherever a German circles and destroys, there must a God fall, and a World be violated. Destruction is the task of the German, and the smashing of the temporal his eternal role. Here there is no fear or despair: He not only drives out the fear of the spiritual, and this and that reverential fear, but he drives out all fears, even reverence itself and the fear of God.

Escape, you timorous souls, from that inward fear of God contained in your love of God, escape from that fear which you neither have words nor common thoughts. Hegel is unmoved by your pleas, for he has transformed your God into a corpse, and so has turned your love into abhorrence. The "Trumpet" has sounded out the true purpose of the Hegelian system—which, hidden under its Old Testament formulations and hesitant expressions, is that "modern thinking, in all of its anxiously contrary movements still rests firmly upon the presupposition that truth and error can be reconciled." "Away!" calls out the "Trumpeter," in angry scorn against all such thinking, "Away with this lust for reconciliation, with this sentimental slop, with this crooked and false worldview: only the One is true, and if the One and the Other were set together, the Other would fall into nothing. Do not come to us with this anxiously sophistical timidity of the Schliermachian school or that of the Positive Philosophy; away with this foolishness, which only wishes reconciliation because error lives within them, and they haven't the courage to tear it out of their hearts. So tear it out, and throw away those whose forked tongues like those of snakes, filled with quick flatteries and mediations, away with them!—even if is a witty diplomacy. Your honest voice, heart, and nature are louder and stronger than that spirit-paralyzing diplomacy.

The Trumpeter, as he should be, is a righteous serf of God, and so rejects Hegel's God as surely the as devout Turk of Allah would seek every means against Hegel, the blasphemer

The *Preface* is devoted to this diplomatic perversion, in which the "Old Hegelians" are greeted with the words: "They always have the word of reconciliation on their mouth—but "adders" poison is under their lips."

But now, we "will face them with the mirror of the system and see if they can recognize themselves in it. We will find out! They will be compelled to answer! They must answer. We pledge before the fact that Göschel, Gabler, Rosenkranz, and particularly Henning—and the rest will answer, for they are guilty before their government . . . the time has come when further silence is a crime."

A "philosophical school" has also developed which would refute Hegel with a "Christian and positive philosophy." However, having only love for itself, it has, on its own, proceeded to oppose the foundations of Christian truth—it has had as little success and influence among the believers as among unbelievers. If we complain, and the government looked about for a doctor, did it find one among these positive philosophers? Has the government trusted a cure to one of them? No! Others are sought out! A Krummacher, a Häavernick, a Hengstenberg, a Harless, must be placed before the breach!

A third set of opponents to Hegelian philosophy, the Schliermachians, are equally dismissed: "They are themselves hooked upon the lure of the Evil One, for they would like to present the appearance of being philosophical themselves. Yet they do nothing to encourage this appearance. They deserve the word: "I know your work, that you are neither cold nor hot. I would thou wert cold or hot. To then because thou art lukewarm, and neither cold nor hot, I will spew thee out of my mouth." Their enthusiasm for the "churchly life" is indeed recognized by the Trumpeter, but to him they are not "earnest, fundamental, comprehensive and diligent enough." They have even found "nothing to set against the blasphemous declarations" of Bruno Bauer (*die evangel. Landeskirche Preussens und die Wissenschaft*).

But finally, it came to Leo, "who first had the courage to publicly step forth against this Godless philosophy, to formally accuse it and to make the Christian-minded government take notice of the pressing danger threatened by this philosophy to the state, Church and to all morality." But Leo is also rebuked insofar as he was insufficiently stern, and his work still "penetrated with some secular leavening," which provided him with much hair splitting. The conclusion is cheaply constructed with psalms anathematizing the Godless.

The *Introduction* [to the Trumpet] reveals to us the real intention of the raging man: "The hour has now struck in which the last, the worst, and the proudest enemy of the Lord will be brought to earth. This last enemy is also the most dangerous, these "Wild Men"—these people of the Antichrist—have dared to declare the non-existence of the Eternal Lord, and this in the full light of day, in the market, before all Christian Europe, in the light of the sun which has never shone upon such wickedness. They have practiced an idolatrous adultery with the Whore of Reason while they have murdered the Anointed of God. But Europe, once filled with Holy Zeal, strangled the Whore, and then bound itself into a Holy Alliance so as to cast the Antichrist into chains and to once again set up the eternal alters of the True Lord.

But then came—No!—but then was scented, nursed, protected, sheltered, indeed honored and paid, a man who was stronger than the French, that enemy from without which had been conquered, and he gave new foundation to the principles of Hell, and raised them into the power of a law. Hegel was called forth and fixed at the center of the University of Berlin! He had, with the attractive powers of philosophy over German youth, secured his introduction.

One cannot believe that this mob, with which the Christian state in our times is compelled to struggle against, is fixed upon any other principle or other teaching than that set out by the Master of Deceit. It is certainly true that this younger school of Hegelians is quite different from that first which gathered itself about its master, for this younger school have openly cast away all godliness and modesty and struggle openly against Church and State. They have inverted the cross and threaten to upset the throne itself—such opinions and deeds of which the older school might appear incapable. But if the older school did not rise up to these things, to this devilish energy, it was only the result of chance circumstance, for fundamentally and in principle, if we go back to the actual teaching of the master, the latest disciples have added nothing new—they have only torn away the thin veil which briefly concealed the thought of the master have revealed—shamelessly enough—the system in its nakedness."

Accepting the charges against Hegel's system, it is now incumbent upon us to examine more closely the actual contents of the book. The reason for this is that in order to present a review of the work that is not lost or wasted upon the reader, and so it is requisite that the order of the work itself be directly laid out. We know of no better way to do this, since the author's memory might not have taken in all of the significant passages in Hegel's work that could have been criticized.

In addition, as announced on page 163, the *Trumpet* is to be followed with a second part, which will show "how Hegel would prove that the character of the religious consciousness, a particular phenomena of self-consciousness, arises out of the inner dialectic of self-consciousness," and at the same time "Hegel's hatred against religious and Christian art and his disintegration of all positive legal codes."[58]

And so, for the satisfaction of the reader who takes a lively interest in the questions of our time, and who would not allow this book to be ignored, and who might find material which might have been missed, we will now avail ourselves of the opportunity to survey the thirteen chapters of this book.

In the first chapter, *"The Religious relation as a Substantial"* the Trumpeter presents Hegel as one who has "drawn a twofold cover over his work of destruction." One is the cover under which Hegel, who speaks countless times of God, and under which he almost always appears as if he understands God as that living God, Who was before the world exited, and so on. The older Hegelians (a Göschel at their head) stay at this viewpoint. But there is yet a further cover which is set up: that religion is a dialectical substance-relationship, in which the individual is related to the universal, which as substance, or—as it is said—absolute Idea as to that which has power over it. Accepting this, the individual spirit will abandon its particular uniqueness and set itself in unity with the absolute Idea. The most powerful spirits (Strauss and others) have handed themselves over and are captured by this view. "But," it is finally said, "more dangerous than this [Pantheistic] view is the thing in itself, which is immediately present to every open and expert eye if it but exerts itself to a certain extent: this is set forth as the understanding of religion as being nothing more than an inward relationship of self-consciousness to itself, and that all powers, which exists as substance or absolute idea are but appearances differentiated from self-consciousness, being merely religious images objectified out of self- consciousness."

After this, the content of the first chapters is evident. (2) The Ghost of the World Spirit. (3) Hatred Against God. (4) Hatred of the Established Order. (5) Admiration for the French and Contempt for the German. (6) The Destruction of Religion. (7) The Hatred of Judaism. (8) Partiality for the Greeks. (9) Hatred of the Church. (10) Contempt of Holy Scripture and Sacred History. (11) Religion as the Product of Self-consciousness. (12) The Dissolution of Christianity. (13) Hatred Against Fundamental Scholarship and the Usage of Latin. (As the Trumpeter has it, "a comic supplement").

The announced second part, for which the author might wish a comprehensive memory, since he lacks no other talents, should be immediately reviewed after it appears, for then, perhaps, something might be found and added to what he has already written. Now, finally, why is it that we should honestly consider this book a Mummery? Perhaps because no God fearing person can be so free and intelligent as the writer is. "Who cannot have the best, is truly not the best!"—

NOTES

1. The work, in two volumes, was published by the Berlin firm of "Allgemeinen deutschenVerlags-Anstalt." In 1967, a photocopy reproduction of the original work was published by Aalen: Scienetia Verlag. These are the only editions. All translations from the German are those of the author of this article.

2. MEW, 28 (Berlin: Dietz Verlag, 1963), 33. A reference to the Stirner's earlier role as teacher in a Berlin school for girls of wealthy families.

3. *Max Stirner: Der Einzige und sein Eigentum und andere Schriften* (München: Karl Haner Verlag, 1968), 280.

4. University of Michigan Press, 2001.

5. Ibid., 151.

6. John Henry Mackay, *Max Stirner: Sein Leben und sein Werk* (Treptow bei Berlin: B. Zack's Verlag, 1910), 213. The excellent recent translation of Mackay's work by Hubert Kennedy, *Max Stirner: His Life and His Work* (Concord, CA: Peremptory Publications Concord, 2005), with its informative introduction is recommended.

7. MEW, 37, p. 293. (repeated footnote 100)

8. Gerhard Beck, *Die Stellung des Menschen zu Staat und Rechte bei Max Stirner* (Koln: 1965).

9. Bonn; Bouvier Verlag Herbert Grundmann., 1979.

10. Kast, xii.

11. Hist. II, pg. v.

12. The term "Constitutionalist" soon became another term for "Revolutionary."

13. Geoffrey Bruin, *Revolution and Reaction: 1848–1852* (New York: Van Nostrand, 1958).

14. The French revolutionaries established a short-lived "Revolutionary Tribunal," in 1793.

15. Hist. II, pg. viii.

16. Hist. II. Pg. viii.

17. *The Ego and Its Own*, 99–100.

18. Hist. I, p. 193.

19. Hegel, *Philosophy of Right*, 5–6.

20. Thomas Knox, in "Translator's Notes" to *Philosophy of Right*, 301.

21. Hist., II, p. 30.

22. Hist. II, p. 20.

23. Hist. II, p. 49.

24. Hist. II, p. 31.

25. Hist. II, p. 19.

26. A few weeks before Stirner's article appeared, Frederick Engles discussed the *Spenersche Zeitung* [*Berlinische Nachrichten von Staats- und gelehrten Sachen* in an article which he wrote for the *Rheinische Zeitung*. In his article Engles rightly criticizes the claim made by the *Spenersche Zeitung* that it was a liberal newspaper.

27. Likely based upon the Hegelian conception of self-consciousness as "being in and for itself." A key conception which led many of his followers into a radical humanism or atheism.

28. A bit of word-play, as a "*Knüttel*" was a physical club, and not a not a social "Club."

29. In 1839, David F. Strauss was invited by some liberal officials in Züurich to fill a Chair of Theology at the University. Hearing of this, the orthodox clergy and

conservative government officials generated such opposition that in time even a public demonstration was held opposing the appointment. The invitation was rescinded.

30. Kölnische Zeitung. From 1842–1843 it published a number of articles by Karl Marx.

31. In the first chapter of *Der Einzige*, Stirner writes of how a child can stand up to the "Father's stern look" and by this "obdurate courage" secure its own maturity and freedom.

32. Stirner's Der Einzige narrowly avoided being confiscated by the Prussian censors who thought that it had been earlier censored by the Saxony censors in Leipzig. When they found out this was not the case it was then disregarded by the Prussian censors as being too absurd to censor. Bauer's 1843 book. *Das entdeckte Christentum* was confiscated and destroyed except for one copy, discovered in 1927, which was then reprinted.

33. Jean Paul Richter (1763–1825) a well-known author of humorous novels and stories born in Bayreuth—as was Stirner.

34. Stirner's irony is here particularly apparent.

35. A very obscure and secretive society, active in the late seventeenth century, which had Rosecrucian and hermenutic interests. Little is known of them, it seems that Stirner is engaged in a bit of humorous scholarship.

36. See Bauer's 1843 essay "*Die Fahigkeit der heutigen Juden und Christen, frei zu warden [On the Capacity of today's Jews and Christians to become free]* in Sass, pp. 175–96.

37. Jacob Balde (1604–1668) a Jesuit known for the patriotic tone of his popular poetry.

38. Johann Joseph von Görres (1776–1848), author, who defended the authority of the Roman Church.

39. Suggestive of the French Revolutionary "Pantheon" and the "Goddess of Reason."

40. Ultras, "Ultra-Royalists," were a reactionary faction in the French parliament during the Bourbon Restoration from 1815–1830.

41. Cf. Oscar Wilde, "Innocence is like a delicate exotic fruit; touch it and the bloom is gone."

42. A character in the novel who was wrongly accused of murder.

43. A *bajadere* was a temple dancer in the European vision of legendary India being popularized by the first translations of Indian classic literature into European languages.

44. An unnamed small-time crook, a brutal and dangerous character.

45. A working class woman, a "grisette" who is friendly with Marie.

46. The son of a gangster.

47. A Notary whose greed has caused a more than a few families to become impoverished.

48. A victim of Ferrand's machinations.

49. Talleyrand's remark that the restored Bourbon rulers had "*learned nothing and forgotten nothing*."

50. Luther's statement, he is cited as an example someone possessed by a "fixed idea." The citation also appears in *Der Einzige und sein Eigentum.*"

51. A possible reference to Bruno Bauer, known as the "Critic" ...

52. Published in 1831, the book took an unusual approach for the time. It described the black, Atar Gull, as being clever enough to rely upon the white prejudice of taking blacks as stupid. This allowed Gull to take bloody revenge upon them for the slave trade.

53. A clear expression of the triadic dialectic of Hegelianis.

54. (1429–1481) also known as "Mohammad the Conqueror." Mahmd II not only expanded the Ottoman Empire but was also known as a reformer and patron of learning.

55. In 1839 a series of wide-ranging Turkish governmental decrees were enacted, liberalizing and reforming the judicial, military, and educational policies. Mohammad II was seen as the precursor of these reforms.

56. The full English translation of Bauer's *Posaune des Jüngsten Gericht uber Hegel den Atheisten und Antichristen: Ein Ultimatum* appeared as *The Trumpet of the Last Judgment Against Hegel The Atheist and Antichrist.* The translation, by the author, was published in 1989 by the Edward Mellen Press, Lewiston, New York. The *Trumpet* translation is introduced with a 57 page section dealing with the life and work of Bruno Bauer. It is fully annotated, with all Bauer's citations from Hegel referred to the original sources.

57. From Goethe's *Faust*, Pt. 1.

58. *Hegel's Lehre von der Relilgion und Kunst: von dem Standpuncte des Glaubens aus beurtheilt* (Leipzig: Otto Wigand: 1842).

Bibliography

Althusser, Louis. *For Marx*. New York: Random House, 1969.
Apter, David, and James Joll. *Anarchism Today*. New York: Doubleday, 1972.
Arvon, Henri. *Aux Sources de l'existentialisme: Max Stirner*. Paris: Presses universitaires de France, 1954.
Avineri, Shlomo. *Moses Hess: Prophet of Communism and Zionism*. New York and London: NYU Press, 1987.
Bakunin, Michael. *Bakunin on Anarchism*. Edited by Sam Dolgoff. Montréal: Black Rose Books, 1980.
Barnikol, Ernst. *Das entdeckte Christentum im Vormärz: Bruno Bauers Kampf gegen Religion und Christentum und Erstausgabe seiner Kampfschrift*. Edited by Ralf Ott. Scientia Verlag, 1989.
Bauer, Bruno. "Charakteristik Ludwig Feuerbach." *Wigands Vierteljahrsschrift* 3 (1845): 123–145.
———. "Die Gattung Und Die Masse." *Allgemeine Literaturzeitung, Monatsschrift*, no. 10 (1844).
———. *Feldzüge der reinen Kritik*. Frankfurt am Main: Suhrkamp, 1968.
———. *Hegels Lehre von der Religion und Kunst von dem Standpuncte des Glaubens beurtheilt*. Leipzig: Wigand, 1842.
———. *Hegels Lehre von der Religion und Kunst von dem Standpunkt des Glaubens aus beurteilt*. Aalen: Scientia Verlag, 1967.
———. "Lebenslauf." In *Bruno Bauer: Studien Und Materialien*, edited by Ernst Barnikol. Assen: Van Gorcum, 1972.
———. *Russland Und Das Germanentum*. Berlin: Neudr. d. Ausg, 1853.
———. *The Trumpet of the Last Judgement Against Hegel the Atheist and Antichrist: An Ultimatum*. Translated by Lawrence Stepelevich. Lewiston, NY: Edwin Mellen Press, 1989.
Beck, Gerhard. *Die Stellung Des Menschen Zu Staat Und Recht Bei Max Stirner*. Köln: Universitat zu Köln, 1965.

Berlin, Isaiah. *The Life and Opinions of Moses Hess*. Cambridge: Cambridge University Press, 1959.
Berthold-Bond, Daniel. *Hegel's Theory of Madness*. Albany, NY: State University of New York Press, 1995.
Bigler, Robert M. *The Politics of German Protestantism: The Rise of the Protestant Church Elite in Prussia, 1815–1848*. Berkeley: University of California Press, 1972.
Blake, Trevor. *Max Stirner Bibliography*. 127 House, 2016.
Bolin, Wilhelm. *Ludwig Feuerbach, Sein Wirken Und Seine Zeitgenossen. Mit Benutzung Ungedruckten Materials*. Stuttgart: J.G. Cotta, 1891.
Brazill, William J. *The Young Hegelians*. New Haven: Yale University Press, 1970.
Bruun, Geoffrey. *Revolution and Reaction, 1848–1852: A Mid-Century Watershed*. New York: Van Nostrand, 1958.
Butler, E. M. *The Saint-Simonian Religion in Germany: A Study of the Young German Movement*. Cambridge: Cambridge University Press, 1926.
Calasso, Roberto. *The Forty-Nine Steps*. Translated by John Shepley. Minneapolis, MN: University of Minnesota Press, 2001.
Cherno, Melvin. "Feuerbach's 'Man Is What He Eats': A Rectification." *Journal of the History of Ideas* 24, no. 3 (1963): 397–406.
Cieszkowski, August. *Gott Und Palingenesie*. Berlin: E.H. Schroeder, 1842.
———. *Prolegomena Zur Historiosophie*. Berlin: Veit und Comp, 1838.
Cieszkowski, August von. *Selected Writings of August Cieszkowski*. Translated by Andre Liebich. Cambridge: Cambridge University Press, 1979.
Cohn, Norman. *The Pursuit of the Millennium: Revolutionary Millenarians and Mystical Anarchists of the Middle Ages*. Oxford: Oxford University Press, 1957.
Cromwell, Richard S. *David Friedrich Strauss and His Place in Modern Thought*. Fair Lawn, NJ: R. E. Burdick, 1974.
Deleuze, Gilles. *Nietzsche et la philosophie*. Quadrige Grands textes edition. Paris: Presses universitaires de Fran, 2010.
Desmond, William. *Hegel's God: A Counterfeit Double?* Burlington, VT: Routledge, 2003.
Dobbins, John, and Peter Fuss. "The Silhouette of Dante in Hegel's Phenomenology of Spirit." *Clio* 11, no. 4 (1982): 387–413.
Engels, Friedrich. *Feuerbach: The Roots of the Socialist Philosophy*. Kerr, 1903.
———. *Ludwig Feuerbach and the End of Classical German Philosophy*. Moscow: Progress Publishers, 1946.
———. *Ludwig Feuerbach and the Outcome of Classical German Philosophy*. New York: International Publishers, 1941.
Erdmann, Johann Eduard. *A History of Philosophy: German Philosophy Since Hegel*. Translated by Williston Samuel Hough. London: Swan Sonnenschein, 1890.
Ferguson, Kathy. "Why Anarchists Need Stirner." In *Max Stirner*, edited by Saul Newman, 167–88. New York: Palgrave Macmillan, 2011.
Ferguson, Kathy E. "Saint Max Revisited: A Reconsideration of Max Stirner." *Idealistic Studies* 12, no. 3 (1982): 276–92.

Feuerbach, Ludwig. *Gedanken Uber Tod Und Unsterblichkeit*. Nurnberg: Adam Stein, 1830.

———. *Kleinere Schriften, I*. Edited by Werner Schuffenhauer. Vol. 8. Gesammelte Werke. Berlin: Akademie-Verlag, 1970.

———. *Kleinere Schriften, II*. Edited by Werner Schuffenhauer. Vol. 9. Gesammelte Werke. Berlin: Akademie-Verlag, 1990.

———. *Kleinere Schriften, III*. Edited by Werner Schuffenhauer. Vol. 10. Gesammelte Werke. Berlin: Akademie-Verlag, 1990.

———. *Principles of the Philosophy of the Future*. Translated by Manfred H. Vogel. Indianapolis: Bobbs- Merrill, 1966.

———. *Principles of the Philosophy of the Future*. Translated by Manfred Vogel. Indianapolis: Hackett, 1986.

———. *The Essence of Christianity*. Translated by George Eliot. New York: Harper, 1957.

———. *Thoughts on Death and Immortality*. Translated by James A. Massey. Berkeley: University of California Press, 1981.

———. *Vorlesungen Über Das Wesen Der Religion*. Edited by Wilhelm Bolin and Friedrich Jodl. Vol. 8. Sämtliche Werke. Leinen: Frommann-Holzboog, 1960.

Fleming, Kurt W., ed. *Recensenten Stirners. Kritik Und Anti-Kritik*. Leipzig: Verlag Max-Stirner-Archive, 2003.

Franchi, Stefano. "Telos and Terminus: Hegel and the End of Philosophy." *Idealistic Studies* 28, no. 1/2 (1998): 35–46.

Fromm, Erich. *Marx's Concept of Man*. New York: Frederick Ungar, 1961.

Gebhardt, Jürgen. *Politik und Eschatologie: Studien zur Geschichte der Hegelschen Schule in den Jahren 1830–1840*. Munich: Beck, 1963.

Gooch, Todd. "Ludwig Andreas Feuerbach." In *The Stanford Encyclopedia of Philosophy*, edited by Edward N. Zalta. Metaphysics Research Lab, Stanford University, Winter 2016.

———. "Max Stirner and the Apotheosis of the Corporeal Ego." *The Owl of Minerva* 37, no. 2 (2006): 159–90.

Hardimon, Michael O. *Hegel's Social Philosophy: The Project of Reconciliation*. Cambridge: Cambridge University Press, 1994.

Harris, Horton. *David Friedrich Strauss and His Theology*. Cambridge: Cambridge University Press, 1973.

Haym, Rudolf. *Hegel Und Seine Zeit*. Berlin: Rudolph Gaertner, 1857.

Hegel, Georg Wilhelm Friedrich. *Encyclopedia of the Philosophical Sciences in Basic Outline: Part 1: Science of Logic*. Translated by Klaus Brinkmann and Daniel O. Dahlstrom. Cambridge: Cambridge University Press, 2010.

———. *Lectures on the History of Philosophy, Volume 1*. Translated by E. S. Haldane. Lincoln, NE: University of Nebraska, 1995.

———. *Lectures on the History of Philosophy, Volume 3*. Translated by E. S. Haldane. Lincoln, NE: University of Nebraska, 1995.

———. *Lectures on the Philosophy of World History*. Translated by H. B. Nisbet. Cambridge: Cambridge University Press, 1975.

———. *Phänomenologie Des Geistes*. Hamburg: Felix Meiner, 1987.

———. *Phenomenology of Spirit*. Translated by A. V. Miller. Oxford, UK: Oxford University Press, 1977.

———. *Philosophy of Mind*. Translated by W. Wallace, A. V. Miller, and Michael Inwood. Oxford: Oxford University Press, 2007.

———. *Philosophy of Right*. Translated by T. M. Knox. Oxford: Oxford University Press, 1952.

———. *The Difference Between Fichte's and Schelling's System of Philosophy*. Translated by H. S. Harris and W. Cerf. Albany, NY: State University of New York Press, 1977.

———. *The Encyclopaedia Logic: Part I of the Encyclopaedia of the Philosophical Sciences with the Zustze*. Translated by T. F. Geraets, W. A. Suchting, and H. S. Harris. Indianapolis: Hackett, 1991.

———. *The Science of Logic*. Translated by George Di Giovanni. Cambridge: Cambridge University Press, 2010.

Hellman, Robert James. *Berlin: The Red Room and White Beer: The "Free" Hegelian Radicals in the 1840s*. Washington, DC: Three Continents Press, 1990.

Helms, Hans Günter. *Die Ideologie der anonymen Gesellschaft: Max Stirners "Einziger" und der Fortschritt das demokratischen Selbstbewusstseins vom Vormärz bis zur Bundesrepublik*. Köln: Verlag M. Du Mont Schauberg, 1966.

Henderson, James P., and John B. Davis. "Adam Smith's Influence on Hegel's Philosophical Writings." *Journal of the History of Economic Thought* 13, no. 2 (1991): 184–204.

Herwegh, Georg. *Einundzwanzig Bogen aus der Schweiz: Erster Theil*. Zurich: Verlag des Literarischen Comptoirs, 1843.

Herzl, Theodor. *Tagebücher, 1895–1904*. Vol. 2. Berlin: Jüdischer verlag, 1922.

Hess, Moses. *Briefwechsel*. Edited by Edmund Silberner. 'S-Gravenhage: Mouton and Co, 1959.

———. *Die Europäische Triarchie*. Leipzig: Otto Wigand, 1841.

———. *Die heilige Geschichte der Menschheit von einem Jünger Spinozas*. Stuttgart: Hallberger'sche Verlagsbuchhandlung, 1837.

———. *Die Letzten Philosophen*. Darmstadt: C. W. Leske, 1845.

———. "Die Philosophie Der Tat." In *Einundzwanzig Bogen Aus Der Schweiz*, edited by Georg Herwegh. Zurich: Literarischen Comptoirs, 1842.

———. *The Holy History of Mankind and Other Writings*. Edited by Shlomo Avineri. Cambridge: Cambridge University Press, 2004.

Hondt, Jacques d'. *Hegel in His Time*. Lewiston, NY: Broadview, 1995.

Hook, Sidney. *From Hegel to Marx*. Ann Arbor: University of Michigan Press, 1962.

———. "Karl Marx and Moses Hess." *New International* 1, no. 5 (1934): 140–44.

———. *Towards the Understanding of Karl Marx: A Revolutionary Interpretation*. London: Victor Gollancz, 1933.

Huneker, James. *Egoists: A Book of Superman*. New York: Scribner, 1921.

Immerman, Karl. *Werke*. Edited by Robert Boxberger. Vol. 5. Berlin: G. Hempel, 1883.

Joseph, H. W. B. *An Introduction to Logic*. Oxford: Oxford University Press, 1916.

Kamenka, Eugène. *The Philosophy of Ludwig Feuerbach*. Routledge & K. Paul, 1970.
Kast, Bernd. *Die Thematik des "Eigners" in der Philosophie Max Stirners: sein Beitrag zur Radikalisierung d. anthropologischen Fragestellung*. Bonn: Bouvier, 1979.
Kierkegaard, Søren. *Journals and Papers*. Vol. 5. Indianapolis: Indiana University Press, 1978.
———. *Letters and Documents*. Princeton: Princeton University Press, 1978.
———. *Søren Kierkegaards Skrifter*. Edited by Niels-Jorgen Cappelorn. Vol. 19. Copenhagen: Gad, 1997.
Kojève, Alexandre. *Introduction to the Reading of Hegel: Lectures on the "Phenomenology of Spirit."* Edited by Allan Bloom. Translated by James H. Nichols. Ithaca, NY: Cornell University Press, 1980.
Koltun-Fromm, Ken. *Moses Hess and Modern Jewish Identity*. Bloomington: Indiana University Press, 2001.
Koyré, Alexandre. *Etudes sur l'histoire de la pensee philosophique en russie*. Paris: Librairie J. Vrin, 1950.
Kühne, Walter. "Neue Einblicke in Leben Und Werke Zieszowskis." *Jahrbücher Für Kultur Und Geschichte Der Slaven* 6, no. 1 (1930): 54–66.
Lämmerman, Godwin. *Kritische Theologie Und Theologiekritik: Die Genese Der Religion-Und Selbstbewusstseinstheorie Bruno Bauers*. München: Chr. Kaiser Verlag, 1979.
Laska, Bernd. "Max Stirner Archiv Leipzig – Max Stirner." Accessed October 16, 2019. http://www.max-stirner-archiv-leipzig.de/max_stirner.html.
Laska, Bernd A. *Ein dauerhafter Dissident: 150 Jahre Stirners "Einziger" : eine kurze Wirkungsgeschichte*. Nurnberg: LSR-Verlag, 1996.
Lauth, Reinhard. "Einflusse Slawischer Denker Auf Die Genesis Der Marxschen Weltanschauung." *Orientalia Christiana Periodica* 21 (1955).
Lenin, Vladimir Ilyich. *Collected Works*. Vol. 18. Moscow: Progress Publishers, 1975.
Leopold, David. "Max Stirner." In *The Stanford Encyclopedia of Philosophy*, edited by Edward N. Zalta, Winter 2019. Metaphysics Research Lab, Stanford University, 2019. https://plato.stanford.edu/archives/win2019/entries/max-stirner/.
———. "The Hegelian Antisemitism of Bruno Bauer." *History of European Ideas* 25, no. 4 (July 1, 1999): 179–206.
Liebich, Andre. *Between Ideology and Utopia: The Politics and Philosophy of August Cieszkowski*. Dordrecht: Springer, 1979.
Lobkowicz, Nicholas. "Karl Marx and Max Stirner." In *Demythologizing Marxism*, edited by F. J. Adelmann. The Hague: Springer, 1969.
———. *Theory and Practice: History of a Concept from Aristotle to Marx*. Notre Dame, IN: University of Notre Dame Press, 1967.
Loewenberg, Jacob. *Hegel's Phenomenology*. LaSalle, IL: Open Court, 1965.
Löwith, Karl. *Die Hegelsche Linke: Texte aus den Werken von Heinrich Heine, Arnold Ruge, Moses Hess, Max Stirner, Bruno Bauer, Ludwig Feuerbach, Karl Marx und Sören Kierkegaard*. Stuttgart-Bad Cannstatt: F. Frommann, 1962.

———. *From Hegel to Nietzsche*. Translated by David E. Green. New York: Columbia University Press, 1964.
———. *Von Hegel zu Nietzsche*. Hamburg: Felix Meiner Verlag, 1995.
Lukacs, Georg. *The Destruction of Reason*. Translated by Peter R. Palmer. London: Merlin Press, 1980.
Mackay, John Henry. *Max Stirner: His Life and His Work*. Translated by Hubert Kennedy. Concord, CA: Peremptory Publications, 2005.
Mah, Harold E. *The End of Philosophy, the Origin of "Ideology": Karl Marx and the Crisis of the Young Hegelians*. Berkeley: University of California Press, 1987.
Marasco, Robyn. *The Highway of Despair: Critical Theory After Hegel*. New York: Columbia University Press, 2015.
Marx, Karl. *Capital*. London: Penguin, 1976.
———. *Das Kapital: Kritik Der Politischen Ökonomie, Erster Band*. Vol. 10. Karl Marx, Friedrich Engels Gesamtausgabe (MEGA) 2. Berlin: Dietz, 1991.
———. *Early Writings*. Translated by T. B. Bottomore. New York: McGraw-Hill, 1964.
———. *Karl Marx, Friedrich Engels Gesamtausgabe (MEGA)*. Berlin: Dietz, 1975.
———. *The Eighteenth Brumaire of Louis Bonaparte*. New York: International Publishers, 1994.
Marx, Karl, and Friedrich Engels. "Manifesto of the Communist Party." In *The Marx-Engels Reader*, edited by Robert C. Tucker. Oxford: Oxford University Press, 1998.
———. *Marx/Engels Collected Works*. Vol. 38. London: Lawrence & Wishart, 1982.
———. *Marx/Engels Collected Works*. Vol. 48. London: Lawrence & Wishart, 2001.
———. *Marx-Engels-Werke*. Vol. 1. Berlin: Dietz, 1967.
———. *Marx-Engels-Werke*. Vol. 3. Berlin: Dietz, 1962.
———. *Marx-Engels-Werke*. Vol. 27. Berlin: Dietz, 1967.
———. *Marx-Engels-Werke*. Vol. 28. Berlin: Dietz, 1973.
———. *Marx-Engels-Werke*. Vol. 37. Berlin: Dietz, 1967.
———. *Marx-Engels-Werke*. Vol. 40.2. Berlin: Dietz, 1967.
———. *The Economic and Philosophic Manuscripts of 1844*. Translated by Martin Milligan. Amherst, NY: Prometheus, 1988.
———. *The German Ideology*. London: Lawrence & Wishart, 1965.
———. *The German Ideology*. Mansfield Centre: Martino Fine Books, 2011.
———. *The Holy Family*. Moscow: Foreign Languages Press, 1956.
Massey, Marilyn Chapin. *Christ Unmasked: The Meaning of The Life of Jesus in German Politics*. Chapel Hill: The University of North Carolina Press, 1983.
Mautz, Kurt Adolf. "Die Philosophie Max Stirners Im Gegensatz Zum Hegelschen Idealismus." *Philosophical Review* 46, no. n/a (1937): 681.
McAnear, Michael. "Max Stirner, the Lunatic and Donald Trump." *American International Journal of Contemporary Research* 8, no. 1 (2018): 8–11.
McLellan, David. *The Young Hegelians and Karl Marx*. First edition. London, Melbourne: Macmillan, 1969.
Mehring, Franz. *Karl Marx: The Story of His Life*. Ann Arbor: University of Michigan Press, 1962.

Moggach, Douglas, ed. *The New Hegelians: Politics and Philosophy in the Hegelian School*. New York: Cambridge University Press, 2006.

———. *The Philosophy and Politics of Bruno Bauer*. Cambridge: Cambridge University Press, 2003.

Moller van der Bruck, Arthur. *Das Dritte Reich*. Edited by H. Schwartz. Hamburg: Hanseatische Verlagsanstalt, 1931.

Munk, Frank. "Communist Heresies: Hopes and Hazards." *The Western Political Quarterly* 22, no. 4 (1969): 921–25.

Newman, Saul. *Max Stirner*. New York: Palgrave Macmillan, 2011.

———. "Stirner and Foucault: Toward a Post-Kantian Freedom." *Postmodern Culture* 13, no. 2 (May 6, 2003).

Pals, Daniel L. *The Victorian "Lives" of Jesus*. San Antonio, TX: Trinity University Press, 1982.

Paterson, R. W. K. *The Nihilist Egoist: Max Stirner*. New York: Oxford University Press, 1971.

Pinkard, Terry. *Hegel: A Biography*. Cambridge: Cambridge University Press, 2001.

Rawidowicz, Simon. *Ludwig Feuerbachs Philosophie: Ursprung Und Schicksal*. Berlin: W. de Gruyter, 1964.

Reimarus, Hermann Samuel. *Fragments*. Translated by Ralph S. Fraser. Philadelphia: Fortress, 1970.

Rockmore, Tom. *Before and After Hegel: A Historical Introduction to Hegel's Thought*. Indianapolis: Hackett, 2003.

Rosenkranz, Karl. *G. W. F. Hegel's Leben*. Berlin: Duncker und Humblot, 1944.

Royce, Josiah. *Lectures on Modern Idealism*. New Haven: Yale University Press, 1919.

Ruge, Arnold. *Aus früherer Zeit*. Vol. 4. Berlin: F. Duncker, 1862.

———. *Briefwechsel und Tagebuchblätter aus den Jahren 1825–1880*. Weidmann, 1886.

———. *Zwei jahre in Paris: Studien und erinnerungen*. Vol. 1. Leipzig: W. Jurany, 1846.

Ruge, Arnold, and Theodor Echtermeyer, eds. "Hallische Jahrbücher Für Deutsche Wissenschaft Und Kunst." Verlag Detlev Auvermann, 1972.

Russell, Bertrand. *History of Western Philosophy*. London: George Allen and Unwin, 1947.

Safranski, Rüdiger. *Nietzsche: A Philosophical Biography*. Translated by Shelley Frisch. New York: W. W. Norton & Company, 2003.

Santayana, George. *The German Mind: A Philosophical Diagnosis*. New York: Crowell Co., 1968.

Schelling, Friedrich Wilhelm Joseph von. *Erste Vorlesung in Berlin. 15. November 1841*. Stuttgart: Cotta, 1841.

Schiereck, Larry Alan. "Max Stirner's Egoism and Nihilism." Master of Arts, San Diego State University, 2015.

Schultze, Ernst. "Stirner'sche Ideen in einem paranoischen Wahnsystem." *Archiv für Psychiatrie und Nervenkrankheiten* 36, no. 3 (January 1, 1903): 793–818.

Schweitzer, Albert. *The Quest of the Historical Jesus*. Translated by W. Montgomery. New York: Macmillan, 1968.

Silberner, Edmund. *Moses Hess: Geschichte seines Lebens*. Leiden: E.J. Brill, 1966.

Stepelevich, Lawrence. "Max Stirner and The Jewish Question." *Modern Judaism* 34 (February 1, 2014): 42–59.

Stepelevich, Lawrence S. "August von Cieszkowski: From Theory to Praxis." *History and Theory* 13, no. 1 (1974): 39–52.

———. "Bauer, Bruno (1809–82)." In *Routledge Encyclopedia of Philosophy*. London: Routledge, 2016.

———. "Ein Menschenleben: Hegel and Stirner." In *The New Hegelians: Politics and Philosophy in the Hegelian School*, edited by Douglas Moggach. New York: Cambridge University Press, 2006.

———. "Hegelian Nihilism: Karl Werder and the Class of 1841." *Philosophical Forum* 46, no. 3 (2015): 249–73.

———. "Making Hegel into a Better Hegelian: August von Cieszkowski." *Journal of the History of Philosophy* 25, no. 2 (1987): 263–73.

———. "Max Stirner as Hegelian." *Journal of the History of Ideas* 46, no. 4 (1985): 597–614.

Stirner, Max. *Der Einzige Und Sein Eigentum*. Stuttgart: Philipp Reclam, 1972.

———. *Der Einzige und sein Eigentum und andere Schriften*. Edited by Hans G Helms. München: Carl Hanser Verlag, 1968.

———. *Die Geschichte der Reaction*. Berlin: Allgemeine Deutsche Verlags-Anstalt, 1852.

———. *Kleinere Schriften Und Seine Entgegnungen Auf Die Kritik Seines Werkes, "Der Einzige Und Sein Eigenthum" Aus Den Jahren 1842–1848*. Berlin: John Henry Mackay, 1914.

———. *Stirner's Critics*. Translated by Wolfi Landstreicher. Berkeley: Cal Press, 2012.

———. *The Ego and His Own*. Translated by Steven T. Byington. New York: Boni and Liveright, 1918.

———. *The Ego and His Own*. Edited by James J. Martin. New York: Libertarian Book Club, 1963.

———. *The Ego and Its Own*. Edited by David Stirner. Translated by Steven Tracy Byington. Cambridge, England; New York, NY, USA: Cambridge University Press, 1995.

———. *The Unique and Its Property*. Translated by Wolfi Landstreicher. Baltimore: Underworld Amusements, 2017.

Strauss, David Friedrich. *Das Leben Jesu*. Leipzig: Brockhaus, 1839.

———. *Hermann Samuel Reimarus Und Seine Schutzschrift Für Die Vernünftigen Verehrer Gottes*. Leipzig: Brockhaus, 1862.

———. *In Defense of My "Life of Jesus" Against the Hegelians*. Translated by Marilyn Chapin Massey. Hamden, CT: Archon Books, 1984.

———. *Streitschriften zur Vertheidigung meiner Schrift über das Leben Jesu und zur Charakteristik der gegenwärtigen Theologie*. Tübingen: C. F. Osiander, 1837.

———. *The Christ of Faith and the Jesus of History: A Critique of Schleiermacher's Life of Jesus*. Translated by Leander E. Keck. Lives of Jesus Series. Philadelphia: Fortress Press, 1977.

Toews, John Edward. *Hegelianism: The Path Toward Dialectical Humanism, 1805–1841*. Cambridge: Cambridge University Press, 1985.

Tucker, Robert C. *Philosophy and Myth in Karl Marx*. Cambridge: Cambridge University Press, 1961.

Woodcock, George. *Anarchism*. Cleveland: World Publishing, 1962.

Zagorin, Perez. *How the Idea of Religious Toleration Came to the West*. Princeton: Princeton University Press, 2003.

Zychlinski, Frank Szeliga Zychlin von. "Der Einzige Und Sein Eigenthum Vom Max Stirner: Kritik." *Norddeutschen Blätter: Eine Monatsschrift Für Kritik, Literatur Und Unterhaltung*, März 1845.

Index

Althusser, Louis, 149
Arvon. Henri, 5

Bakunin, Michael, 22–23, 25, 32, 53, 66
Baldisonne, Riccardo, 3
Ballerstadt, Heinrich, 30
Bauer, Edgar, 73, 95, 99–100
Benjamin, Walter, 149–50
Bentham, Jeremy, 4, 122, 145
Bettina von Arnim, 36, 113
Burke, Edmund, 163–64

Chernyshevsky, Nikolay, 117

Deleuze, Gilles, 5, 25, 157, 159
Descartes, Rene, 7
deVolney, C. Francois, 81
Dupis, Charles Francois, 81

Echtermeyer, Ernst T., 67
Eichhorn, Karl von, 22
Eliot, George [Marian Evans], 87, 122
Erdmann, Johann, 6, 64, 109, 115

Ferguson, Kathy, 4–5
Fichte Johann Gottlieb, 13–14
Fischer, Kuno, 46, 113
Forster, Frederich, 21

Fromm, Eric, 148–49

Gabler, Georg Andreas, 20–21, 31, 63–65, 195
Goethe, Johann, 40, 66, 73, 136

Heine, Heinrich, ix, 103–4, 112, 122
Hellman, Robert James, 147
Helms, Hans C., 1, 29, 162
Hengstenberg, Ernst Wilhelm, 17, 195
Heraclitus, ix, 14, 38, 60, 138–39
Hertzen, Alexander, 15, 66, 72, 117
Herwegh, Georg, 34, 112
Hook, Sidney, 5, 144
Huneker, James, 38
Hyppolite, Jean, 159

Immerman, Karl L., 67

Joachim of Flores, 70
Joll, James, 4

Kamenka, Eugene, 118
Kapp, Christian, 32
Keller, Gottfried, 112
Kennedy, Hubert, 118
Kiekegaard, Soren, 23, 32, 67

Kojève, Alexander, 158
Kűhne, Walter, 77

Laska, Bernd, 35, 159
Lenin, V.I., 3, 15, 117
Leo, Henrich, 16
Lessing, Gotthold E., 80, 83
Lobkowicz, Nicholas, 154
Löwith, Karl, 6–7, 11, 24, 47, 84, 115

Mackay, John Henry, 28, 31, 35, 37, 165
Marheineke, Philip Konrad, 21, 31, 80
Marklin, Christian, 82
Marsco, Robyn, 4
Mauthener, Fritz, 5
Mautz, Kurt, 5
McLellan, David, 5
Mehring, Hans, 5, 158
Michelet, Karl, 32, 64–66
Moleschott, Jacob, 118

Neander, Karl, 31
Newman, Saul, 3–6, 46, 59
Nietzsche, Frederick, 6, 38, 67, 87, 157–59

Paterson, R. W., 53
Paulus, Heinrich, 83–84
Pinel, Philippe, 49
Pisarev, Dmitry, 53, 117
Proudhon, Pierre Joseph, 4, 52, 175

Rawidowiz, Simon, 117–18
Reimarus, Hermann, 83–84

Richter, John Paul, 199
Ritter, Carl, 31, 33, 110
Ritter, Henrich, 31
Robespierre, Maxmillien, 102
Rosenkranz, Karl, 22, 113, 115, 195
Ruge, Arnold, 23, 33–38, 66, 100, 102, 112–13, 126–28, 168
Russell, Bertrand, 144
Rutenberg, Adol, 34, 37, 65

Safranski, Rüdiger, 158
Santayanna, George, 38
Sass, Hans-Martin, 98, 104
Say, Jean-Baptiste, 35, 135
Schelling, Friedrich, 22–23
Schleiermacher, Friedrich, 22, 31, 66
Schultz, Johannes, 19, 22
Schweitzer, Albert, 81, 84, 104
Smith, Adam, 35–36, 52, 135
Spinoza, Baruch, 54–55, 73, 122–28, 136–39
Szeliga, Franz Zychlin, 59, 97–100, 127, 132

Trendelenburg, Friedrich, 21, 33
Turgesnev, Ivan, 32, 66, 117

Vatke, Wilhelm, 17, 31
Vogel, Manfred, 109, 112
Voltaire, 80, 100
Von Altenstein. Karl, 18–19, 22

Wagner, Richard, 112
Werder, Karl, 32, 64–66
Wiegand, Otto, 59, 97, 104

About the Author

Lawrence S. Stepelevich is professor emeritus of philosophy at Villanova University. He is a former president of the Hegel Society of America and was the executive editor from 1977 to 1996 of their journal, *The Owl of Minerva*. His work, *The Young Hegelians: An Anthology*, was his first extensive study of the radical students of Hegel.

www.ingramcontent.com/pod-product-compliance
Lightning Source LLC
Chambersburg PA
CBHW050904300426
44111CB00010B/1375